William Thomson

Sermons preached in Lincoln's Inn Chapel

William Thomson

Sermons preached in Lincoln's Inn Chapel

ISBN/EAN: 9783744744737

Printed in Europe, USA, Canada, Australia, Japan

Cover: Foto ©Lupo / pixelio.de

More available books at **www.hansebooks.com**

LINCOLN'S INN SERMONS

LONDON
PRINTED BY SPOTTISWOODE AND CO.
NEW-STREET SQUARE

SERMONS

PREACHED IN

LINCOLN'S INN CHAPEL

BY WILLIAM THOMSON, D.D.

CHAPLAIN IN ORDINARY TO THE QUEEN, PROVOST OF THE QUEEN'S COLLEGE, OXFORD,
AND PREACHER TO THE HONOURABLE SOCIETY OF LINCOLN'S INN

LONDON
JOHN MURRAY, ALBEMARLE STREET
1861

NOTE.

To the " Sermons preached at Lincoln's Inn," a few have been added which were preached elsewhere. They resemble the rest in tone and object; and the variety of occasion may be a relief to the reader.

CONTENTS.

SERMON		PAGE
I. THE CHRISTIAN'S VIEW OF TIME	. . .	1
II. CONSTANT PRAYER	. . . .	17
III. CHRIST OUR HIGH PRIEST	. . .	30
IV. THE CHARACTER OF PILATE	. . .	47
V. IMMORTALITY	. . . .	62
VI. THE POWER OF THE ATONEMENT	. .	78
VII. THE CRUCIFIXION	. . .	96
VIII. THE RESURRECTION	. . .	109
IX. THE HOLY SPIRIT	. . . .	124
X. GOD IN NATURE.—I.	. . .	138
XI. GOD IN NATURE.—II.	. . .	155
XII. THE HOLY TRINITY	. . . .	174
XIII. THE CONVICTION OF SIN	. . .	188
XIV. THE NATURE OF SIN	. . . .	202
XV. THE DECEITFULNESS OF SIN	. . .	216
XVI. SIN IN THE REGENERATE	. . .	232
XVII. THE LIGHT OF THE WORLD	. . .	247
XVIII. FAITH AND SIGHT	. . . .	263

CONTENTS.

SERMON	PAGE
XIX. THE TEMPLE OF GOD	278
XX. THE NIGHT COMETH	298
XXI. THE CHARACTER OF DAVID	310
XXII. PROVIDENCE AND FREE-WILL	325
XXIII. LOVE OF THE BRETHREN	342
XXIV. THE DOOM OF JERUSALEM	356
XXV. SHE IS A SINNER	373
XXVI. THE SECOND TEMPLE	390

ERRATUM.

Page 117, last line, for ii. 63, read i. 16.

SERMONS

ETC.

SERMON I.

THE CHRISTIAN'S VIEW OF TIME.

PSALM xc. 3, 4.

Thou turnest man to destruction; and sayest, Return, ye children of men.
For a thousand years in thy sight are but as yesterday when it is past, and as a watch in the night.

THERE is no reason to doubt that this psalm is "a prayer of Moses, the man of God," as the title in our Bibles describes it, although the name of Moses does not occur in the inspired words themselves. If we assume that it was written by him in the wilderness, after the sore pilgrimage of eight and thirty years which the children of Israel were condemned to drag out there, then the meaning of many of its words starts forth with a new distinctness. The houseless congregation, to whom such words as *home* and *country* had become dim traditions, begin their prayer to God, "Thou hast been our dwelling-place;" they acknowledge that they are outcasts from an earthly home because He, in His anger, has cast them out from Him. They confess that their sins have been the cause; and they pray that He will return, and make them glad according to the days wherein He has afflicted them. They have seen and suffered His wrath only too long; now let His glory and His beauty be made known unto them. And the prayer is a presage of the end of their pilgrimage, and of their forgiveness and their settlement in the land that God had given them.

This psalm, then, is one of the oldest of the inspired utterances. It is the prayer which is read over the mortal dust of some hundreds of the children of men every week in London alone. And, so used, none of us finds it antiquated. The lapse of 3000 years has not made it necessary to discard this clause and that. Words that described the relation of the children of Israel to the eternal God, serve still to express the devotion of English hearts turning to God in their sorrow. As these grand words are uttered the curtain that hangs round our life seems to draw back, and we see, beyond, depths that we dreamt not of. From time and the slow succession of events, from the minutes and hours that seem so long and so many, we turn to God, whose eternal nature was as it now is, even when the world was formed, and to whom a thousand years are no more than the middle watch of the night is to a sound sleeper. Nations that seem established for ever, are carried off down the roaring cataract of time; men full of pride, and glory, and power, grow and perish like grass; and God alone remains unchangeable, the same yesterday, to-day, and for ever. " Thou turnest man to destruction; and sayest, Return, ye children of men. For a thousand years in thy sight are but as yesterday when it is past, and as a watch in the night. Thou carriest them away as with a flood; they are as a sleep: in the morning they are like grass which groweth up. In the morning it flourisheth and groweth up; in the evening it is cut down, and withereth." Now, without attempting to grasp the whole of a subject which, indeed, comprehends a complete view of human life, let us only speak at present of one part of it, *the Christian's view of time.*

We have no other measure of time than the succession of acts or events. What time may *be* is another and deeper question : I only say that we measure it by what we can do or observe in it. Our sense of duration arises from our being placed in a world where there are so many trains of events that succeed each other in a regular order. Summer and winter, morning and evening, the waxing and the waning of the moon, the intervals of bodily activity and of sleep, are so many events that mark the course of time ; they are as it were the motion of the hands on the great dial of the universe, to tell us how much of life has flown, but not how much remains. Within ourselves measures of time are provided, by which our activity is the means of ascertaining duration. We resolve to go hither or thither; and our going follows on our resolution; and then weariness warns us that our steps have been many; and all along successive purposes of the mind and successive acts of the body prompted by them, make us conscious that time is passing: and how much time, we have learnt by experience to estimate roughly, by knowing how many resolves or actions can pass before us in a day or an hour. Even when the sluggard folds his hands to do nothing, he has in himself an obscure sense of the passing of time, which tells him the difference between a minute and an hour. His heart beats within him almost as regularly as the pendulum of the clock; and all the processes of vegetative life go on within him. He does not count them nor observe, but still he is obscurely aware of something that goes on through all his frame, and its progress serves as an obscure measure of time. If then time is valued by events, it follows that a being differently made from us would form a different notion of time, according as he differed from us in rapidity of thought and action. If the will were twice as swift to decree, and the hand and foot twice as nimble to execute, if all the bodily functions were quickened in proportion, then the space of time that lies between sunrise and sunset would serve to include twice as much of life as it does for one of us; and the sense of time would not be the same as ours, because it would be founded on a far quicker succession. Even to the same man in different conditions, the word time means two different things; and it is a proverb that joy quickens and pain clogs the march of time; because the excitement of the one calls us off from observing those facts within and without us that are given us for a measure; and in the other, the mind is painfully conscious of each successive moment, counting every throb and studying all the shades and degrees of suffering. In fewer words, whatever distracts, renders us less observant of the states that measure time, and so appears to cheat us of time itself; whatever quickens our self-observation, multiplies the acts of the mind, and so appears to prolong it. The Psalmist himself tells us of a time that is for us as though it were not; we sleep through the watch of the night, living but observing nothing; and though our heart, the balance spring of life, intermits not, though the watchful hosts of heaven move on, then as evermore, round the polar star, we know not when we wake that the watch has passed, except by an inference. Those hours have been stolen out of our existence, and given up as to death. In the sick man's chamber they seemed an age; to the healthy sleeper they reckon not even for a moment. So that without pronouncing any opinion here upon a mere speculative question, What is time? we may decide that we measure time by the succession of events, and that such a measure must vary with the number of events, and the intensity of our observation. And when we speak of a given interval of time, say for example of last year or last month, we do not in fact speak of something which is necessarily the same in amount and value for all, but of something which varies in value according to the nature and activity of each.

There are two consequences of this, both of a very practical kind, one relating to the divine nature and the other to our own life, which may serve to excuse these remarks.

In those words "a thousand years in Thy sight are but as yesterday when it is past," the Psalmist has thrown a light upon the nature of God such as a volume of reasoning could not have kindled. With God there are no measures of time. With us time is the name we give to the duration of a certain succession of thoughts and efforts, each of which for a moment held full possession of us, each of which cost us a certain pain, and contributed a little to the weariness which at last took shelter in repose. The Most High does not and cannot so govern the world. He does not look away from the earth to add fuel to the sun; He does not leave one nation of the earth neglected whilst He works mighty social changes in another. That is the mode by which a finite creature would labour: but we cannot conceive Him who has been our dwelling-place from one generation to another working under such limitation and constraint. When the sculptor determined to make a statue he fixed upon the quarry whence the stone should come, he indicated the part of the stratum whence the purest blocks might be hewn, and whilst the workmen were getting it out, and the ship was bringing it, he matured the design by degrees, and moulded it in clay, not without trials and alterations that tasked him severely. The excellent work comes forth at last; but he alone whose hand wrought it knows what pains it has cost. And all those acts following singly one upon another have occupied perhaps a year of the artist's short life. But if you would know how the world was made and is governed — if, at least, you would have a dim apprehension of what you never can truly know, — you must discard all those notions of pain, and hope protracted, and efforts that succeed each other and wait for each other. You are now upon holy ground, in the presence of One to whom a thousand years are but as a watch in the night, to whom it is one thing to will and to do; on whom all things in heaven, in earth, and under the earth wait daily and hourly for their being, and would perish if He forgot them for a moment. All that we mean by time must now be left out of the account. The preparation of the earth for man's habitation, has occupied thousands upon thousands of years; the history of the Jewish nation from its rise to its ruin has taken up many centuries; the life of one man only fills a few years' space. But all these have been moulded by God's hand, not a hair of any head has fallen to the ground without Him. And one has not cost more effort than another: the thousands of years during which the world has been shaped on one unchanged plan have been as the days "few and evil" of the individual man's life. There is no forgetfulness, no casting aside of an unfinished work for some other. It is no wonder, when we consider who the Agent is, that the first stones, so to speak, of the world's foundation bear plain marks of the same hand that crowned at last His finished work with man; that the first living creatures, entombed long since under the slow accretion of ages, are formed on the same laws of life and growth as those that begin their existence to-day. It would be a longer and more tedious task, if a man were the worker, to build a world than to guide a wayward nation through its fortunes: but what means *longer* or *shorter* when there is no labour, nor waiting, nor weariness, but only the streaming forth of an omnipotent will? Dare we say that it cost more to construct the universe than to guide the footsteps of one man during the short year that has just closed? There is time with God, and He has made fixed measures of it for our use; but those constraints which are put upon us by time do not touch His nature who is the Ancient of Days, the "Age of Ages." And we must try to follow the Psalmist in freeing our conception of the Most High from such false limitations. For it is not a question of ingenious thought but of love and devotion that we are now considering. God is spoken of as our dwelling-place, as a place to hide us in, as one who gives us shelter when we seek it, as one to whom the wanderings of our feet are none of them unknown;

yet we cannot think of Him in this light, so long as we represent Him to ourselves as painfully striving to compress into cycles and centuries the great tasks allotted to them, and in the preoccupation of great works forgetting us and our little needs and feeble prayers. If we know Him as one to whom a thousand years are but as yesterday when it is past, then our yesterday and our to-day rise in importance as the longer period sinks. And we may fly to the shadow of His wings, confident that when we pray to Him "So teach us to number our days that we may apply our hearts unto wisdom," we are not adding another voice to a confusion of sounds which His ear only partly hears, not trying to divert to us an attention pledged already to some other work. For the watch in the night through which we slept in security was as important as a thousand years to Him. With Him nothing is great or little, long or short. His power watches at the sleeper's pillow (nay, must watch or he would perish); and the great universe cost Him no more thought or trouble to construct than did the task of holding that soul in life for a few defenceless hours till the morning comes again.

God is eternal; He is omnipotent; He is infinite; and these words, vague to us though their meaning must be, imply that no finite thing, no measured interval of time, but shrinks into nothing in respect of Him. Alike the orbit of the sun and the cradle of a child occupy an insignificant portion of that space which is itself too small to be considered when compared with His immensity. Pray to Him then, for His ear is free for you; treasure up your minutes, for His hand measures out to you every one of them; lay you down in peace and take your rest, for it is He only that makes you dwell in safety. And let the very greatness of His operations remind you that nothing is for Him great or little. The same care that presides over the universe protects the sparrow in the hedge and the grass in the field; not more care or less, but for each the fullest measure that it requires.

There is another side to this subject. What is the true measure of time *to us?* I know that the outward measures are accurate enough, and when a man says to his friend "Another year is gone," they understand a certain space which can be precisely computed; but if acts and activity are the true measures of time for us, and not the hands on the clock, nor the changing path of the sun, then it may be well doubted whether in fact we do know at the end of a year what or how much it is that has gone away from us. A year of earnest work in the way of duty and for the cause of God, a year of amusement, a year marked by tasting first, and then drinking deep of, the foul cup of some new sin, a year marked by a great change of character for the better, in which he that once served sin has made up his mind, through God's help, to serve it no more; any of these may be included under the phrase, "Another year has passed." Out of the looms of time a measured portion of the web of our life has come; the measure the same for all, the texture and the tints how different! Nay, are there not even single minutes in which the scattered lights of our thoughts are gathered into one focus, and burn an indelible imprint into the soul? A man went once to Damascus, and a light from heaven struck him blind, and the Spirit of Christ, more penetrating than that light, sent deep into his conscience the unanswerable question, Why persecutest thou me? The man was St. Paul, and that minute bore in it the germ of the church of the Gentiles, and of *our* knowledge of the Redeemer. A careless student was walking with his friend, when a flash of lightning struck the friend dead, and awoke the student out of his worldliness. Luther was the student, and the Reformation that spread through the half of Europe began from that terrible instant. Minutes like these are not to be reckoned only at their value as fractional portions of a year. Time has a quality as it has quantity. Our years, my friends, are not each matched with each like so many cups or platters turned off from the potter's wheel. And this it is which makes time so unspeakably precious to us. We cannot be sure that a single day or year may not carry in it the decision of our eternity. There may be no great sign or wonder to tell us so; to all around the weight of another year upon us may seem no greater than in time past. But every part of us is growing. Habits are strengthening, feelings growing calmer, the advice of others losing its influence over us, the circle of those who might have the right to advise is fast contracting. And it is surely possible that when we are only conscious that a year is gone, our whole life, so far at least as life is a state of probation admitting of change and improvement, may have passed away with it. Well does the Prophet commence the prayer of this Psalm, the latter half of it, with the words, "So teach us to number our days, that we may apply our hearts unto wisdom!" Our days are not merely to be counted, but estimated according to the worth of them in respect to divine knowledge. Our years, be they few or many, are all that stand between us and eternity. The hour that passes by unimproved, might have been capable, for aught we know, of bearing witness to some earnest resolve, some saving prayer, some conquest over temptation; and such inward changes fashion the soul into the aspect that it shall wear in an eternal life that is close before us. We are too apt to fancy that years pass over us changing us but little, that whatever bodily effect time may have had upon us, the moral effects are too slight to notice; we are not much better or worse, not much nearer heaven or hell, for twelve months more of acting and suffering. Such an opinion contradicts the word of God, nay, contradicts our own experience. Terrible is the power of a bad habit over a man; it is hard to cope with in its beginnings, it is often, to human power at least, unconquerable when it has become confirmed. By degrees it destroys shame and remorse, it withdraws the pleasure that then allured us, and an imperious master has us in his grasp, instead of a light companion. Let no one suppose that he has kept company with a sin for a whole year, walked with it, conversed with it, ate, drank, and slept with it, lived for it and in it, and still come out no worse from that atmosphere of pollution. He does not feel more sinful, nay, he is easier in his conscience than of old; and that is his curse! The very feeling of remorse is leaving him: the moral part of the man is stiffening already with a present death.

And does not the Word of God tell us that this is so? Does it put forth three kinds of life that a man may lead, or only two? Besides the saved and the lost, are there also those who are neither saved nor lost? When the Apostle says "We are of God, and the whole world lieth in wickedness" (1 John v. 19), he knows no third condition. Nor does he who has told us that "Whosoever will be a friend of the world, is the enemy of God." (James iv. 4.) Nor does our Lord himself, when he presents to us the last judgment, and the separation of all men into two classes, the righteous on the right hand and the wicked on the left; when He even describes the surprise of the indifferent that they should be judged so severely. "Lord, when saw we thee an hungred, or athirst, or a stranger, or naked, or sick, or in prison, and did not minister unto thee?" (Matt. xxv. 44.) What was there in their lives, they thought, that had any bearing upon Christ at all? They had lived out their days as they found it easiest, and now they hear that every one of those dull, sluggish, godless days is a crime. The broad mark of distinction between a Christian and an un-Christian life is that the thoughts, the affections of the one are turned to what shall come hereafter, whilst the other looks not beyond the limits of this present world. And therefore, however hard the sentence may seem, those who are not with God are against Him; those who are not seeking their salvation through Him who was born, died, and rose again for us, are in the way of being lost for ever.

There are, then, no indifferent men, nor are there any indifferent years of life. The past year has its public history, its tidings of discovery, of warlike struggles, of political change; but besides all this, a record might be made of struggle, and change, and progress in every single heart of us that are here. It is strange, if this be granted, that so little account is made of a year. There is a story of a man that was let down by a rope over a rock to gather sea birds' eggs; and whilst he was hanging as between heaven and earth, he saw one or two of the little strands of the rope begin to part under his weight; another and another gave way, if relief could not be brought before the last should crack, he must be dashed to pieces. You can conceive how the man's very frame grew old, even with minutes of such agony as that. But at the twelfth stroke of the hour which parts two years, a little fibre of the cord cracks asunder that holds us suspended over eternity. They will all snap by degrees. The man that I spoke of was drawn up in time, none were ever rescued from the fall out of time into eternity. But the terror of it is only for those who have no sure hope in God. "Because thou hast made the Lord which is my refuge, even the Most High, thy habitation; there shall no evil befall thee, neither shall any plague come nigh thy dwelling. For He shall give his angels charge over thee, to keep thee in all thy ways. They shall bear thee up in their hands, lest thou dash thy foot against a stone." (Ps. xci. 9-12.)

This, then, is the Christian's view of time. Time is no limitation on the power and working of God; for a thousand years in his sight are but as yesterday when it is past, and as a watch in the night. And again it is no certain measure of man's condition to ascertain how many years of life have passed without taking into account the moral changes that they have wrought in him. Let those who have done nothing for God, but have only counted the years of life, without *weighing* them, begin to walk in His fear and obedience; let them see that sin is a heavy weight round our neck, and that only the cross of Christ through faith in His blood can remove it; let them try to live according to the self-denying loving life that has been set out as their example; let them seek the good of others, knowing that wherever a suffering brother is, Christ is there; and let every one, even amid the most urgent claims of an engrossing profession, find time to say daily in his own heart those solemn words of Job, " When a few years are come, then I shall go the way whence I shall not return."

SERMON II.

CONSTANT PRAYER.

ACTS x. 2.

A devout man, and one that feared God with all his house, which gave much alms to the people, and prayed to God alway.

THESE words are the description of Cornelius, a Roman officer, the servant of a pagan emperor; and though they imply no doubt that he was at heart a convert to Judaism, it does not seem that he had resigned his post or neglected its duties. They describe the highest kind of religious character; a man ruling himself and his household in the fear of God, a man whose whole life was a prayer to God.

What are we to understand by these words "And prayed to God alway?" When we are bidden to "pray everywhere" how are we to comply? Cornelius did not neglect his duties in order that he might seclude himself to pray. Many of us are devoted to a laborious profession; and it can hardly be meant that we are to cast that aside to consecrate ourselves to God in a state of devout leisure. Are such words as these "And prayed to God alway" to be taken in their literal meaning? If not, are we to understand that always means no more than frequently or regularly? Or is it the word "pray" that is to bear a wider sense than that in which it is usually understood?

It is clear at the outset that prayer sometimes means more than the asking from God those things which we need. To go no further than the Prayer Book at our hand, the "Order for Morning and Evening Prayer" consists not merely, nor even chiefly, of petitions, but of confessions of sin, praises, the reading of God's word, and the giving of thanks. In the Acts of the Apostles, when the seven Deacons were about to be appointed, the Apostles said "we will give ourselves continually to prayer, and to the ministry of the word" (Acts vi. 4); but here, too, prayer must have stood for every kind of communing of the soul with the Almighty. It is doing no violence to language to define prayer as the intercourse of the human spirit with the Divine. Whether a man desires to receive grace from God, or feels thankful for benefits, or meditates on God's power and knowledge and justice, or upon his own past offences against the divine law, or upon the deeper meanings of that law and their application to his own daily life, we may say that he prays to God. For the soul is then walking as in the presence of its heavenly Father, conversing with Him, speaking to Him the language of faith and love. And as thoughts like these are not of necessity confined to the bedside, but may be a light in the heart in the midst of daily affairs, it is at least conceivable that a man occupied by a profession as Cornelius was, may yet be engaged in prayer (so to speak) *always;* may bring in the thought of God upon each new event that claims his attention; may make it his earnest wish and desire that all his life should go on as under the eye of his Divine Master. Such a man I conceive Cornelius to have been. Brought up under idolatry, he has not dwelt in the Jewish land without recognising the superiority of the worship of the one true God, as the Jews possessed it. There was nothing very inviting in the low morality of the Jews at this time, in the mechanical rules which the Pharisees put in the place of the weightier matters of the law; but the heart of Cornelius was open to the truth, and the one true God claimed that heart for his own. Whether this centurion was openly a proselyte, a proselyte of the gate as it was termed, or not, matters little; he was at heart a worshipper of Jehovah, as any pious Jew would be. And when the Gospel began to be diffused throughout Judæa and Samaria, he had heard of it and thought about it; and it was the subject of his prayers to God that he might be able to know the right concerning it; and God listened. "Thy prayer is heard and thine alms are had in remembrance in the sight of God." He was told where to find a teacher who would guide him into the truth after which his soul was yearning; and he heard it and believed. Such was Cornelius — a man whose daily life, and each event of it, was full of the consciousness of God; a man who keenly heard every bidding of the heavenly Master whom he served; a man to whom life was not the mere routine of a soldier's duties relieved by indulgence in pleasures; but a divine gift, full of earnest worth and meaning, to be used upon an earth of God's creation in the midst of His creatures, every one of them divinely sustained. It is possible to lead a praying life. It is possible to make God the counsellor of all the actions. Cornelius did it. He prayed to God alway. The stated devotions were not wanting; but the life itself was a prayer in action. He was a man seeking God not in words only, but in all that he did. And in our busy practical times, we can only hope to pray to God always in that sense. Pressing duties encroach on meditation; their urgency engenders habits foreign to meditation. Too fast for our sight flash the thousand wheels of the great social machine, on which we are whirled round as a small part. Those constrained faces knit with anxiety that haunt you in the streets, those lips whispering busily to themselves in the crowded thoroughfare, those thousand vehicles locked in confusion at the confluence of streets, with all the occupants goaded to impatience by the words "Too late;" they all remind us of the impetuous age in which we live. Who can pray to

God always amidst such dire confusion? Do not despair even of that. Amidst the money-changers' tables you cannot pray as in the precincts of the Temple. But there is a kind of work that becomes a prayer: *Laborare est orare*. From the most active life in this great city may be daily floating up, for aught we know, to the throne of the Most High, an incense of worship more pure than any that issues from the quiet chamber of the pious recluse. I do not speak of acts of mercy and almsgiving only; that there is a prayer in these all would admit. They are an imitation of, and therefore a longing after, the loving Son of God, who is our Example. But in matters of mere business occasions arise, and daily, on which the principles of religion may be brought to bear. Thus in the intricacies of commerce an opportunity offers itself of taking advantage of another. It is unfair, fraudulent; but then it is secret. A knowledge of business would make it possible so to wrap up the guilt of the transaction that detection shall be impossible. The worldly man, hiding even from himself the true character of his act, seizes such an opportunity. The Christian, who lives as under the open eye of God, finds no temptation in the secrecy of the sin. He knows that God would have him to be just, though it be to his own hindrance. He desires to act as if on the tables of Sinai was written "Thou shalt not" against this particular form of evil. In a word he "inquires of the Lord;" not in a church, not perhaps at that moment on his knees in his own chamber; but in his bank or his counting-house he enters into the closet of his own heart, and shuts the door against temptations, and there in secret communes with God, and acts upon the light so derived. Is it a violence to language to say that the man has prayed and been heard? He bent not the knee, but he made the spirit of self bow down before One that ought to rule him. He wished for guidance, and he is guided.

Or take another kind of case. No one can shut his eyes to that hideous feature of our social state, that a large number of one sex dwells in the midst of it, sealed already with the signet of destruction; shunned, like the Judæan lepers, by all who would keep their name unstained. Under our eyes they bear about daily the load of moral and physical ruin. They are lost. But where are the strong wills that cruelly overruled them to their destruction? Where are those whose knowledge of the paths of sin guided their foolish feet to the flowery edge of the pitfall and cast them down? The balance of eternal justice is not unequal; and when the sins of men are weighed against the sins of women, those not these will carry down the scale. There will be no alleviation of this enormous evil, until the true offenders arraign themselves before the divine justice, and are convinced of sin. But see how differently two men will act under this kind of temptation. He who is accustomed to live for the present, knows no better heaven than an elysium of the senses. The occasion of sin is found, he hurries into it with a mind that recks of neither past nor future. Than this act of wrong-doing murder is not more horrible. But he sees it under other aspects. There is a purple tint in his eyes that gives a glow of beauty to the hateful treachery; his ears are not shocked even by the lying promises he utters. The sorrowful sighing of the outcast, the wailing of her bereaved mother he hears not now; they shall be hereafter. So are the ranks of the lost recruited; and women are punished for a sin in this world which men do, and which will not be arrested till men stop it. Yet even now there are men of another sort. What is a moment's pleasure to the Christian compared to the thought that he will offend God, will grieve or perhaps quench the Holy Spirit within him, will give over to Satan the soul of another as dear to Him that died for men as his own can be. So he sees the sin as sin; he prays that he may be able to stop his ears to the temptation, he flees from it. He manages to strip it of its false colour and attractive form; and to see it in its real ugliness and hatefulness, as a foul act of treachery to another, as a thorn that will pierce his own heart and rankle there, as a chain that he will feel the bitter weight of for years if he give way. Is not this struggle for moral freedom in the nature of a prayer? For it is the endeavour to fight in the strength of God against a temptation which in his own strength he could not resist.

If it be said that in the common use of speech such cases are rather examples of reflection or of resolution than of prayer, let it be remembered how close is the connection between this kind of moral conflict and direct prayer to God. Let any one resolve to walk on straight towards the guiding star of duty, and he will discover at once how miserably unfitted he is for an undertaking so difficult. Not a day but must bring him some perilous temptation to remind him of his weakness. Not a day but recalls his attention to the constant struggle between good and evil within him; "for the flesh lusteth against the spirit, and the spirit against the flesh, and these are contrary the one to the other." (Gal. v. 17.) He cannot conform his mind to the image of Christ, any more than a statue can shape itself out of the marble block in which it lay buried. He cannot "put on as the elect of God, holy and beloved bowels of mercies, kindness, humbleness of mind, meekness, long-suffering . . . charity which is the bond of perfectness." (Col. iii.) He cannot climb that ladder of Christian graces, by adding "to faith virtue, and to virtue knowledge, and to knowledge temperance, and to temperance patience, and to patience godliness, and to godliness brotherly kindness, and to brotherly kindness charity." (2 Pet. i.) He could as soon climb up to Heaven to pluck down the stars that glitter there, as gather these Christian virtues for himself. But God can do all for him. It is in striving to act, that the sense of utter dependence on God is brought home to him. How natural then to ask! The empty earthen vessel made conscious of its need, must desire to be filled from the fulness of the heavenly fountains! When he remembers the strict injunctions of God's word to be holy, he must ask help of Him who is and who maketh holy. And thus it is that the active man may be the man of most prayers. For a prayer is an earnest wish sent up from our heart to the throne of grace; and earnest wishes will be frequent in proportion as real straits more frequently beset us. Cold and lifeless in comparison with these cries of the soldier out of the thick of the battle, would be the elaborate orisons of the saint upon his pillar, or the hermit in his cell. For amongst men, and in aiding men, or striving with them, do we the disciples find our education; as our Master made the scene of his ministry in the midst of the men whom He would serve. The soul in retirement has often grown sickly with over-consciousness of itself, and invented needs and called for help against phantoms of its own creation. But the trials that surround us in our daily duties are those which God has made for us; and to Him we turn for strength to surmount them.

Is it too much to say, Christian hearers, that the great need of our time is that of men whose life is full of prayer? There are not wanting men of piety; but they often stand on the margin of the seething mill-stream of life and shriek out warnings against the dangers they cannot share. There are many whose activity and industry are almost pushed to a disease. But this active life and the piety of heart to guide it, are as rare a combination as they are precious in an age like this.

How are we to cultivate this habit of constant prayer? Believe in the first place one of the most obvious of theological truths,—God is present everywhere. "Whither shall I go," says the Psalmist, "from thy spirit; or whither shall I flee from thy presence? If I ascend up into heaven thou art there: if I make my bed in hell thou art there." (Ps. cxxxix.) But we need *not* flee. The spirit of the law echoes in that sublime psalm. David speaks in fear and wonder of the omnipresent God. But the spirit of the Gospel breathes through those words of our Lord,—"If a man love me, he will keep my words, and my Father will love him, and we will come to him, and make our abode with him." (John xiv. 23.) "God is present with us," is the fundamental truth of all religion; "through Christ who became one of us," is the addition which Christianity makes to it. Do we suppose that this huge city, where hundreds of thousands struggle daily that they may live, is a social chaos, looked at from afar by God, but not by Him directed? Do we suppose that on the stage of Europe, kings are suffered to play their part, and define or obliterate the boundaries of states, without the permission of the King of all the earth? As well suppose that chance guides the stars in their harmonious courses. God exists; and to exist is to know, to will, to govern. Turn then to Him : make frequent approaches to His throne, at any time, in any place ; ask His help for any undertaking ; and if it is one which you dare not bring before him, abandon it. Such a practice, to use the words of Bishop Taylor, "reconciles Martha's employment with Mary's devotion, charity and religion,—reconciles the necessities of our calling, and the employments of devotion. For thus in the midst of business you may retire into your chapel—your heart —and converse with God by frequent addresses and returns." And the fruits of this practice will be justice and uprightness in action, forbearance towards others, kindness towards the helpless, love towards all. It would be too much to say that this state of mind can be completely realised. Not Cornelius, not even the Apostles, had so learnt to pray to God always that the world had lost all power against them. Yet, my brethren, aim at no lower mark than this. Trade grows dishonest, morality is debased, crimes are frequent, poverty suffers. And God has given to the men of this generation power against these social mischiefs ; power of the same kind, and from the same source as that which Jesus speaks of : " These signs shall follow them that believe. In my name they shall cast out devils. They shall speak with new tongues. They shall take up serpents, and if they drink any deadly thing it shall not hurt them ; they shall lay hands on the sick, and they shall recover." (Mark xvi. 17, 18.) Men that in this latter time of the world shall resolve to believe in Christ, and act as if the belief meant something — you shall cast out the devils of fraud, and lust, and cynical selfishness; you shall speak the new language of the law of God; you shall take up the serpents, money and pleasure, and cast them away safely; you shall drink the draught of a money-getting or a legal or a political career, without being poisoned by covetousness, or sophistry, or selfish ambition. And as you buffet your way through the temptations of the world, your firm grasp shall give strength to the morally weak and sick. Your voice shall cheer some fainting brother; your character shall prove to him that a life founded on the belief in God is possible, and when achieved is beautiful. Your work will thus be worship; and the example of your life will be one long pleading on behalf of the Master whom you serve. Do not undervalue the opportunities for meditation and prayer that can be saved from the imperious claims of labour. Especially keep the seventh day free for its proper uses. The Redeemer shrank not from the daily intercourse, the daily conflict, with the men whom by His incarnation He had made His brethren. But in the night upon the solitary mountain He communed with His Father, and brought back strength for the morrow's labour. The same great Christian writer who said, that "to labour was to pray," has given us elsewhere the converse of the proposition, — "He knows how to live aright, who knows how to pray"—*Recte novit vivere, qui novit orare.*" And both are true. But when the worshipper rises from his knees and opens his door and goes out to do his work in the world, his prayers are not concluded. He cannot bring his life into harmony with his prayers, except by living always as in prayer, by walking evermore with God; "fearing him as a judge, reverencing him as a Lord, loving him as a patron, obeying him as a Father.

SERMON III.

CHRIST OUR HIGH PRIEST.

(Preached in Westminster Abbey.)

———✦———

Hebrews ix. 11, 12.

Christ being come an high priest of good things to come, by a greater and more perfect tabernacle, not made with hands, that is to say, not of this building; neither by the blood of goats and calves, but by his own blood he entered in once into the holy place, having obtained eternal redemption for us.

Let us carry back our thoughts to one particular day in the history of the Jewish people. On the tenth day of the Jewish month Tishri, in the autumn of the year preceding the death of our Lord, the people of Jerusalem were gathered together, fasting, at the Temple, to witness the most solemn act of their religion. Caiaphas the high-priest ministering alone, having washed himself, arrayed himself in white linen garments, instead of the splendid vestments of his office, and went up to make atonement for the people's sins. A bullock and two goats were provided as offerings. He slew the bullock and one of the goats, the bullock for his own sins, and the goat for those of the people. Then he entered into the most holy place of the Temple, within which, except on this day, he never might set his foot, first with incense, then a second time with the blood of the bullock and of the goat. And he sprinkled the blood of the victims on the lid of the ark of the covenant, and he sprinkled it also seven times on the floor of the most holy place before the ark. Then he came forth into the court of the Temple and laid his hands upon the remaining goat, in token that he laid upon its head the sins of all the people. It was then led away into the wilderness and released, and the special ceremonial of the day was at an end.

Although this sacrifice was one among many in the Mosaic system, it is in fact the key to them all. It was the most sacred festival known to the law. It was called the Great Day of Atonement. It is known now to Jews as "the great day," and even as "the day," the crowning day of all the sacred year. Only on that one day did the people fast entirely from sunset to sunset. It was, to use the words of the Law, "a sabbath of rest" to them (Lev. xvi. 31); no work could be done upon it. And when we find that the day of all days, for so was it considered, was a day set apart to the work of reconciliation with God, we possess in that fact a key to the whole drift and purpose of the Mosaic dispensation. It was a ministry of reconciliation : it was a system framed for men deeply conscious of sin, and yearning after atonement. And every act in that remarkable ceremonial was directed to express that idea. The preparatory washing by which the priest purified himself; the white linen robe, symbolical of purity and holiness, the offering which the priest made for his own sins, as if to show that no man, not even God's high priest, was free from the universal pollution, that no man could pretend to be pure, and thus set himself up to redeem his brother ; all these proclaimed to the Jewish nation, " None is holy save one, the holy one of Israel ; and from him alone can men be made holy, and after his holiness they should seek earnestly." The bullock that was offered, was the usual sacrifice for the sins of the priest, and the goat was the usual offering for those of the people. But in this sacrifice alone there were two peculiar acts, which gave it a more solemn emphasis ; the one, the high priest's entering into the Most Holy Place, to carry as it were the symbols of the people's penitence nearer to the very presence of the Most High ; and the other, the sending off into the wilderness of the scape-goat, carrying with it the sins from which this act of worship has just delivered the people. Both the chief ideas of every sacrifice are brought out most strongly in this one ; the drawing near to God, and the deliverance from sins thereby effected. A nation rested from all its labour, abstained from food, sent its representative into the Temple to say in its behalf, by acts if not by speech, "All we like sheep have gone astray! Gather back thy scattered flock lest we perish in the wilderness." Of all the acts in the history of ancient people, the Jewish day of atonement must have been the most striking. For two profound religious truths, that God is pure and that man is sinful, are here proclaimed in act and in symbol. They are the two fundamental truths of religion, and the day of atonement was a day devoted to the revival of them. Admire, if you will, the struggles of a nation seeking freedom, follow out in history the steps of a great man building up an empire by arms and wisdom; but the grandest spectacle of all no heathen nation can offer you, the sight of a people prostrate before God their king, earnestly desiring, not conquest, not wealth, but reconcilement with their God, from whom their sins had put them asunder.

But we are considering the day of atonement in one particular year, the year preceding the crucifixion of our Lord. And here we must look at this day of sacrifice, not in the intention of it, but as it was in fact. Caiaphas was the high-priest; we shall hear of him again, as taking an unconscious share in another sacrifice, urging the Jews to put Jesus to death, on the ground that it was expedient that one man should die for the people. Caiaphas had been made high priest by Gratus, the Roman governor, who went before Pilate, and who in a short time had deposed no less than four high priests from their office, as if to show the Jews that their most sacred functionary had become the very puppet of an emperor's underling. Caiaphas, the fifth in succession, would have shared the same fate but that Gratus was recalled, and Pilate took his place; and he preferred other modes of oppression to that of deposing the priests. The very vestments of the high priest were now kept by the Romans, as a kind of hostage for their good behaviour[*]; and delivered out to them seven days before the three great festivals, and before this fast day, to be purified from the pollution of heathen contact, before they could be worn. Close to the temple stood a certain tower; it had been built by a high priest, but now bore a heathen name, given in compliment to a heathen emperor; and in that tower of Antonia the priestly robes were kept, under the custody of a Roman garrison; and some mocking officer gave them out for use, with a smile at the Jewish superstition, and took care to demand them back when the festival was over. That tower that overlooked their sacred Temple contained the arms that would repress the Jews if they attempted to re-vindicate their own national life; and the mocking eyes, which, despising whilst they witnessed the most solemn rites of their religion, checked and damped the ardour of the worshippers. That was not the worst. This day of atonement presupposed on the part of the worshipper a temper of sincere humility; and the religious teach-

---

[*] Josephus, Antiq. xviii. 4, 3.

ing of the Jews had now passed almost wholly into the hands of the Pharisees. What they were we know from the testimony of lips that cannot lie. " All their works they do for to be seen of men. They make broad their phylacteries, and enlarge the borders of their garments. And love the uppermost rooms at feasts, and the chief seats in the synagogues, and greetings in the markets, and to be called of men Rabbi, Rabbi." (Matt. xxiii. 5, 6, 7). To be as the Pharisees were, to appear outwardly righteous unto men, but to be full within of hypocrisy and iniquity, was to be as unfit as possible for bending low on the great day of sacrifice, bowed down with the consciousness of sin, and penetrated with the majesty and the holiness of God. A time-serving high priest, kept in his place only by due subservience to a heathen power, a body of teachers hardened by the worst form of spiritual pride, a strong leaven of unbelief, brought in by the contact and the rule of unbelievers; such were some of the elements of the Jewish community on the last celebration of the day of atonement, in the 29th year of our era, as commonly reckoned. And who can wonder that in all those who shared the worship of that day in true humility and penitence, there arose a strong yearning for some better thing? The life of that high act of worship had departed out of it. At no time could the blood of bulls and of goats have purified the souls of men from sin, inborn and actual. But this day of atonement was part of the covenant which Jehovah made with his chosen people, was one of the conditions on which he would continue their king. But now the lines of the covenant between Him and them were growing daily more obscure, the hedges that once fenced off the chosen people from the rest of the world were broken down. With the death of Herod, nearly thirty years before, the sceptre of Judah had departed, and her crown had been cast down to the ground. Hardly to be called a people, hardly to be suffered to worship, what marks remained to her of the divine protection? But the pious Jew pondered still upon the recollections of the past, and in the prophecies of that past, he found the presage of a better future. When would it come? When would the night pass, and the dawn of the Sun of Righteousness, with healing on his wings, appear? How long, O Lord, how long?

But I have said that this was the last celebration of the day of atonement. How can this be true? Did not the Temple stand for forty years after this, and did not its worship go on? Yes: the thunder-storm did gather over the city for so long before the shattering bolts came out from it to her destruction. And yet it was in a sense the last celebration of the day of atonement. Before another year had come round, the sacrifice of One towards whom all the law and the prophets pointed had been accomplished; One had entered into the holy of holies, who made the work of all other high-priests vain and needless. Lift up your eyes unto the hills of Galilee, you that are going away from the ministrations of the day of atonement with your souls unsatisfied, for from thence cometh your help. There, perhaps upon this very day, a young man, surrounded by a band of twelve chosen friends, is telling them that he must shortly go to Jerusalem, to offer up Himself as a sacrifice for the sins of men. A few days hence, He will be here in Jerusalem, treading the very court of the Temple, celebrating the Feast of Tabernacles like any other of His countrymen. You may see Him and hear Him speak. The great High Priest of his people shall suddenly come to His Temple, and none shall know Him. Caiaphas shall hear of Him; nay, words of prophecy shall be put into his evil lips about Him, yet he shall not see in Him the Priest that supersedes himself. Pilate shall speak to Him yet shall not recognise a King greater than his own Roman master. Yet here, in that young man, is the High Priest of God to offer sacrifice for all the world. Here is one that shall enter not "into the holy places made with hands, which are the figures of the true; but into heaven itself, now to appear in the presence of God for us." (Heb. ix. 24.) It was the last time that the day of atonement was celebrated in deed and in truth. The bullock and the goat were slain year after year, and high priests, the successors of this one that helped to murder the Lord of Life, put on the robes of purity and humiliation, and entered into the holy of holies, and the scape-goat felt the priest's hands upon its head, and was led out into the waste; but all the meaning was gone out of the service. To Jerusalem it had been said, "Your house is left unto you desolate." Jerusalem that killed the prophets, had filled up the measure of her iniquities by killing the sinless Son of God.

For, six months after this, happened another day of atonement, another day that might well be called "the great day," "the day." If you had asked Caiaphas what took place upon it, he would have told you that a certain Galilean teacher had so taken possession of the minds of the common people, that they followed him in multitudes. He would have said that apprehending some civil disturbance, which would have compelled the Romans to interfere, and to draw still closer the very narrow limits of their independence, he had thought it right to advise that the interests of the people should be preferred to the rights of one man, and that this Jesus of Nazareth should be put to death; that they had crucified Him, scattered his followers, condemned His doctrine, and that probably they should hear of Him no more. But how shall *we* regard that day of atonement, my Christian hearers? It is not merely a man that we see, borne down by the weight of the cross, His strength withered with a long night of suffering and insult, tottering out to Golgotha to be put to death after the manner of a convicted slave. It is not merely one act of injustice out of the many which the Jews had perpetrated against godly men that excites our indignation. To think thus is to know Christ after the flesh. The death-day of Jesus was the great day of atonement, prepared from the time of Adam's sin, prefigured from the date of Moses' law, in all the sacrifices, and especially in this high solemnity of the scape-goat. There was the priest, who had laid aside the vestments of his celestial splendour, who stood arrayed in the white linen robes of his own innocence. And the cross is the altar that shall be sprinkled with the victim's blood; and Golgotha is the Temple where the offering shall take place. And he that is the priest shall be the victim too; nay, both victims, for He shall lay down His life like the goat of sin-offering, and shall bear on His head the sins of the people like the scape-goat. And He shall enter into the holy of holies, even into heaven itself, to carry up the blood of the sacrifice into the very presence of the Father; and at the moment when this work of exceeding love is accomplished the veil of the visible Temple is rent in twain, from the top to the bottom, in token that the true holy of holies, even heaven itself, is no longer closed against those that would enter in. It was a token too, that the time of Jewish probation was at an end, that the favouring presence of Jehovah must be looked for no longer in their Temple. From the time when the guilt of that blood fell upon the city, the forty years that remained to it were but so many years of retarded doom. Priests shall sacrifice, but the smoke of the incense, and the steam of blood comes not up to the throne of God. The Temple, of which the decoration had been proceeding for well nigh half a century, and was still going on, stood firm and looked beautiful; but the sentence of Jesus, that by and bye not one stone of it should stand upon another, had shaken its foundations, and each day was but one more counted towards the term of its destruction. Over the unconscious city brooded the irrevocable ruin. He that would have been the King of the Jews, and was called so in mockery by his persecutors, has become the terrible Judge of the Jews, and the King and Priest of the whole earth. In the words of inspiration, "This man, after he had offered one sacrifice for sins for ever, sat down on the right hand of God; from henceforth expecting till His enemies be made His footstool. For by one offering He hath perfected for ever them that are sanctified." (Heb. x.)

My Christian hearers, one of the marks by which the religion of the Jews is distinguished from all false religions is that it confesses its own incompleteness. It offers up sacrifices, and at the same time its prophet says, "To obey is better than sacrifice, and to hearken than the fat of rams." (1 Sam. xv. 22.) It gives forth an external law, hard to obey and full of pains and penalties; and its prophet utters God's promise for the future of a law that should be within the heart, "I will give them an heart to know me, that I am the Lord: and they shall be my people and I will be their God: for they shall return unto me with their whole heart." (Jer. xxiv. 7.) Its worship is carried on by a caste of priests; but the prophet says to all the faithful people, "Ye shall be named the priests of the Lord: men shall call you the ministers of our God." (Is. lxi.) The coming of the Lord Christ to His Temple should not have taken by surprise the ministers of a religion that had been full of this consciousness of its own defects and of longings for the full brightness of the day of which it was but the twilight and the dawn. In the Lord Jesus all that elaborate system is summed up and completed. None of the great truths which the Jewish religion expressed but finds in Him its fulfilment. You cannot say that He is the priest and not the offering, or the offering and not the priest. You cannot say that the sin-offering or the peace-offering alone represents Him. Does not the whole New Testament tell us in every page that He came to set at one God and man — the Creator and the creature whom sin had murdered? It is true that the analogy between the Mosaic offerings and the death of Christ is more exactly drawn out in the Epistle to the Hebrews than in the other books of the New Testament; but every Gospel and Epistle sets forth Jesus as the Mediator between God and man. And the great atoning act has taken place. The day of atonement, *the day*, has come. The priest has slain the offering for sin and has passed within the veil, and for us, the great human congregation, He is making intercession in the most holy place, even at the very steps of the Father's throne. Vital to every one of us is the question — How are we taking our part in this great act of worship, this mystery of restoration? Have we a real faith in the need and the effects of the Redeemer's death? The services of our church are leading us on to a special recollection of His sufferings. Have we the faith to recollect them aright — to stand on the temple-floor of Golgotha, looking in earnest towards the blood-sprinkled altar of the cross, looking upwards towards the inscrutable veil, behind which our High Priest has disappeared? Can we say with all our hearts — God is great and pure! My sins are a sore burden too heavy for me to bear! For when we feel the greatness of the gulf that separates us from God, the sinful from the sinless, then, and then only, can we believe in (just because we need the belief) the great High Priest who has made a bridge over the gulf for us to pass over. Oh, let us beware of turning this great truth of our religion into a lie by holding it in insincerity. Never on this earth was there a more deplorable spectacle than the Jewish day of atonement presented after the death of Jesus had rent the veil of the Temple and doomed the city to ruin. They patched up the rent, and high priests that were servants of an emperor rather than of God, performed the ceremony of the atonement. And Pharisees came there saying, "We are not as other men are;" and Sadducees came that looked for no future life at all; and the people came, who had learnt to reverence their blind guides more than God himself; and the high priest went solemnly into the holy place from which God in his just indignation had departed. And all the service of the day of atonement was vain—was utterly lost; for the hearts of the people were not there and the face of God was averted from it. It was a miserable sight. It was an annual fraud put upon themselves by those misguided souls. But was it more deplorable than when a Christian congregation meets for worship, that is, for the recollection of the mercies of their Redeemer, and many are there who have brought their sins with them and have not the will to forsake them? Look up in true faith, oh Christian people, to your High Priest, clad in white robes, standing before God to make intercession for you. Upon his head all your sins were laid: in Gethsemane he felt their weight and bowed beneath it. Turn your eyes neither to the right nor to the left; there is no other priest, no other Temple, no other victim than He. No human priest or guide can stand in white robes to intercede for you; all are spotted and tainted with sin. Ask not that sorrowful mother, who saw her son suffer without being able to help herself or him, ask her not to take your prayers and carry them to the ears of her son: no such power is hers. She stands by his cross the weakest of the weak, needing help from God as you and I need it; and the High Priest turned from the altar and from his holy work, to commend that helpless woman to a disciple's care. A word of prayer from your lips, if you *mean* the word you speak, will reach the ear of your High Priest as readily as one from those of his virgin-mother. And what He has done for you is complete: if you were to slay sheep and oxen till the rivers ran with blood, that would not touch one sin which He has not already found the medicine for. Let the love of that divine Person, your King, your Prophet, your Priest, your Sin-offering, your God, your most loving Friend, possess you completely. Say out of the depths of your contrite heart,—What shall I render unto my Lord, for all His benefits to me? And your conscience will answer, I will receive the cup of salvation which He offers me. Since He has brought me with so dear a price, I will give myself to Him. Is it supposed that this casting of our burden of sin upon the Lord will cause indifference to sin and a want of earnestness in striving with temptation? The thought of the man Christ Jesus sacrificing Himself for our sins cannot but make us, if it is a real thought, thoroughly hostile to sin and haters of it. The Lord died for me! Was not the disease terrible that needed such a cure, and ought I not to loathe it? Shall I, believing that He did so die, blacken again the soul that He has washed white as wool by plunging into sins anew? Shall I dare to whisper the impure suggestions into the soul of another for whom He died as He did for me? Shall I play the very part of Satan against Him, destroying what He saves, casting down what He builds up? It were better for me that I had not been born. Shall I pass through life as if there were no such things as sin and salvation — as if it were all one long day of buying and selling, eating and drinking, laughter and gossip, when I know the great fight that on Calvary was fought and won, when I know who it is who has passed behind the veil to plead with God for the souls of his people? Never can the sight of the cross make one who looks on it careless about sin. When the conscience feels the comfort of being at peace with God, when he that labours and is heavy laden comes to the Saviour and finds rest, he cannot turn that new-found peace into a license to relapse. He says to himself, God has shown me mercy, has taken me out of the mire, has made His son a sacrifice for my transgressions. How shall I show my thankfulness? I will bring out my darling sins, my cherished vice,—the sinful wish that nestles in my bosom very near my heart — and I will slay it before him. Not for atonement, for He alone has atoned; not to make a merit for myself, for all that I am or can be is His; but in order that I may show my sympathy with His loving work and my belief in its reality, I will slay before Him the dearest and inmost sin of my soul. My impure desire, my indolence, my worldly wishes and feelings, my envy and wrath — all shall go from me, because He has shown me the exceeding sinfulness of it. Having boldness to enter into the Holiest by the blood of Jesus, by a new and living way which He hath consecrated for me, through the veil, that is His flesh, and having Him as my High Priest over the house of God, I will draw near with a true heart in full assurance of faith, having my heart sprinkled from an evil conscience and my body washed with pure water.

SERMON IV.

THE CHARACTER OF PILATE.

MATTHEW xxvii. 24, 25.

When Pilate saw that he could prevail nothing, but that rather a tumult was made, he took water, and washed his hands before the multitude, saying, I am innocent of the blood of this just person: see ye to it. Then answered all the people, and said, His blood be on us, and on our children.

IN that Creed in which Christendom has been accustomed to sum up its faith for about eighteen centuries, two names are mentioned; and, with the exception of Mary, the mother of our Lord, they are the only names admitted of those who have borne the form of man. The one is that of the Son of Man and King of Glory; the other that of one of the most miserable of the human race. The one is the Saviour of the world, and the other the ruler who allowed him to be murdered. The one is Jesus Christ; the other is Pontius Pilate. Nowhere in the world, till the day of judgment shall overtake it, will a Christian congregation recall the fact that Christ suffered without holding up Pilate as the instrument. And of one who represented for eleven years the terrible might of Rome to the prostrate Jewish nation, it may be said that almost nothing is now known, except that he put to death One whom the Jews spoke of as the carpenter's son. In ten thousand congregations this very day, in this country, has the crime been commemorated. There is something strange and awful in this unsought pre-eminence in infamy. There is something awful in the fact that a crime which he sought to disavow, was really perpetrated through him; that it proved to be the greatest wickedness the world had ever seen, although Pilate knew it not; and that this unhappy man, after he had ended his earthly troubles by the death of a suicide, should never be allowed to sink into the dark oblivion that he courted for himself when he ended his spoilt and frustrated life. Down all the ages echo the words of condemnation,—Crucified under Pontius Pilate; crucified under Pontius Pilate.

What account shall we give of this fact? Some will say that chance threw a weak man into a situation where even a strong one might have tripped. Is it not rather that Pilate is set before us as a conspicuous instance of the peril of living without principle—without God in the world? What we call *chance* is but the shadowy side of certainty : all facts are certainties to the Omniscient. When we see the steps that bring them round, we call them effects; when we do not, we try to call them chances. Not one person of all those who stood about the Cross came there by chance. The prison-doors neither closed nor opened upon Barabbas by chance, nor did the high priest speak, nor the soldiers revile, nor the treacherous heart of Judas grow black as the night into which he hastened towards the betrayal; nor did Peter follow and then deny him, nor John stand beneath the Cross with Mary, nor Joseph and Nicodemus bring the spices and prepare the tomb by chance. In our common daily life that we lead now there is no room for chance. Surely there was none *then*, when the sacrifice of the Lamb of God was drawing to its consummation! Pilate reaped as he sowed; it was not chance that made him shrivel like a leaf before the fiery trial, but it was the sinful life of the man — the absence of those qualities which made even some pagans trusted and esteemed. And the inspired account does not give us here a remarkable instance of the power of chance — God forbid! but it sets a mark for ever on one particular form of sin, for a beacon to us and to our children. Wherever there are those who strive neither to be for Christ nor against him, wherever there is a conviction of sin stifled for want of moral courage to avow it, wherever the array of past sins throngs upon us to make the right choice we fain would make impossible, there is Pilate's sin repeated.—Crucified under Pontius Pilate; and crucified afresh under us!

All that we know of Pilate's career, beyond what the Gospels reveal to us, may be recalled in a few words. He was the sixth of the Roman governors of Judæa; the Jews detested him, as cruel, treacherous, and oppressive; he brought the Roman ensigns, with their "graven images" of Cæsar, into Jerusalem, and when the Jews remonstrated at this breach of their law, he tried to coerce them into submission. He made an aqueduct with the sacred money of the Temple; and when the Jews again rose in indignation, his soldiers, mingling with the multitude with hidden daggers, slew many of them. A similar act of cruelty towards the Samaritans caused his recall. He was disgraced and banished; and then, brooding over his misfortunes, he became his own executioner. This rough sketch may seem at first to resemble but little the delineation put before us in the Gospels. There is a man fierce, cruel, intractable; here, one full of weakness and perplexity. There he plays the part of the oppressor; here he trembles and obeys. The Jews were not allowed to exercise the power of life and death; they found Christ guilty by their law, and brought him to Pilate that their verdict might be followed by a sentence of death. Thus Pilate stood to the Jews in the position of a court of appeal; if the sentence of death which they demanded was unjust, it was his most obvious duty to refuse to confirm it. Yet how he tries to abdicate the powers of a judge, and to throw the responsibility upon them! When the multitude had chosen Barabbas to be released unto them instead of Jesus, Pilate asked, " What shall I do then with Jesus, which is called Christ ? They all said unto him, Let him be crucified. And the Governor said, Why, what evil hath he done ? But they cried out the more, saying, Let him be crucified." He found no fault in him ; yet, instead of speaking as a judge, " I have examined him ; I find no fault in him ; and I am here to protect such persons, nay, and to protect you, from dipping your hands in the blood of the innocent," he made them, heated to madness as they were by their anger against Christ, the judges in his stead. "What evil hath he done ?" And this appears in another place,— when Pilate, still willing to release Christ, went forth to the multitude, and said unto them : " Behold I bring him forth to you, that ye may know that I find no fault in him. Then came Jesus forth, wearing the crown of thorns and the purple robe. And Pilate said unto them, Behold the man!" Still there was the same fear of offending them, the same dread of saying too much! He wished the sight of Jesus to plead with them instead of his words. The suffering Saviour, His body bent and crushed with anguish, after the agony in the garden had withered His frame as with old age, wearing the crown which the soldiers had put on in mockery, was a sight to move their pity more than their anger. Behold the man! Is this poor, persecuted, crushed creature one whom you need fear ? Will he make himself by force a king? Judge for yourselves whether there is any danger here! But why did he fear to speak thus? Why did he leave it to them to conceive the pity which he might have powerfully suggested? The multitude were not always so hostile to Jesus: if they were now shouting, "Crucify Him," they had lately cried, "Blessed is he that cometh in the name of the Lord." A few words, let them only be bold and just, may turn that tide of fury back again. He is neither brave nor just. The occasion is lost. He washes his hands, as a sign that he has nothing to do with the death of the Lord, and then delivers him up to their will. He washed his hands, indeed; but could he clear them of their guilt? He has perverted justice; he has deserted the cause of the opprest. Not all the rains of heaven would cleanse those hands; the blood of the Lord of Life is upon them. It is the only occasion of his bad life in which we read that he showed pity; but just because he felt the first motions of faith in the Redeemer was his guilt the greater.

But there is in truth nothing in the Gospel account which is repugnant to the representation of Philo and Josephus. A man of the world without principles is described in both. Nowhere can we fasten on Pilate one single conviction, whether moral or religious. When he came in contact with firm belief in others he was utterly perplexed. When the Jews had remonstrated against bringing the effigies of Cæsar into the city, he threatened them with instant death; but the Jewish historian tells us that they bared their throats to the sword, saying "Death is better than that our laws should be broken." And the weak spirit was overcome by a courage so unintelligible;—how could men be willing to die upon a question of images?—and he laid his cruel threats aside, not without admiration, and carried back the obnoxious ensigns to Cæsarea.* His one principle of action was that he should shine as Cæsar's satellite, and that the Jews should look upon his borrowed light with trembling reverence. To do his work as his imperial master would have it done was his ruling desire. And it is not clear that he was unsuccessful in this. For ten years he managed to govern the most stubborn people of all the tributaries of the empire for a master hard to please. His picture is drawn by Josephus in the most unfavourable colours, because he had given a severe shock to Jewish feelings. Yet perhaps from the Roman point of view he had merits as a governor. Where he saw his way clearly he was firm. His cruelty and harshness appeared, perhaps, the best means of restraining a most turbulent race; and so were adopted deliberately. Pilate was a man then devoted to his own profession, doing his best to satisfy the master whom he served, and hoping to be rewarded in time with a higher command. But the Jews knew well the weak point in his position, and the power which it gave them

---

* Josephus, Antiq. xviii. 3, 1.

over him. When they saw that he sought by every means to set Christ at liberty they began to work upon his fears; "If thou let this man go thou art not Cæsar's friend; whosoever maketh himself a king speaketh against Cæsar." He must not appear before the emperor to defend himself against a charge of favouring a rebel: his footing was too insecure; he must submit to anything rather than that. And so he delivered Jesus to their will. The sin, however, did not receive its reward. Not many years after he *was* complained of, was ruined by it; and, with the sudden crumbling down of that professional reputation which he had taken such pains to establish, for which he had been cruel and weak by turns, his heart turned to stone within him; all that he lived for was gone, that light of favour, which was his only light, was withdrawn; and the wretched man, groping in the darkness of his despair, found no way for himself but that of self-destruction.

Is there no word of warning for us in all this sad account? We have heard this morning * the history of that great act which was in Christ an all-sufficient sacrifice, to the Jews a terrible crime, to the world a great salvation. And that is the subject which more or less will occupy our minds during the present week. I will suppose that no one has turned his eyes again upon his suffering Lord without being somewhat moved in heart. The betrayal, the false

---

* Sixth Sunday in Lent.

accusations, the buffetings, the desertion of his followers, the denial of Peter, the dragging from tribunal to tribunal, the preference of Barabbas, the crown of thorns, the bitter death of the cross—these are facts which, unless our hearts are insensible indeed, must touch them deeply. For He was wounded for our transgressions, He was bruised for our iniquities, the chastisement of our peace was upon Him, and with His stripes we are healed. I will suppose that we never stand in thought beside the Cross without some measure of love and thankfulness towards One who has so loved us. Is it not just to warn us to measure the depth of such feelings, and to show us how terrible it is to believe in Christ *only a little*, that Pilate is suffered to stand so prominent on the final scene? Instead of thinking this Roman governor a monster without parallel, I am persuaded that characters of that type are the commonest that can be found. The man who, much occupied in his own worldly engagements, becomes convinced, by some means of God's sending, that Christ is truly the Son of God and our Redeemer, yet has not the moral courage to take that truth home to his heart and let it fashion all his life without regard to what others may say of him,— is that a character hard to discover? To say "I find no fault in him;" to wash the hands from participation in His blood; to set up over Him "The King of the Jews," and refuse to take it down; such was the Christianity of Pilate; and I fear that many men go no farther. It will not be out of place then to speak of the worth of *moral courage*, of that quality which enables a man to hold fast, and avow, and follow up a conviction when he has found it. Look again then at the two persons who are now before us, if you would understand the dignity of moral courage. Look at the Governor and the Prisoner. Pilate sat upon his seat of judgment, with his guards around him, the delegate of the mightiest of the kings of this world. Life and death were in his words; for it seems that he wielded more power than was usually entrusted to a Roman procurator. He could say to one Go, and to another Come, and to another Do this, and he would be most strictly obeyed. But was there any real strength under all this show of strength? No; look again. His belief in the innocence of Jesus draws him one way; his fear of the Jews another. He serves a capricious tyrant; if the Jews accuse him, all his power may vanish like a dream when one awaketh. So that he is not free to act. Anxious and uncertain, he goes from Jesus to the Jews, from them back to Jesus, not knowing himself what he will do at last. There is no strength in him.

Look, on the other hand, to Jesus of Nazareth. He had nothing to lose but his life, not even his garments; for the soldiers had already set their minds upon them. No signs of power were about Him. "Behold the man!" He had a crown and a robe indeed, but they were given Him in cruel sport. Wounds and stripes were His only attendants.

His lovers and His friends stood aloof, and His kinsmen afar off. And the suffering was permitted to reach even to His soul. He began to feel that strange hiding of his own divine power from himself for a time which made Him cry at last, " Why hast Thou forsaken Me?" Yet in all His loneliness, His sorrow unspeakable, there was a great strength. He was not tost to and fro between two opinions. He was not truckling to the Jews for fear. Fear had scattered His disciples, but He was dauntless. He was finishing the work which had been appointed Him ever since the sin of the first man. The Cross indeed was bitter, but He went his way towards it without regard to mockery, anger, or persuasion.

And Pilate, as we have seen, did the sin without even receiving the poor wages he had promised himself. The worst that could have happened to him, if he had obeyed his better impulse and set the Redeemer free, overtook him as it was. Recall, and banishment, and death were his recompense. And Christ, who made Himself humble, is now exalted. He was poor and in misery, and is now the Lord of the whole earth. The sepulchre that received Him could not hold Him long; He broke the gates of brass, and cut the bars of iron in sunder. Weak as He seemed, how many thousands now put their trust in Him as their only strength! On His Cross, the very place of His lowest humiliation, how many look with wonder and love as the key of their salvation!

And this contrast is a fair test of the difference between the worth of moral courage and of cowardice. Everywhere the want of earnest belief is felt to be a weakness, and the strong conviction prevails, and wins over by its own strength, without argument.

You have begun to feel, my Christian friends. Dare to be convinced. Fear not, lest you should be led too far. You are touched with the love of Jesus. He has in some way knocked at the door of your heart, be it by such inspired words as have been read to us to-day, by the loss of some friend, by a long sickness, by gratitude for some special prosperity. Be not content to let such a feeling die out without profit, without becoming a better man by means of it, and leading a renewed life. The customary visit to the usual pew, the customary subscription, the old routine of brief and hasty prayers, these cannot satisfy a heart consecrated to a new life, a better way, a heavenly hope. Christ tries you not by the measure of other men; He proposes to you the example of His own life; He offers us for our imitation His perfect and uniform devotion to His Father's work. If from the fear of being singular we dare not follow Him whom we know to have the right to lead us, then Pilate's sin is repeating itself in us. Many a man is turned from the right by some individual tempter; but there is one powerful tempter, whose efforts are less thought of, and that is society itself — that lukewarm, languid, supercilious, hard, indifferent looker-on, whom so few dare to offend, even by too much devotion and activity. And one great reason for turning daily to that great Example, beside whose Cross we have been to-day, is that our standard of duty may be high in spite of the temptations to bring it down to the social average. Those rules of life, mean and scanty, by which men act are dinned into our ears from sunrise to sunset; the higher and nobler views of life, which perhaps we formed on our knees in the morning, are pared down and blotted out by a thousand strokes, small yet effectual, inflicted during the day. Let us, then, search the Scriptures. Let the ideal of that noblest life, that most loving death, be printed deeply in our memory. Will not this alone rebuke our petty aims, our affection for things below? Shall we not see from this, if God's Holy Spirit gives us grace to see, that a life of self-sacrifice is beautiful, and a life of self-interest base? Shall we not grow to think little of the precepts of the world, when we are learning at the feet of the world's Redeemer?

Thus much as to our aspirations after good. If we trace the history of any one of those who has fallen into open, flagrant sin, it will be found, nay, it is proverbially confessed, that the want of moral courage, of power to resist, is the chief ingredient in the sinner's ruin. It was that which added to Pilate's career its worst sin; for the sin by which he has become infamous was the one with which his own choice had the least to do. It was that which betrayed even Peter into backsliding. It is that which to this day the vicious, the fraudulent, and the dissolute plead as their poor excuse. Terrible position for an immortal soul, for one that must one day stand before the judgment seat, that his safety from some enormous sin depends upon what we call the chance of his meeting temptation! A man rises in the morning, not knowing whether good or evil shall befall him, he meets the tempter, who offers him some scheme of impurity or wickedness which they are to join to commit, and he comes back at night with the chain of hell riveted round his neck. There may be in a congregation many of these children of chance, who, if the temptation is well-chosen and the moment opportune, are sure to fall. Are we in that position of extreme peril? How careful, then, should we be to avoid the occasions of sin, and the evil companions that know our weakness, and the pursuits which would take us too near our danger. Hopeless, indeed, would these reflections be, if we did not know that God has promised strength to them that ask it. Weak man or woman, trembling on the verge of sin, afraid of the precipice, yet afraid to flee from it, it is as sure as that God's word is true that you may draw back from the ground that is crumbling under your feet. Pray to the God of heaven and earth, who breathed into you the breath of life, who sustains and loves you even now, that He will infuse into you the spirit of a new courage, that He will purge out from you the miserable fear of man's opinion, that gives some harder associate such a terrible power over you. You may yet learn to say with a good courage what the Psalmist has said (Ps. xxvii.), " The Lord is my light and my salvation; whom shall I fear? the Lord is the strength of my life; of whom shall I be afraid? When the wicked, even mine enemies and my foes, came upon me to eat up my flesh, they stumbled and fell. . . . Wait on the Lord: be of good courage, and he shall strengthen thine heart: wait, I say, on the Lord."

SERMON V.

IMMORTALITY.

Psalm xvi. 8, 9, 10.

I have set the Lord always before me: because He is at my right hand, I shall not be moved.
Therefore my heart is glad, and my glory rejoiceth: my flesh also shall rest in hope.
For Thou wilt not leave my soul in hell; neither wilt Thou suffer Thine Holy One to see corruption.

Although this passage refers unquestionably, on the authority of St. Peter and St. Paul, to the resurrection of Christ Himself, it applies also, through Him, to every member of Christ's body; for He was raised to be the firstfruits of them that slept. We take part in His security and His rejoicing: the death which He overcame we vanquish; from the corruption that could not hold Him shall we be delivered. We may appropriate the words to ourselves, though in a lower degree: we may say in them that we have an assured hope of immortality founded upon our trust in God.

And most of us assume that this hope is active within us, without taking account of the strong temptations, practical and speculative, which often concur to assail it; and never, perhaps, more actively than at this time. There is indeed a temptation which is knit up with our practical virtues. For almost all the discoveries and institutions of which we are accustomed to make our boast as a nation have been the fruit of a strong and exclusive devotion on the part of those who have effected them. The concentration of the powers of different men upon the objects which they have severally proposed to themselves as the end and aim of life, has enriched our libraries with treasures of thought, and our homes with a thousand conveniences and ornaments, and our political system with wise institutions, such as a careless dreaming people, murmuring in their sleep that all was vanity, could never have attained. But do we not feel, one and all of us, that the intensity of our interest in the present is dangerous to that higher interest which we profess when we say that we believe in "the Resurrection of the Body and the Life Everlasting?" Do we not feel that it tends to increase upon us; that the visible begins to occupy us more and more, and to expel the distant and the unseen from our thoughts? Do we not learn to praise, as something practical and positive, the habit of living in and for the present, and to shrink from other and deeper thoughts as visionary and unsubstantial? At first we throw ourselves into the stream of earthly endeavour without distrust, believing that we can swim at pleasure to the firm shore, and there rest on hopes that are surer than those of this world. But we are carried on against our will. The duties of a profession, the charge of a family, the growing love for our own line of activity, possess us more and more. The days seem too short and too few for our engagements: if we could have a wish it would be that the sun and moon might stand still, as over the fight in Ajalon, that we might prolong the day sufficiently for the enlarging sphere of our occupations. And so it comes to pass that the life everlasting is from many minds, and those not the worst or most depraved, entirely excluded as a subject for earnest thought and belief.

If, indeed, the evidence for the soul's immortality were of the same kind as that for our earthly existence; if a future state were as certain and plain as sleeping and waking, buying and selling, hunger and thirst; then the paramount claims of an awful eternity would cause the brightest prospects and highest interests of this mortal life to shrink into a small compass. But it is not so. God has been pleased to withdraw eternity a little away from us, to make the soul's separate existence capable at least of some question, where men have a mind to doubt. And whilst the visible world has a kind of truth and certainty about it, for we can touch and handle it, and make impressions upon its parts, and feel it reacting on us in pleasure and pain, when we turn to the life invisible there is much darkness and shadow, which revelation has not wholly lighted up, which bare reason cannot enlighten at all. That human soul which manifests itself in a feeble consciousness, that ebbs and flows with our bodily states, that is suspended in sleep, disturbed in illness, utterly subverted in insanity, that at last *seems* to fail because a sluggish material heart sends a supply of blood somewhat too scanty to a material brain, can it indeed live for ever? Flickering as it is, will it outlast the sun and stars and shine for evermore? Seated deep in this wonderful human frame, will it disentangle itself from that in its dissolution, and, like a winged dove, flee away to some other place of rest? These are questions which cannot be asked without awe and wonder. And when we begin to raise them, the speculative temptations of which I spoke endeavour to influence the reply. We are not all aware, perhaps, how actively and how generally materialistic views of the human mind are now being put forward in this and other countries. Some physiologists would have us regard the mind only as a function of the body: they indicate the organ with which it is more especially connected; they dwell upon the facts which seem to show that mental power fluctuates with the bodily states; they prove that bodily organs not directly the seat of thought sympathise with the brain, and by their disorders disturb its functions; they lead us, if they can, to the conclusion that thought is but a secretion of the brain (I quote words actually employed), and that consequently when the body perishes, or the brain fails and decays, thought will cease for ever. Now there is no reason to fear that this revolting conclusion will ever become part of the general belief. Even in times when the doctrine of immortality rested upon far weaker grounds than it does now, men escaped by means of an evidence within themselves from accepting the doom of annihilation. But that it has disturbed the faith of some, I am well assured. Let it be said at once, then, that however specious this kind of reasoning may be in its appeal to obvious facts, it rests upon a great fallacy, that of assuming that a thing necessarily has its origin where it is first made manifest. By this line of proof it might be shown that light is created in the moon, just because light is manifestly present there, and although it came from the sun we did not see it on the passage. Or it might be proved that magnetism is created in the bar of iron where it shows its effects, although the whole world certainly, and probably the whole solar system, is concerned in the production of that force which is made sensible to us by the little magnet we hold in our hands. All that such facts really prove is that the brain is the organ of thought, the appropriate instrument by which, in its present state, the soul forms relations with the world around it. And in order to prove that thought is not only manifested but created in the brain, we should require at least some evidence of the fitness of matter to produce or become mind, against which the presumption is at the outset overwhelmingly strong. The bodily organs have the power to secrete, that is, to separate, certain substances from the body; but the very word implies that in some shape these substances were ascertainably present before the separation took place; there has been an alteration by means of the organ, but not a creation. And who can pretend to say in what shape the poetic image, or the yearnings of maternal love, or the patriot's fiery resolution, existed in the human frame before the brain separated and produced them? No two things are more opposed and contrasted than mind and matter: no two things are more different in all the laws and conditions that affect them; and therefore that one can pass into the other ought to be the very last proposition that should be assumed without proof.

But the mind, rejecting the material theory of its own nature, finds another difficulty in an opposite direction. True; mind and matter are diametrically opposed, and though it has pleased the Creator to link them together, and to give to matter a certain power to modify the manifestations of mind, and to mind a certain influence over matter, the one can never become the other, neither can the one be so bound up in the other as to be subject to its laws of growth, change, and decay. It would follow, then, that whilst my frame is created from the dust of the ground, my soul must be a spark from the divine mind Himself. He planted in me this image of Himself; He made it possible for me to do what the lower creatures cannot do, to look upon Him and know Him. And so my soul cannot perish, because He of whose nature it is a part is eternal and unchangeable. But how it shall exist, is a harder question. It is easy to assure myself that it does not perish; that when the material part of us mixes with the dust or floats in exhalations through the air, the spiritual part will return to its own place. But will it preserve its personal unity? Will that which is implied in the word *I*, with all its hopes and aspirations, its affections, its remorse, its growth in goodness, possess its personality still? Will it be as the separate water-drop, or will it be mingled indistinguishably in the ocean of an infinite Mind from whence it was taken? For the whole moral importance of the doctrine of immortality turns upon this, How shall God be indeed a rewarder of them that diligently seek Him, if the separate personal existence of His servants is obliterated in the grave? This was the point which Plato's beautiful speculations on immortality missed. It is what Aristotle, in contending only for the immortality of the universal reason, formally abandoned. This is what the Christian must not part with, for it is the whole secret of his life, that seeking God heartily in this life, he, the same person still, shall find Him in another; and that he shall stand before the throne of his Lord at the last day, to give account of all things done in the body, feeling conscious that they are all *his* acts still, because he is still a separate person, brought nearer to God now than when he walked upon the earth; and the new life just beginning is a continuation of the earthly life that ended with the grave.

How, then, are we to keep fast the precious hope of everlasting life? How are we to be sure that the soul will continue to exist, and that it will preserve its personality, and that its life will be consciously felt to be the continuation and the sequel of this present earthly state?

Now, besides that which appears to be at once the true argument and the simplest, many others have been proposed. It could not well be otherwise. Any one that thinks at all, has sought at some time or other to ascertain the grounds of his hope of a future life. Whether we are born to play for a few hours upon the stream, and then to perish in the first shower, or are the heirs of a heritage which shall suffer no loss, even in the dissolution of worlds, when the elements shall melt with fervent heat: here is an alternative in which the interests of all are bound up. What wonder, then, if men have striven by different methods to prove to themselves and others that the hope that is in them of a future life is not groundless? Thus one has maintained that the soul is a distinct element, having nothing in common with matter, and therefore independent of its conditions; that as an element it is a simple substance, incapable of being resolved into other substances, and therefore incapable of destruction. According to this view, just as we believe that even after the great change of death, the material elements somewhere remain, neither increased nor diminished, even by the weight of a hair, so the spiritual element returns to its proper region without the smallest loss. To the objection, that if the material elements do not perish, they undergo great changes, and pass into new combinations and forms of being, it is answered, that the soul cannot be capable of such changes, but must continue to exist in and by itself, since there is nothing else of the same kind with which it could combine, or into which it could be transmuted. There are undoubtedly minds to which arguments like these carry conviction: but in calling the soul an element or simple substance, what should have been proved is rather assumed; and the denial of the materialist, who regards the mind as the compound result of several bodily processes and conditions, would bar this argument as against that form of unbelief.

Another argument, far more persuasive and practical, maintains that the powers and virtues of men, often frustrated, never quite perfected in this life, are of themselves a sign that there is a future life in which they will be matured, since God will create nothing in vain. And if this be taken, not so much for a proof as for a consoling reflection, nothing can be more important towards understanding the dealings of God with man. We are in a world full of surprises: what we call *casualties*, of war or of peace, are daily cutting short the lives of some of us. The uncertainty of life is a theme which poets think they have worn out, which even the preacher handles sparingly. A great battle is fought; a ship perishes at sea; a hundred or a thousand lives are brought to a close. Yes; but those thousand men that yesterday were in the world, but now are not, were a thousand scholars in the school of the Almighty. Parents had watched them; teachers had stored them with precepts of duty; families looked on them as their strength and support; their minds were full of plans that wanted years for their fulfilment, of knowledge that had taken years to grow, and of which the harvest was scarcely begun. Is it easier to suppose that a little water oozing through a plank, or a little powder kindled in a tube, has brought utterly to nothing the power, and knowledge, and growing experience of the man that dies, or that hereafter in some way they will be carried on to completeness and turned to account? A general instinct decides for the latter.

But there is a ground more secure, on which we may rest our hopes of immortality; and it is to be found in our knowledge of God and of his moral law.

The man that has begun to obey God feels that he shall not die but live. Whoever foregoes his ease for his duty, whoever prays, or suffers for truth, or labours to make truth and justice more known and observed among men, has set to his seal that God is true, and that there is a life hereafter, to which he stands in relation, of which he forms a part. If it were not so — if we could suppose that St. Paul, for example, the brave soldier, the unwearied messenger of Christ, in whom the things hoped for were a real substance, and the things not seen were evidently proved, was deluded in his hopes of a future rest and a crown of glory, and that all that remained of him after death would be to be sought for in the shifting wind and the senseless dust and the rains of heaven, — then all trust in God would vanish, and the life of man would be a juggling game, in which the best play for something that is not, and the worst cheat them by snatching the real stakes whilst their eyes are turned away; for all who shape their lives with a view to a higher life are deluded; and the ignoble crew who say, "Let us eat and drink, for tomorrow we die," have seized the true philosophy of life. You will say that virtue is its own present reward; and that is true. But the reward is one strictly connected with a continuance of being, and with the hope of the fruition of God in the state that shall be. Strip the good man of that future, and you utterly confound the present. Tell the first martyr that his vision of the heaven opened, and of the ineffable glory within, is the creation of a brain over-wrought, which a few moments will dissipate; tell Paul and Silas, when in the Philippian gaol they pray and sing praises to God, that it depends on their judges to terminate at pleasure all their communion with God for ever; and you confound all the powers of the soul at once. What seemed their truth is become a lie; what seemed their strength is their weakness, against which the basest accidents may prevail; what seemed their hope is darkness: to Him that seemed the object of their love they shall never approach.

If there should be any one who hears me to whom have been suggested doubts as to the future life, I would commend to him this truth, that the more we live for that life the more strong will be our conviction of its reality, and the more content we shall be to expect it, even though we cannot bring down its mysteries to the present measure of our understanding, or represent to our minds fully the features of that unknown country. And this will explain a paradox that must already have struck some minds. One might expect that if doubts can be raised about the immortality of the soul, they would be most besetting where signs of the decay of nature were most evident. One would think that when the last stage of life was come, and, hovering between life and death, the soul seemed sometimes to exist, and sometimes to have perished, and the clear speech of reason was turned into muttering or raving, all these shocking signs would bring to a crisis the doubts of the bystanders, if any such existed, and that prayer would not be offered for one who seemed to have reached the very end; whose personal existence seemed to be dissolving visibly in the decay of the bodily powers. And yet it is not so. Never are the prayers of men more fervent than when their own life, or that of one they love, is trembling in the doubtful scales. Never is the glance into a life beyond the grave more clear and earnest, than when death and the grave seem most likely to prevail. It is not by the dying bed that the sceptic would think of saying, "The lamp is going out — the oil is exhausted — there is no more hope here, for death is the end of all." No: doubts are strongest when the sense of life is strongest too ; when the will forms resolutions as though no death could subdue it, and the activity of our thought and persistence of our memory are promises of the long continuance of existence. But in the one case God is greatly needed, and so his love and justice are seen, because men look for them with sorrow and yearning, and it is felt that He will not leave the soul in hell, nor suffer any of the least of His holy ones to see corruption. In the other, men rely on their own strength, and try to stand alone, as gods, knowing good and evil : and then the promises of God and his attributes, which are the surest evidence for our immortality, are hid from their sight.

Do not then let us complain that the sense of eternal life is weak within us because of deficient evidence. The life of the soul was meant to be its own evidence. But we are created for a present life and for a future : if we have thought only of the former, and steeped our souls in it, and glutted our thoughts with gain or praise or sensual pleasure, what wonder if our vision of the latter grows dim? To live as if there were a world hereafter, this is not to prejudice our reason, nor to put fetters upon our convictions; it is to restore the due balance between the seen and the unseen, to counterpoise the scale in which this present life is weighed, wherein we have thrown, perhaps, the whole weight of our thoughts and wishes. And here the excellence of the Gospel of Christ appears. Christianity is not the first to teach the doctrine of immortality; but the precepts of our Lord are the best and only practical teaching for one who would live as an immortal being. I remember to have read how some of those who perished in the French Revolution, in which they had themselves acted a part, passed their last night upon earth in striving to resuscitate their hopes of immortality, of which the false philosophy current at that time had cheated them, by going over such arguments as those in the Phædo of Plato: and the tumbril of the executioner arrived whilst the problem was yet unsolved. Few spectacles are more sad than this. The hope that they could afford to trifle with in life, they felt after in the hour of death. But a month of Christian obedience to their divine Father would have taught them more of the nature of their own souls than all the reasoning that pagan teachers ever wove together. If we seize Christ's promises and live in them, the belief in immortality will become a part of us; and in the hour of death we shall not be suffered to fall into doubts about that to which we have an inward witness in ourselves. Let us then pray to God to infuse into our life an earnest purpose. Let us live for something beyond what the present life, its wants, and its duties require. Let us exclude from it all that is plainly contrary to the hopes of a Christian. Luxury and waste will fill us with the pride of this life. Lust will fear to think upon a future judgment, wherein it must be condemned. Too great anxiety about our present pursuits will leave us no room for better thoughts. The constant habit of private prayer, the use of the holy communion, which is a seal and pledge of our resurrection to everlasting life, and the thoughtful study of God's holy word, will keep alive the relation between us and our Father, through Him who has overcome death. Then through all fears and under all the fluctuations of life, something sure will be found on which the feet may rest. Shall I doubt of the immortality and eternal personality of my own soul? the good man may say. The mind may sometimes, indeed, be crossed by a difficulty about it, and I may have no final complete answer to the objector who doubts it. But God has spoken already to my heart, and I believe that He *is*, and that He will not cast me out. He will not hold up before me false lights and false convictions to mislead. My faith in Him has enabled me to understand this life and its purposes, but not except in connection with another. "I will bless then the Lord, who hath given me counsel; my reins also instruct me in the night season. I have set the Lord always before me : because he is at my right hand, I shall not be moved. Therefore my heart is glad, and my glory rejoiceth: my flesh also shall rest in hope. For thou wilt not leave my soul in hell: neither wilt thou suffer thine Holy One to see corruption. Thou wilt shew me the path of life: in thy presence is fulness of joy; at thy right hand there are pleasures for evermore."

SERMON VI.

THE POWER OF THE ATONEMENT.

(Preached on Good Friday.)

———✦———

John xix. 30.

When Jesus therefore had received the vinegar, He said, It is finished: and He bowed His head, and gave up the ghost.

The services of this week have prepared us to stand, as we do to-day, at the cross of the Redeemer who died for us. And these are His dying words, — "It is finished." They are not words of surprise at an unforeseen calamity; they are not the exclamation of an unthinking agony. Something that was to be done before that priceless life could be laid down is finished; and He sees that it is so, and bows His head and gives up the ghost. And thus the last act of His life is bound up with all that went before. When He was twelve years old, He said, "Wist ye not that I must be about My Father's business?" At the beginning of His ministry He said that He was come to fulfil the law and the prophets; He told

Nicodemus that He must be lifted up, even as Moses lifted up the brazen serpent in the wilderness, "that whosoever believeth in Him should not perish, but have everlasting life." As His ministry drew towards its cruel termination, He warned the disciples more than once of what should follow. On the night of His betrayal, in that self-consecrating prayer in which He as priest offered Himself to God as victim, He said, "I have glorified Thee on the earth; I have finished the work that Thou gavest Me to do."[*] Through his life, from first to last, runs the thread of one steady purpose. To live and die for men was the lot which He had chosen when He sat upon the right hand of the Father. He did live for them; He did die for them. He bore their griefs, felt their sins, suffered for their sakes insult, and stripes, and death. There were written upon His heart, so to speak, the words, "I must work the work of Him that sent Me while it is day: the night cometh when no man can work." But when the night of death came He was able to say, "It is finished."

My Christian brethren, the one subject of this day, on which a preacher cannot choose but speak, is the sufferings of Christ for men. And I propose to speak first of the nature and power of those sufferings, and then of their influence upon our own life and conduct.

Now it is essential that in our minds the sufferings of the Lord Jesus should stand quite apart, distinct

[*] John xvii. 4.

from all other cases recorded in history, where good intentions, and pure conduct, and fervent love for mankind, have been punished with obloquy and death. Whereas the death of the martyred sage or self-doomed hero changes for good a small surrounding circle of beholders, whose moral nature is touched and elevated by the spectacle, and there the influence stops, in the sufferings of our Lord every child of man, whether standing close to the foot of the cross or as far off from it as the world's orb will give him space, whether living in those last days of Jewish probation and first of human deliverance, or not yet for a thousand years to be born into the world, possesses a real interest, which cannot be abdicated by shutting the eyes or stopping the ears, which may be claimed and used or thanklessly ignored, but which in either case is the most important possession that a man can call his own. It is indeed no common sorrow that the evangelists mean to describe to us. In the words of Jeremiah, applied by Jewish and Christian writers to the Messiah, "Is it nothing to you, all ye that pass by? Behold, and see if there be any sorrow like unto my sorrow, which is done unto Me, wherewith the Lord hath afflicted Me in the day of his fierce anger." He, the man of sorrows, drank of a cup whose bitterness we can never know. He was beaten, pierced with thorns, and nails, and a spear; His body was made a mark for all scorn and insult. But this was not His sorrow. These were nothing to the grief of His soul. "A wounded spirit who can bear?" Who knows what was the strength of that deadly sorrow and agony, whose outward token was the bloody sweat in the garden of Gethsemane? The whole weight of human transgressions, a mountain reaching up to heaven, was laid upon His spirit to crush it. And where were the comforts that men turn to in their heavier trials? There were none for Him. Did He turn to His own countrymen, those whose sick He had healed, and whose dead He had restored to life? They cried aloud for His death, with curses on themselves and on their children. Did He look around for His disciples? They forsook Him and fled. Did He lift up His thoughts to heaven to gather strength to wrestle with His agony? There was even thence no consolation. His union with the Father was not dissolved indeed; but the vision and influence of it were taken away. There never was any sorrow like that which made Him cry, "My God, my God, why hast Thou forsaken Me?"

Is this sorrow nothing to us? But for our sins our Lord would never have suffered. Every sinner threw in the weight of his own transgressions, by itself enough to destroy him, to make up the enormous aggregate of the griefs which the Saviour bore. And let us remember that to Him sin was not an invisible evil, lurking under smooth words and plausible actions. He "knew what was in man;" knew how great the diseases were that needed the physician's aid. He saw all the world as it was; He measured the guilt, past, present, and to come, which His blood must cleanse away. The Pharisees might make broad their phylacteries, make clean the outside of the cup and platter, fast and give alms to be seen of men, and these arts might deceive men. But Christ saw the inward uncleanness, that they were like whited sepulchres, which indeed appear beautiful outwardly, but are within full of dead men's bones and all uncleanness. In every man that lived, no matter what his endowments, what the love and admiration that pursued him, there was this inward corruption and ugliness of sin ; and the eye of the Saviour saw it. Even in the infant, that seemed so pure and clung so lovingly round its mother's neck, there was a seed of evil from which the rank flower and poisonous fruits of sin would unfold themselves with years. Think what it was for Christ, who so loved the world as to give His life for it, yet who was too pure even to look upon iniquity — think what a sorrow it was to see all men as painted sepulchres, beautiful without, full of uncleanness within. Then, again, He did not bear our sins as we bear them. With us, the hardened conscience feels not their weight ; the inward eye closes to them of its own accord. The burden we bear about within us is unfelt because it is constant, even like the pressure of the atmosphere on our material bodies. We are full of disguises ; we call evil good, and cheat ourselves into a false estimate of our real condition. But Christ could not so lighten His sorrow. He bare all sins, and knew how grievous every single sin was to bear. He perceived that the wages of sin is death; and so bore the weight of ten thousand thousand deaths, even of the whole punishments of the world, in His single person. The sorrows that we feel, then, for our sins, He endured; nay, even the greater sorrows we ought to feel, if we knew the enormity of our own offences.

Now this is no overwrought picture of our Redeemer's sorrow; it is by no mere metaphor that we say that He bore our sins. For how, I ask, can you understand that awful scene under the olives of the garden of Gethsemane, that night when the cup of suffering in the hand of our Lord was filled up for Him to drink, upon any theory of ordinary grief and fear, except indeed by making the Master weaker than His disciples? If we are to regard our Lord only as exhibiting in that darkest hour of His life a pattern of absolute resignation to the will of God, we are constrained to ask how it comes that He must struggle so terribly with fear and agony, when Stephen and many another martyr have met their fate full of high courage. If we regard Him only as a teacher about to be put to death by those who hate His doctrine, we seem to see one afraid to die for what he knows to be the truth, although the records of the Church shew many who have died with songs of joy for their beloved Master. No, my brethren; it is plain that the evangelists set forth the agony of Christ as different in kind as in degree from all common sorrow. Not as at the grave-side of Lazarus does He add His tears to the general grief, one among many; but withdrawn from all eyes, with not even the broken reed of human sympathy to lean on, He wrestles in the darkness with mysterious apprehension and anguish, such as you cannot classify under any of the ordinary emotions, whilst His three elect disciples fall to sleep. St. Mark says, "He began to be sore amazed;" and the Greek word would mean almost "began to be surprised and terrified." And then the words of His prayer, "O, My Father, if it be possible, let this cup pass from me: nevertheless not as I will, but as Thou wilt," from one who has all along known and taught that His departure must be through suffering and death, indicate a profound perturbation of spirit. Either the evangelists mean to display here a struggle and a suffering, great, terrible, preternatural, different altogether from what other men are called to bear, or to exhibit one who has been so very strong, suddenly prostrated with fear at the mere approach of death. Who can doubt between these two? We know they do not mean to depreciate the Lord of life. It is not, then, that the moral courage is less, but that the anguish is infinitely greater. You can understand the agony in the garden, if you suppose that there Christ was able to gather up into Himself the spiritual interests of all the human race, if you think that as in Adam the root of the sinfulness of all was contained, even so in Christ the sin of all was extirpated. You can understand it if you suppose that besides the sympathies of a man, He had the knowledge and power of God, to hold, as it were, in his hand the interests of all mankind; but not, I think, on any lower view. Look not here for a teacher like the pagan Socrates, beguiling the last hours of life in cheerful talk; nor for mere patient tolerance of human calamity, like that of Job; nor for a martyr like Stephen, hastening across the gulf of death that separates him from his seen Lord. Look rather upon a great and unique warfare, fought for us against sin and the powers of darkness; and wonder not that unusual symptoms of awe, terror, and suffering should mark a transaction that stands quite alone, quite above our understanding.

There are those who shrink from confessing the atoning effect of the Saviour's death, because they think that anything in the nature of a sacrifice, any offering in which one suffers for the sins of others, is at variance with the strict justice of the divine nature. But there are two words in this objection which are used without any very accurate measure of their meaning; the words *justice* and *sacrifice*.

Who amongst us can look abroad upon the complex facts of social life, and say that he understands the plan of the divine justice? Men say that it is unjust that one man should suffer for another; however willing may be the sufferer, however he may put aside the rights of his own innocence, it is revolting to our reason to suppose that God will or can accept such a sacrifice as effectual towards the forgiveness of the guilty. Yet I suppose there is nothing in human history more plain than that men suffer the natural punishments for things of which they are not guilty. We speak as if the Saviour's sacrifice were the only fact hard to be accepted in the divine economy, as if an objection established against this one tenet would leave all the rest of the divine government plain and easy to be understood. That is not the case. How do we make it just that all from their birth should need atonement, that they should be incapable of holiness? How do we account for the ruined health and morals of the children where the father has been licentious? how for the devastation of whole countries in a warfare waged upon the quarrel of kings? how for the calamities which shipwreck, and earthquake, and contagion bring on the unoffending? how for the light and prosperity enjoyed by European races, whilst the African nations grovel in degradation? Men are not, and cannot be, regarded only as free and responsible units, each planted apart from all his neighbours and thoroughly independent of them all; as perfectly free on the one hand, and on the other, completely responsible for all their acts without help or hindrance from any other. Man has his individual life; but he is also one of a family, of a city, of a nation; and his lot is bound up with that of others in all these relations. When the shells are crashing through the roofs of the bombarded town, they will shatter alike the warrior and the man that longs for peace. When the pestilence that walketh in darkness and destroyeth in the noonday is marching through our streets and alleys, it mows down alike those whose careless habits have encouraged the disease, and those who have purged their dwellings from those pollutions on which infection feeds. The Most High is just indeed; but He is also a jealous God, visiting the sins of the fathers on the children. Through such enactments does His justice work itself out. One day we may understand His ways and learn that His moral government proceeds on laws as beautiful and as harmonious as those which regulate the world of nature. But in the meantime let us not argue upon God's justice as if we understood it thoroughly. So far from its being a paradox that another should exercise an influence over our moral being, examples of such an influence will occur to every one. And a being quite separated from all other natures, and owing nothing of his character or his actions to others around him, cannot even be conceived of as existing under our human nature. If it is unjust that your sins, out of which you cannot help yourselves, should receive great help from another whose you are, in whom as the Word and Wisdom of God you live and move and have your being, why are you allowed to profit by other men's toil and labour in anything whatever? All that you are and have has come from others, now through the most wearing labour, now through perils that have even cost life itself. There is therefore nothing repugnant to the known facts of God's government in the belief that one may exert an influence over others, both for good and evil; it is not utterly abhorrent to the divine justice that one should be permitted to lift off the weight of others' sins, unless it is also abhorrent to it that sins should be transmitted from father to child, or the profligate be allowed to entice the innocent to share his sin. The power of others over us is one of the most difficult forms of that obscure enigma — the existence of evil in the world. But of all solutions the least satisfactory to my own mind would be that which allowed it for evil and denied it for good; which admitted that the sins of the first Adam may be inherited, but denied that the second Adam could relieve them; which was able to say, "In Adam all die," but found it a blasphemy against the justice of heaven to add, "Even so in Christ shall all be made alive."

But in speaking of the Redeemer's sorrow, the word *sacrifice* must also be used not loosely, but in its own appropriate meaning. Now it will be seen that the sacrifice which Christ was able to offer for us was a sacrifice in a far higher and holier sense than that which any other high-priest could offer. For what was the sacrifice in all other religions but something *merely* vicarious, something connected with the offerer in no closer degree than that he raised it in his field or bought it with his money, or at least esteemed it precious? The links of connection were external and mechanical between the worshipper and his victim, and so the effects of the offering could not be moral, really reaching to the purifying of the soul. The effects would be external and conventional too, as in the Mosaic system, where the offering preserved indeed the worshipper in his position as a citizen of the Jewish polity, but could not take away the inward guilt of his offence, nor make him perfect. There was offered for us, not a ram caught in a thicket, not a pair of doves bought in the outer court of the temple; but One who, bearing the divine nature and power, claims us as His, holds us in His hand, and will not let us be plucked forth; who, in a word, stands united to us in a relation such as no mere man can stand in to any other man. It is on the altar of Calvary that this Lamb of God, able to take away the sins of the world, meets our eyes. The sorrow that He feels is no selfish apprehension; it is — although the phrase may shock — it is sorrow for *His* sins, for the sins which He has taken from us into and upon Himself. There was no spot of sin upon that shining soul, any more than there had been throughout His life. But the consciousness of guilt, and the feeling of its enormity, and the pain and anguish of it, poured in upon Him in that hour of darkness, and brought Him down as into the dust of death. When He prayed that if it were possible the cup might pass from Him, it was not the cup of death that amazed Him and almost overthrew Him,—of that He had long spoken calmly to His disciples, and He knew that the cup could not pass from Him;—but the cup that was so bitter was the cup poisoned with guilt. "The sorrows of death compassed Me, and the floods of ungodly men made Me afraid. The sorrows of hell compassed Me about; the snares of death prevented Me."* He shrank from a death of atonement in which the sins of the whole world should be laid upon Him who knew no guilt. No man, not the purest nor most philanthropic, can redeem his brother or give to God a ransom for him; but He is man to suffer and God to take up our interests into Himself. He has the conscience of a man to feel the utter misery and horror of sin; and the power of God to make all our case, even down to sin, His own. It is in this divine power of taking us into Himself that the great mystery of the Atonement appears. For He is God; in Him we live and move and have our being. If He in His compassion says, "I that have holden you up ever since you were born, will now come down and bear for you that which has destroyed you," we dare not say that this is impossible, that it is unjust, that we ought not to be found in Him, but each should stand alone, and bear his sin and sorrow by himself. The plan of mercy may be hard to understand; we may have to wait long before we comprehend it fully. But no other scheme to account for sin and evil, and our deliverance from them, is easier. And those

* Ps. xviii.

words which are so consoling to the weary heart, will be found also more convincing to the enlightened reason the more they are pondered, — " Since by man came death, by man came also the resurrection of the dead. For as in Adam all die, even so in Christ shall all be made alive."

And can a life and a death like this offer us anything that we can imitate? Must not men and angels stand as adoring witnesses of a transaction which they cannot even comprehend? What can we do more than receive the cup of salvation which He has prepared for us? And yet the Apostle says, " Let this mind be in you which was in Jesus Christ." It was the mind of Jesus to consider His life a ministry for God; to say, " I must work the work of Him that sent Me," and to be able to look back at last, and say, " It is finished. I have finished the work that Thou, O God, gavest Me to do." It was His mind to lay down all selfish wishes for honour and comfort which would have interfered with His perfect singleness of purpose. It was His mind to submit in all things to the will of the Father. He felt for all that sinned and sorrowed, and loved them, and strove to help them. In all this He was our example. Nay more, it is His example that has made a life of this kind possible and actual. And those who would come after Him must try to follow Him in this His sympathy with the sinful children of men. To feel for all who sin and suffer is not natural; nay, by an instinct of self-protection we learn to live amidst scenes the most affecting, without allowing them to ruffle our serenity. Whilst the Master was wrestling with the powers of darkness, the disciples slept hard by; and the thoughts that bore Him down disturbed them not at all. Living in this crowded island, which still is but a little corner of the world, it is wonderful how much men contrive to keep out of view for the sake of their own peace. If as we sit here our vision could be enlarged, so that we could see our social state as it really is, how would the calm of our souls be broken up and replaced by horror and amazement! Every night that we press our pillow, the drunken revel with its blasphemy and violence, and the traffic in lust, and the robbery and the murder go on under the silent stars. Here the watching mother prays on her knees to Him whom she has served to keep her firstborn from the evil of a perilous world; and there the object of her prayers is raving in his cups, or casting the pearl of his manhood into a harlot's lap. Misery huddles its rags together and shrinks into a corner, sheltered from the night wind, to benumb itself into an unnatural sleep. To and fro, before the house where pure daughters are nurtured tenderly, paces she who once was a daughter herself, but who now has no mother but shame. "The wicked are like the troubled sea when it cannot rest, whose waters cast up mire and dirt. There is no peace, saith my God, to the wicked." And when the morning comes again, the passions of millions wake up, and seethe and ferment and struggle for the mastery. So that day and night the smoke of sin goes up, as from Tophet, out of the country, nay, out of the very city, in which we live. Every day weak brothers and sisters, pressed with want, beguiled by temptation, cease to cling with desperate hands to an honest life, and drop off into the flood-tide of sin, and are lost. If to sin we try to add the sum total of calamity, the powers of calculation fail. If you could gather into one city the some two thousand houses in England in which deaths will occur within the next twenty-four hours, each with its little group of mourners, you might form some notion of the daily tribute paid to sorrow. "There was a great cry in Egypt, for there was not a house in which there was not one dead." But the sick, the overtasked, the famishing, the ruined, are all to be added to the tale. And all over the world the same elements of misery are combined in varying proportions. Is it not a wonder that we are so happy? Our Lord in the Garden of Gethsemane saw these things, measured their depths, bore the grief of them. God forbid that any of us should have to endure the constant sense of so much wretchedness! It would sear the eye that looked on it. But in this respect, as in others, let us endeavour to take up our cross and follow our Lord. Let us feel a little for the throes and anguish of those amidst whom we live. Let such thoughts soften our pride and sober our gladness. Let our plans for our own pleasure and advancement give way sometimes to efforts to make the mass of suffering somewhat less. Two good results will follow from such a training. We shall be more fit to watch our hour with the Saviour in the Garden of Gethsemane; we shall understand better, though very dimly still, what kind of struggle it was that the High Priest who is touched with the feelings of our infirmities underwent for sin. We shall feel how real, how vast, was the work which, as Mediator between God and man, He performed for us. Sin gives its children pleasure for a season; but if they could see its fruits of bitterness growing in others, poisoning their life, and blackening their hopes; if they could realise the fact that just to eradicate this enormous evil, the Son of God, one with the Father, descended into the lowest abyss of suffering, and out of the deeps cried to the Father for succour, and for a season seemed to cry in vain, then they would begin to deal in earnest with their own corruption, and wrestle in their own Gethsemane, and reach peace through repentance.

On the other hand we shall be ministers of His in lightening the sore burden of our race. It may be little that we can *do*, but the man that can only feel for sin, acquires by that a great power over it. Hardness makes hardness: but the most wicked will own, if but for a time, the softening influence of a kindly word spoken in good will. No one expects us to endure the Saviour's struggle with sin; but can we not watch with Him one hour? Can we not see something of the nature of His struggle, and feel for sin in our degree? To acquiesce in all that others suffer round us, as necessary consequences of civilisation; to leave the child in his ignorance, and the woman in her ruin, and in self-defence to shut out every thought about such enormous evils, is to sleep when we ought to watch. "The spirit indeed is willing, but the flesh is weak." Sin, we know, is horrible; but it is easier to shut it out and rest in peace, as we cannot undo it. Oh, resist that weakness of the flesh. Doubt not that there is a power stronger than sin, that has wrestled with it and overthrown it. Doubt not that the same love which was in Him so powerful to reclaim, will not be without its effect when exhibited by you. Fight sin with his weapons; feel for it, take the thought of it home to you, fill yourself with a sense of its horror, and with a wish to reclaim others from it as from a consuming fire. And out of that conviction speak and act; and you shall find that a power not your own goes with you; and it will soften the rocks of the heart, and make the crooked paths straight, and the rough places plain. You will not reform society: but if one soul owes to you its repentance there will be joy in heaven, there should be joy in you.

SERMON VII.

THE CRUCIFIXION.

LUKE xxiii. 39—41.

And one of the malefactors which were hanged railed on him, saying, If thou be Christ, save thyself and us.

But the other answering rebuked him, saying, Dost not thou fear God, seeing thou art in the same condemnation?

And we indeed justly; for we receive the due reward of our deeds: but this man hath done nothing amiss.

IF we take the accounts of the three Evangelists together, we are led to suppose that at first both these malefactors reviled the innocent one who shared their punishment; but that, during their protracted suffering, the heart of one of them was touched with repentance, and with the conviction that Jesus was indeed the Christ. The sight of His constancy under suffering, and the miracles that marked the awful event, may have both contributed their share to this change in his heart. But of this I do not wish to speak at present. It is the most conspicuous example of dying repentance and forgiveness, and one which offers much food for thought. But let us look now at these two criminals, rather as examples of the offence of the Cross, and of the overcoming of that offence.

The Bible shows us in the history of the Passion, an innocent man put to death for pretended crimes, a sinful and hypocritical people enjoying a full triumph over him, and no interference on the part of the Most High, to put an end to this enormous wrong. That this kind of paradox often occurs in a world where the divine justice is seen indeed, but through a veil which our eyes are too weak to penetrate, has often been admitted without any severe shock to the faith. But the same persons who acquiesce in other examples of the triumph of wrong, cannot easily admit that even our redemption was to be effected by means, which for the moment seemed to show so little the justice or the mercy of God. From first to last, the cross of Christ has been a stone of stumbling to men of various tempers and degrees of piety. How can the Anointed of the Lord suffer on the Cross, or by suffering, benefit those whom He has loved? "Be it far from Thee, Lord," said Peter (Matt. xvi. 22), shocked at the thought of an end so unworthy for one whom he knew to be the Christ. The mockery with which His enemies triumphed over Him on the Cross, was all founded on the impression that the Saviour could not suffer, that God would not permit such a shameful death to overtake Him if He were truly what He pretended to be. "Ah! Thou that destroyest the Temple, and buildest it in three days, save Thyself and come down from the Cross. (Matt. xxvii. 40.) "He saved others, Himself He cannot save" (v. 42). Even the thieves could spare a moment from their own sufferings to cry, "If Thou be the Christ, save Thyself and us." (Luke xxiii. 39.) The disciples lost heart at the strange event, and two of them said, expressing probably the feeling of the whole body, "We trusted that it had been He that should have redeemed Israel." (Luke xxiv. 21.) If John the Evangelist stood near the Cross, and received from our Lord a sacred command, we are to suppose that a strong personal love drew him thither, and not that his mind could accept, any more than those of others, the doom of crucifixion as a wise and necessary part of the divine plan. It is indeed most remarkable how general the belief was, that the Cross could not belong to the Saviour, nor He to the Cross. "He has suffered, therefore are His pretensions vain," seemed to the high priests too logical to need any explanation. It was even a truism to hang a jest on: people do not assume a disputed saying as the basis of a jibe, nor are they apt to jest whilst there is anger or danger. The moment the fatal nails fixed to the tree the body of Him whom they had both hated and feared, all his claims seemed dissipated, and fear and hate became triumph. Bear with me if I say that the haste with which they drew that conclusion, was natural. The suffering of the Lord for our salvation was so complete, the abasement and humiliation so thorough, the marks of failure as a teacher of men and founder of a new kingdom so signal, that there seemed nothing left to fear. They were even astonished at their own success; and their jesting was all the more bitter, that they found that their exaggerated fears had been groundless. They did not expect that Pilate would have yielded so easily; nor that the people would so soon have forgotten their benefactor. The wicked deed seemed so easy and so complete, now that it was done, that they avenged themselves on their own victim, for their own former fears of His power and importance. Bear with me if I say that standing under that wooden cross amongst the vile, and looking at it, we should have felt something at least of the force of the logic on which the priests relied. The cross of Christ, not seen as we see it through the purple twilight of many ages, that softens its dreadful outlines and tinges it with glory, but that cross on which the Son of Man suffered a real and terrible death; got back for all the love that He had been pouring out on the human race, nothing but words and looks of scorn; thirsted, and received vinegar and gall, to assuage his thirst; thirsted still more urgently for the returning dews of divine comfort from heaven, which had ever been His until then, when He hung with the weight of all human sins upon Him, and receiving for that thirst the gall and vinegar of the sense of human sin; would prove a trial to the faith of many of us, if we were brought to witness it with unprepared minds. We look for a king and deliverer; here is a tortured and dying man, who has not been able to deliver himself. We look for a destroyer of sin, we expect to see Satan like lightning fall from heaven; and round about the cross all man's worst passions are broken loose in hideous triumph; and He does not still them nor punish. We look to heaven, hoping that all this may pass like a dream, and the justice of heaven be asserted against an impious defiance of it;— the Most High has seen, for He drops a veil of darkness over the city, as a token of His displeasure;— but the fearful tragedy is acted out, and the Most High interferes no more to avert it than did Baal to vindicate his priests against Elijah. It would have been difficult for one to have inferred until the death of our Lord had actually taken place, what the Centurian said when he saw the portents that accompanied it, "Truly this was the Son of God." (Matt. xxvii. 54.)

And yet under that cross we may safely stand. On those details of suffering on one side, and of blasphemous cruelty on the other, which the Gospels set before us with a fulness that has no parallel elsewhere, we may fix our thoughts. For in spite of all that has been said and felt about the difficulty of accepting the doctrine of the Atonement, you will find that this great fact really claims an interpretation the very opposite of that which the enemies of Christ put upon it. What seems the unrighteous death of an innocent man, is truly the most rigorous exactness of divine justice. What seems the highest triumph of the enemies of God, is truly their condemnation and punishment. Whilst the providence of God seems for a time to sleep, on the contrary it is here affording to the crucified Jesus, an opportunity of showing forth His greatness in His lowest humiliation. These three points I shall endeavour briefly to set before you in the rest of this sermon, praying that God will give us grace and strength to remove out of our way the stumbling-block of the Cross, and to see in the sufferings of His divine Son, His wisdom, His righteousness, and His love.

I. The conviction of sin pricks the hearts of most men at one time or another. Let them take what pains they will to rub out the sharp lines that separate right and wrong, an inward uneasiness refutes from time to time their most ingenious efforts. They cannot but admit, although with various degrees of conviction, that sin is abhorrent to their own conscience, and therefore to God the judge of all the earth. Further, they feel that sin is in a sense indelible: their own sin *is* theirs, although it may have been committed in years long past. The face has changed, the eyes have grown dim, the hair is grey;

there is not perhaps one particle of the frame the same. But ever and again the sins of youth, its sensuality, its hardness, its selfishness, rise up like phantoms out of the distant past; and we know them again for ours. Our mark is upon them: they send an icy pang of remorse through the heart as they have done often before. They have not lost their distinctness, perhaps they are even more painfully distinct, and promise us more clearly what grim companions they will prove to our old age. Now, Christian friends, in these facts (for though they are feelings they are also facts) lies the germ of all practical religion. That sin is accursed of God, and that it is a clinging pollution, imputable for ever (so to speak) to him that commits it, not lessened or changed by length of time, is the belief with which all men must set out on the narrow road to salvation. Other way there is none. The preaching of John warned men to flee from the wrath to come; that of the Apostles at Pentecost awoke their consciences and drove them to ask What shall we do? The sense of sin has ever been the first thought awakened by true religion: and even amongst false religions we can discern a difference according as the distinction between sin and right has or has not been preserved. Now, see how completely the death of the Redeemer has solved this great difficulty, of preserving alive the horror of sin and its imputability; yet at the same time of removing from us the guilt and the punishment of it. Sin shall not go unpunished, for God is just: yet the guilty shall not all perish everlastingly, for God is also full of compassion. On the cross there hangs a sufferer on whom God has laid the iniquity of us all: but who can such a victim be? First, he must be a willing victim, laying down his life of himself freely: for if the punishment even of the smallest sin were inflicted on him as guilty of it, without or against his will, the justice of heaven would be infringed. But next, the victim must be capable of sustaining such a part for the sins of the whole world. A *man* cannot suffer for all men's sins; he cannot open wide his arms and clasp in one embrace of love and sympathy the whole human family. Let him be as philanthropic and devoted as he may, — the effects even of his death as a martyr would have been unfelt beyond his own narrow circle of action. To do a thing which shall affect the whole race of men,— those that have long since returned to the dust, and those that are not yet fashioned out of the dust,— requires surely the same kind and amount of power as that which creates and sustains man. The victim, then, must have the power of God, in order to take up into himself all human needs and sorrows and weaknesses. But if he is to suffer for sin, and so write with his own blood the great lesson that sin shall not go unpunished, he must also be man to suffer as one of us and for us.

Such, then, is the sacrifice that has been transacted on the earth before our eyes. The Son of God has come down from heaven, has taken on Himself all our sins, freely and out of His exceeding love, and in His pains we see how fierce is the anger of God against sin. Just when God's justice appears to have forgotten itself in allowing an innocent man to perish, is that justice most conspicuous in providing a precious sacrifice capable of taking away the sins of the world. Think not, oh my friends! of the bodily pangs that wrung that pure and sensitive frame; think of sin and what He felt and suffered for that. "Daughters of Jerusalem," said our Lord Himself, "weep not for me, but weep for yourselves and for your children." (Luke xxiii. 28.) He asked no sympathy for His bitter pains; no man took His life from Him, but He laid it down of Himself, and He had more than strength to bear all the foreseen sufferings involved in the sacrifice. It was not bodily pain that made Him an object of interest and compassion; when we think of all the agonising pains of disease that wring the wretched frames of men in sick rooms and hospitals, I know not whether we should be right in assuming even to those mighty sufferings an indisputable pre-eminence. "Weep not for me — the cup prepared for me of the Father, have I not fortitude to drink the dregs of it and suck them out?" But He bore our griefs, our sins that were griefs to Him though carried all too lightly by us; He who knew no sins was punished for all. He gathered in upon His own spirit the insufferable sense of all our offences, felt them really as sins, in all their guilt, their loathsomeness, and the dreadful wrath wherewith God looks on them.

II. But, secondly, this act which seemed the triumph of wicked men was really their condemnation. Christ was even then the Judge of men; all the wickedness and weakness of their hearts were laid bare before Him. Even Peter, and Thomas, and John are sifted in this trial, and their different degrees of faith come out into strong relief. Judas and Pilate are thoroughly weighed and found wanting. The chief priests and the multitude had the choice between a murderer and the Lord of Life, and they chose the murderer. The people had before this been favourers of Jesus; but now that the touchstone of the Cross is applied they fail under the test. "His blood be on us and on our children!" It is wonderful how men lay bare before Him the inmost recesses of their guilty spirits. It is not a culprit hanging on a cross that we see, so much as a judge sitting upon a tribunal and revealing the thoughts of many hearts, and condemning them. Well might the Prophet ask, "But who may abide the day of His coming? and who shall stand when he appeareth?" (Mal. iii. 2).

III. And, lastly, it follows that the death of Jesus, instead of being something done in a corner, of which the watchful providence of God took no account, was the fulfilment of a gracious design prepared for our salvation long before, and never for an instant suffered to be forgotten. Promised to Abraham, announced by Jacob, by Moses, by David, described by Isaiah rather with the distinctness of history than under a prophetic veil, the Messiah has come at length; and though he hangs upon the cross and shall lie in the grave, God will not leave His soul in hell nor suffer His Holy One to see corruption. He will highly exalt Him and give Him a name that is above every name, that at the name of Jesus every knee may bow, and every tongue may confess that Jesus Christ is Lord to the glory of God the Father.

We see, then, my Christian friends, that this momentous event which brings us together here to-day, is capable of two interpretations. Viewed as an act of atonement for sin, the wisdom and the righteousness of God are vindicated in it. Only let us bring to the contemplation of it a deep sense of the reality of sin, and we shall read aright this history of our deliverance. And the cross of Christ is just as much a touchstone and a test for us, as it was to those who stood beneath it on Calvary. The sufferings of the Lord Jesus are not laid bare to us in the Gospels with such minuteness of detail, in order that we may gaze on them with idle wonder. The Evangelists, so concise elsewhere, when they approach this final scene describe for us most minutely every throb of suffering, every exclamation of anguish. We see in the garden the agony which was too sacred to be witnessed fully even by the three chosen disciples who were the Lord's companions. The kiss of Judas and the disciples' flight, Peter's denial, and the spitting, and the mockery, and the buffets that marred the meek face of the Redeemer; the scourging, the crucifixion, are all drawn out before us; not a detail seems to be spared. To what end is this recitation of horrors? If they had fallen upon some murdered relative of our own we should have entreated the bearer of the evil tidings to spare us these harrowing incidents, and tell us only the final issue of death or life. In departing from their usual forbearance, the Evangelists I think do not mean merely to shock us into unusual compassion for a great sufferer, but to give us a measure of sin by an account of what was suffered for sin. If upon this sacred day no emotion of sorrow for our own sins has arisen from contemplating that august Sufferer, it would be better to turn away from that spectacle altogether. "Is it nothing to you, all ye that pass bye?" (Lam. i. 12.) Will you dare to look on it unmoved as something in which you had no hand? They are wearing out, with every kind of mental distress and bodily injury, the strength of the Victim. Every taunt is felt; for He has shown how He loves men, and He must therefore be pained at their hate. They are bruising and defiling the face on which hereafter angels shall look with reverence. They are raging against Him, who has passed His life in healing their sick and teaching and comforting them. Is this nothing to us? Our sins brought it about. How should we dare to look on Him whom we too have pierced, and bruised, and pained, without abhorring that within us which is enmity against Him? How shall we cleave to those sins which we can measure now by the vastness of those sufferings? Oh, from this day forth let us mark sin and avoid it! let us look up to the Cross with wonder that One so lofty should have died for us so polluted with our vileness! Giving ourselves up this day to self-abasement and repentance, let us when Easter comes round draw near with joy to celebrate at the Lord's Table the completion of the work of the Redeemer. And daily and hourly let our aspiration to God be—" Deliver us from sin: teach us to watch our footsteps and restrain our hearts from wickedness; for it is an abomination to the pure Son of God, it crucifies the Saviour of the world afresh and puts Him to an open shame."

SERMON VIII.

THE RESURRECTION.

ROMANS xiv. 7, 8, 9.

For none of us liveth to himself, and no man dieth to himself.

For whether we live, we live unto the Lord; and whether we die, we die unto the Lord: whether we live therefore, or die, we are the Lord's.

For to this end Christ both died, and rose, and revived, that he might be Lord both of the dead and living.

Two days ago we were considering the immediate effects of the Crucifixion on those who witnessed it. We saw how it scattered the disciples and extinguished their hopes, and how it filled the chief priests and Pharisees with triumph, as the complete termination of all their fears about the new Prophet who set them at nought. We should have to describe the resurrection and its effects in very different language. The very first news of it awoke the Apostles from their depression: and even Thomas, the most desponding of the whole band, received such convincing proofs of the reality of the great event that no doubts on that point could ever again disturb him. Ten times, at least, did the Redeemer appear before witnesses with the life that He had once laid down and now had taken again; and in four or five of these cases the assembled Apostles were the witnesses chosen. The effects of this were that all their confidence in their beloved Lord was restored; that the cross itself appeared now under a new aspect, and it was no longer so unworthy of the Lord Jesus, now that it was known to be the scene of a new victory. Mocking voices had cried in the midst of His sufferings, "If he be the King of Israel let him now come down from the cross and we will believe him:" but He had done far more than this challenge imposed. He had come up from the tomb, alive and safe, never more to perish. All that had occurred during the last few days, from the hour when they had forsaken Him to the time that He stood amongst them again, had altered entirely their relation to Him. To speak at all with one who had passed through the valley of the shadow of death would be a strange and awful thing; but to be allowed to draw near to One who for them and their salvation had tasted death and conquered it, must have moved the disciples to the very foundation of their being. Accordingly their demeanour towards Him, and His to them, are no longer the same. It is not now the familiar friend taking sweet counsel with them, it is their Lord and Master speaking to them with command.

He stands amongst them and says, "Peace be unto you." He breathes on them and bids them receive the Holy Ghost. He distributes to them His last warnings and injunctions. To Thomas He says, "Blessed are they that have not seen and yet have believed." To Peter He says, "Feed my sheep;" and again, "If I will that he tarry till I come, what is that to thee? Follow thou me." To the whole body he gives the command to go and teach all nations and to bear witness to the facts that they had seen. On their side profound awe and reverence had replaced the affectionate intimacy of an earlier time. Jesus is now their Lord, their King, and their God: the resurrection has taken away all doubt of His power and majesty, where any existed. He was indeed become the Lord of all men, both of the dead and the living. He, as a man, had passed through each state, and for men; and they recognise Him as their Lord. He had fought a great fight for them and won it, and therefore He is their Captain, the Captain of their Salvation. He had put himself at their head in the time of their sorest need, when sin and suffering in this life and the pains of hell beyond the grave made their case almost desperate; and He had remedied their evils, and now they will have Him as their Lawgiver and King. For it is in this sense that the Apostle connects the death and resurrection of our Lord with His title of Lord both of the dead and living. He was God from everlasting, and one with the Father. His connection with the human race begins with the creation of the first man. But Jesus Christ as God and man, as the founder of a new kingdom to be established on earth, dates His title from the events with which that kingdom began. It began from the dawn of that first day of the week, when an angel rolled away the stone from the door of the sepulchre. It began at that empty tomb into which the wondering women looked after they were told that the Lord was risen from it. It began with that resurrection which proved to men that the atoning death of the Lord was not an act of blind devotion, nor a miscalculation of His influence, nor a despairing surrender, but a deliberate sacrifice for the world's sins, and a sacrifice accepted by Him to whom it was offered.

Now observe how simple and how entire was the belief of the Apostles in the power of this fact to compel men to faith and love. All the evidence we possess shows that the Apostolic preaching was of remarkable simplicity, and that the staple of it was, the facts of the Redeemer's life, and especially His death and resurrection. When St. Peter preached at Pentecost, he described who Jesus was, and told them "That God hath made this same Jesus, whom ye have crucified, both Lord and Christ:" and the bare statement of this accusation wrought most powerfully upon them. This perhaps is less wonderful since the hearers were some of those, probably, who had actually taken part in the wicked deed, and conscience was already busy with them. But

Philip in Samaria, and Paul at Damascus, and Peter at Cæsarea all preach the facts of our Lord's life and ministry; and in the last case the crucifixion and the resurrection are those which are expressly insisted on. "We are witnesses," says the Apostle, "of all things which He did, both in the land of the Jews and in Jerusalem; whom they slew and hanged on a tree: Him God raised up the third day and shewed Him openly, not to all the people but unto witnesses chosen before of God, even to us who did eat and drink with Him after He rose from the dead." (Acts x. 39.) It is probable indeed that before the Gospels were reduced to writing they had already taken shape from the preaching of the Apostles, and that in them, but more especially in the three first (for the fourth was not written by its inspired author till the close of the first century), we possess not the texts of the apostolic sermons but the sermons themselves; that the close resemblance of these three arises from their all following the exact line of the apostolic preaching; and that the Apostles considered themselves rather as witnesses than as commentators. In the recitation of the facts of our Lord's life there was power to draw men over to Him, and to make them confess with sincere love and penitence that He was their Lord and their God. The belief which was made the condition of admittance into the new society was the simple acceptance of the fact that Jesus of Nazareth had bound the human race to himself by an unheard of act of love and devotion.

I

And nothing is more remarkable than the attainment of such success by means that seemed so inadequate. They told the Jews that the carpenter's son, whose mother and brethren they had among them, who was neither scribe to teach them the deep things of the Law, nor Pharisee to awe them by the proud assumption of superior sanctity, had been by them crucified and now was risen, and had thereby become the Lord of all men. And many a Jew admitted it; and loved this new-found Saviour, and bowed the knee to the throne of grace in His name; nay, when the time came, was willing to die rather than deny Him. But by degrees the Gospel spread to places where Jewish customs and expectations were almost unknown. It reaches Athens, and even there in that focus of Greek thought and cultivation, St. Paul offers to his hearers the same spiritual food: he tells them of a judgment to come, " whereof" God "hath given assurance unto all men, in that he hath raised Him from the dead." (Acts xiii. 31.) Yet this was not rejected with general derision; some mocked indeed, others wished to hear more; but some believed at once. We open our Bibles, and the first epistles which meet our eyes are those to a Church at Rome and to a Church at Corinth; and in both these cities we find that the risen Jesus is known as the Lord of the dead and the living, is working in many hearts, is loved, and trusted, and adored by many, and the fact that it is so is spoken of by the Apostle with the same calm confidence in its reality

as we might speak of any transaction of our daily
life. Wonderful power of one single event! Even
in those early days the resurrection of a man, plainly
announced by thirteen witnesses, with none of the
forces to aid it that usually work great social revolutions, is actually changing the fortunes of the world.
What followed in later days we know too well.
Rome, perversely tolerant of every religion except
the true, became suspicious of the Christians. Bitter
persecution, sometimes emanating from the Emperor
or his deputies, sometimes from popular fury, did
the utmost to extirpate the remembrance of the
name of the crucified and risen Redeemer. The
emperor of the world was trying his strength
against that of the Lord in heaven. In one of these
persecutions, Polycarp, of Smyrna, is brought before
the pro-consul, who says, "Come, curse Christ, and
I will set you free." "Eighty-six years," answers
the old man, "have I served Him, and I have received only good at His hands! Can I curse Him,
my King and my Saviour?" Christ, then, is a real
Master; working in Heaven for and upon such a
servant as this, as truly as any human ruler can
work on earth. And in the end the emperor wholly
fails; when the Church is left at peace, its good deeds
speak to those without and allure them; when it is
persecuted, the blood of martyrs, shed upon the
ground, springs up in crops of Christian men. And
at this day throughout all the countries where law
and freedom, and cultivation and commercial enter-

prise, mark the highest and fairest branches of the human stock, Christ is acknowledged as the Lord. Very imperfect, indeed, is their devotion to Him, and many their backslidings; but still in His name every knee bows and every prayer is offered; His Cross is looked up to as the altar of sacrifice, His power and spirit are the admitted sources of all spiritual life. The Apostle's words are verified, " To this end Christ both died and rose again, and revived, that he might be Lord both of the dead and living." (Rom. xiv. 9.)

Hitherto we have taken a merely external view of this great phenomenon, because in that way we best see how great a wonder it is. There is the crucifixion, the obscure crime of a city about to perish; and here are the chief nations of the earth, eighteen centuries later, going softly and sorrowfully because of that crime, and again rejoicing because the death that it wrought has been vanquished. Christians, however, must not rest content with the external aspect only.

Now first among the causes of the Gospel's triumph — if it be not rather the sole cause — is that the belief in the crucifixion and resurrection was not a bare profession, but a real inward life. That some new principle was really working in and fashioning the minds of believers, is always assumed by the Apostles, and not in the way of a heated enthusiasm, in which the mind projects the colours of its tainted eyesight upon the facts it sees, but as calmly as we could speak of the transactions of the parliament, the law-court, or the exchange. Writing to the Corinthians, St. Paul does not endeavour to *persuade* them into the belief that they are living a new life in Christ; he speaks of it in the simplest language of fact—" I thank my God always on your behalf, for the grace of God which is given you by Jesus Christ; that in everything ye are enriched by Him, in all utterance and in all knowledge. Even as the testimony of Christ was confirmed in you: so that ye come behind in no gift; waiting for the coming of our Lord Jesus Christ." (1 Cor. i.) This is the strain in which men write to their friends about assured facts; thus would a man express thankfulness for his friend's health or his prosperity, or the advancement of his children, or any of those matters of fact which admit least doubt, and require least argument. And more than one of the apologists of Christianity, as Justin Martyr* and Tertullian†, appeal to the existence of conspicuous Christian virtues amongst them, which even their enemies are expected to admit. Their patience of wrong and of suffering, their strict morality, their unselfishness, their mutual love, contrasted so strongly with the tone of Pagan society, that they were like water-springs in a dry and barren ground. "Christ," says Augustine, "appeared to the men of an old and expiring world, that whilst all around them was fading away, they might receive through Him a new life

* Apol. ii. 63. † Apol. ch. 39.

and youth."* It was the evidence of good works, rather than that of miracles, which attracted new inquirers to the Christian ranks, even whilst persecutions were thinning them. Young lads and tender women, common workmen and slaves, showed that a new spring moved all their actions; and those who came in contact with them, if they had in their hearts any germ of good at all, must have felt the influence of this moral superiority. And can we find any other solution of this change, than the simplest of all, that Christ was keeping his promise of being ever with his disciples? It was God that wrought in them; it was the promised Spirit of God that guided them; it was the Lord of the dead and the living who was sitting at the right hand of God, and helping and communing with those whom the Father had given Him. Or if you persist in supposing them to be self-deluded, why, amongst all the delusions of the ancient world, was this the only one that bore such pure and wholesome fruit? If it is *not* God that works love, joy, peace, long-suffering, gentleness, goodness, then from the highest products of this world we live in, and those which we all feel to be the highest, the divine agency is excluded.

But supposing the divine agency to be admitted, then it follows that our Lord's nature is divine. Not only does He, after His resurrection, accept divine honour, and confer power such as God alone can confer, but His Apostles ascribe to Him beyond

* Neander, Church History, vol. i. sect i.

all doubt divine powers and honours. Now in this is involved the whole question, whether our faith is or is not mixed with idolatry. God cannot have been working for so many centuries in the Church, causing men to bring forth fruits of righteousness, in order to confirm in the earth an idolatrous delusion. The Son of Man must be in the truest sense the Son of God, and Lord and Christ, as myriads of voices have been ever proclaiming Him to be, or else — and the very soul revolts at the alternative — a wrong belief about His person has been winked at and assisted as a salutary lie. Had the Church of Christ been perpetuating that worst of all errors, taking the glory of God and transferring it to another, long since would the fountains of grace have been dried up for it, and the spiritual rains of heaven would have refused to refresh it, until its idolatry was purged away. But we may bow the knee in His name; we may look up to Him on His divine throne, we may say with Thomas, " My Lord and my God," because the steady fulfilment of His promises, and the streams of blessing ever derived from Him by His Church, assure us that His account of His divine relation to the Father is the very truth.

But if we know the Redeemer as a Lord over us by the work which he does amongst us, let us not shrink from the question that evidently follows. *What marks of His work shall we discover in ourselves?* " If ye then be risen with Christ, seek those things which are above, where Christ sitteth on the right hand of God. Set your affection on things above, not on things on the earth. For ye are dead, and your life is hid with Christ in God. When Christ who is our life shall appear, then shall ye also appear with him in glory." (Colos. iii. 1–4.) This is a high strain, and one to which we can hardly brace our minds. Do not, however, suppose that the Apostle speaks of us as if we either are or should be dead to earthly duties. Earthly hopes and principles of action are to be merged in divine hopes: but the daily duties may be actively pursued, and even the rewards of them accepted, by one whose life is yet hid with Christ in God. It is an old taunt to say that if our belief in Christianity were sincere, we should cast aside all other business, and think only of the realities of death, and heaven and hell, for the mind that had once grasped these would be incapable of attending to smaller things. It is specious, but untrue. The Ruler of the world has given us our portion in the work that He is ever carrying on in it: and in order that we may do it earnestly, He has made it seem great in our eyes. The book in your hand may be greater to your eye than a mountain on the horizon; not that it is greater in truth, but that the business of your eye lies now with the present book, and not with the distant mountain. Go and try to ascend the mountain, and then when your concern with it begins, you will find what its dimensions are. The little child that the mother shelters so tenderly, so that the keen east wind shall not touch its cheek, is not so beautiful, or so precocious, or so loving as she would give it out; but God has set that mother one great duty for the present, and it is made engrossing to her that she may do it carefully and well. And so with many of us, the calls of a hard profession may consume our days and nights, and the time we give to it, and that which we give to our spiritual concerns, may bear no proportion to each other; and yet we know that the passions of suitors are matters of a moment, and the words in which we try to do them justice, eloquent and ingenious words, fall dead without an echo, whilst the soul is an heir to eternity. But so has our Maker allotted us our share of duty. If we tried to alter it, and to measure out our time to those things only of which we see the eternal importance, and to reject altogether that which belongs merely to time, we should be bad citizens, and whether we should be better Christians is matter of much doubt. But the problem which we have to solve is to import into our daily work that "life hid in God" of which the Apostle speaks. The grace of Christ, if it be really in us, will exhale like a sweet perfume in all we do. Those long laborious hours of social duties we may not be able to abridge, but can we not show even in them candour and love of others, and truth and justice, and unselfishness and piety? For such graces as these, which were so conspicuous in our Lord are of the things above, on which our affections should be fixed. The time set apart for prayer and communing with God may be short, but it may be devoted to the fervent consecration of ourselves to Him for all the other hours that round off the circle of a day. Here is our shortcoming. Here is the thought that *will* come in. Is the Lord of dead and living in any real sense *our* Lord? Has He that conquered the grave conquered the worldly part in me? Are covetousness, ambition, impurity, indolence, thoroughly put down? Questions such as these are painful to propose, and hard to answer. If we are immersed wholly in the present world, the fashion of which passeth away, if Christ be dead in vain so far as we are concerned, the thoughts that belong to this day may help to awaken us. The mountain on the horizon seems small and dim, but towards it we are travelling, and it grows daily bigger: it is the mountain of heaven that we must scale, and there is a dark and silent valley, invisible at present, through which we must pass before we reach it. Compare the great realities that we have been looking at to-day with the all-engrossing business that draws our attention off them. The subtlest tongue will be silent before long; the most eager strife will cease; the wisest decision will be quoted no longer at most than the kind of right it relates to shall subsist. But we must all appear before the judgment seat of Christ; and at that bar the issue that is decided is for eternity. May He that judges us plead our cause also; and because we shall have acknowledged from our hearts that He is the Lord of the dead and the living, may He wash out our sins with His blood, and say, Thou hast been faithful unto death; I will give thee a crown of life.

SERMON IX.

THE HOLY SPIRIT.

PREACHED ON WHITSUNDAY.

Acts xix. 2.

He said unto them, Have ye received the Holy Ghost since ye believed? And they said unto Him, We have not so much as heard whether there be any Holy Ghost.

In the great city of Ephesus, the chief centre of commerce in the Roman province of Asia, many forms of religion were to be found. Among them, not the least remarkable, was this little band of the Baptist's disciples, who had long since been baptized by John, and had made no farther progress in the truth. Probably they knew not of the death of Jesus, certainly they were ignorant of the power of that death. Of the divine Spirit of truth, the Comforter sent by Jesus from the Father, they had not heard. What place in their estimation the Baptist held, we cannot know; but it seems as if he were more to them than the humble forerunner, unworthy to stoop down and unloose the shoe-latchet of a coming Master. For they sought nothing more than they had received. When the river at Ænon laved their limbs, in token that the old pollution was washed away, and a purer life was to begin, John himself told them that his was no complete work; "I baptize you," he said, "unto Him that shall come after." (Comp. Acts xix. 4.) But Jesus had come and ascended on high, and the Holy Ghost had descended with portents and taken possession of the Church, never to leave it again. And of all this they knew nothing. They had left Judæa probably soon after their baptism, and here they reappear at Ephesus, some four and twenty years later, when the Church has grown to man's estate, still in the infancy of their belief, and repeating their first lesson of the baptism of John. There is a strange historical interest about these twelve disciples, dwarfed in their Christian growth, through no fault of their own, when some who had received the same baptism were now Apostles of Jesus Christ. Other cases there must have been, where seed was sown, and received into good soil, yet without bringing fruit to perfection. Besides those places where the light of the Gospel shone full and clear, scattered rays of light must have pierced to distant regions. The man that had heard John only, the man that had eaten of the new-created bread, one out of five thousand on the shores of the Sea of Tiberias, and had gone after Jesus no farther, the woman that had felt for the sorrow of that other woman that stood near the three crosses, where three reputed malefactors hung, the stranger that had heard the miraculous tongues at the feast of Pentecost, and had inquired no further about them; when we think of these, we can hardly help asking, why, having seen so much, they were not suffered to attain to more. But so God ever deals with us in the school of this world. To some He speaks once or twice; others hear His voice often in repeated calls and warnings. We cannot understand His ways in this: one thing, however, we know, that of us to whom much has been given, much will be required. But the question which St. Paul puts here, is one which, upon this day every one of us may well ask of his own conscience. "Have ye received the Holy Ghost since ye believed?" Do not let anyone suppose that the answer will be in every case the very opposite of that in my text. "We have not so much as heard whether there be any Holy Ghost *for us to receive*," would be an answer in many cases not very far from the truth. For if we were to analyse the idea which many have formed of the power and working of the Third Person in the Blessed Trinity, we should not find that He is looked on as a friend dwelling under their roof, and in their heart, such as the Bible describes Him. He is the being who dealt with Elijah in the awful seclusion of the cave in Horeb. After the Crucifixion, when a great spiritual revolution was to be begun in the earth, He came down and divided Himself, in cloven tongues of fire over the disciples, and divided their speech into the languages of many nations, to convince the indifferent that a great work was begun. But that in this nineteenth century, in the midst of the monotony of our civilisation,— here in London,— here in this little chapel,—the presence of the same divine Spirit in those who love God is as sure as the presence of the air they breathe, or the light wherewith they see one another; this is a proposition which has something startling even for us, who profess to admit it. And it is not because we are indifferent, that we would thus thrust away the inevitable presence. There is something awful to us in the nearness of God. This great fire we think will consume us. If we were to hear the voice of God any more, we should die. Shall God make a temple of that soul in which lusts, like unclean birds, nestle and defile? Shall His light shine there to show the avarice and the malice, and the sloth and indifference, that it were better to hide from any eyes? We should be disposed to say to the Holy Spirit, "Depart from me, for I am a sinful man, O Lord." But we cannot shut the door against Him. As the waters cover the floor of the sea, as the air reaches every corner and presses through every cranny, so is there nothing from which God is excluded. The Spirit of God was present at the creation. (Gen. i. 2; Job xxxiii. 4.) "Whither shall I go from Thy Spirit? or whither shall I flee from Thy presence?" (Ps. cxxxix. 7) asks the Psalmist. All wisdom, and prudence, and excellence of knowledge in men, is ascribed ever in the Old Testament to the same Spirit. Of one man it was said, the Lord "hath filled him with the Spirit of God, in wisdom, in understanding, and in knowledge, and in all manner of workmanship." (Ex. xxxv. 31.) Of another, even of Christ himself, the Prophet says, "The Spirit of the Lord shall rest upon Him, the spirit of wisdom and understanding, the spirit of counsel and might, the spirit of knowledge and of the fear of the Lord." (Is. x. 7.) Without the Spirit, no prophet could ever have spoken. Even upon Balaam the Spirit of God, we are told, came, when he was to utter his message. Those on whom any special blessing has lighted, are said to have received the same Spirit. Where any change or reformation of character is wrought, the same Spirit is said to be at work. "A new heart, also," says Ezekiel, echoing the very words of God, "will I give you, and a new spirit will I put within you, and I will take away the stony heart out of your bosom, and I will give you a heart of flesh. And I will put My Spirit within you, and cause you to walk in My statutes, and ye shall keep My judgments and do them." (Ez. xxvi. 26, 27). And in the New Testament, the Holy Spirit is spoken of as the Spirit of wisdom and revelation, which "searcheth all things, yea, the deep things of God." (Rom. xi. 33.) He reproves, teaches, sanctifies; He can be resisted, tempted, grieved. Put together all that is said of Him in holy Scripture, and you find that it can only meet in one, in the omnipresent, omniscient God. And when you ask, Have I received the Holy Ghost since I believed? you mean, "Have I felt the beginning of His good work in me?" If you have not received Him, yet He is near you; if He dwells not in you to sanctify, He is near you to reprove and rebuke. If He is not correcting your corrupt affections, He is a daily witness of their wanderings. From God you cannot escape; from the dominion of the Holy Spirit you cannot withdraw your own finite spirit any more than you can keep the sun's light from visiting the earth. But it rests with you who are under the loving rule of a most merciful Father, whether you will receive the Holy Ghost as a friend and advocate, or resist him as an enemy. Do not say, "We have not so much as heard whether there be any Holy Ghost." God is above you, and around you; if you would rather live without His presence, because you fear His rebukes of sin, know at least how hopeless the wish is. You could as soon live without the blood of life. Let the words of a heathen philosopher rebuke such an aspiration. "God is near you," says Seneca, "is with you, is in you. A sacred spirit sits within us, the observer and watch of our evil actions, and our good. As he is treated by us, so he treats us. There is no good man without God. Can anyone rise superior to the changes of fortune unless assisted by him? He it is that suggests great and lofty counsels to us. In every good man God dwells."

How shall we know whether the Holy Spirit is dwelling in us? The tokens of His indwelling are such as cannot be mistaken. One of them is, the growing love of our neighbour that He works in us. "Seeing ye have purified your souls in obeying the truth through the Spirit *unto unfeigned love of the brethren*, see that ye love one another with a pure heart fervently." (1 Pet. i. 22.) I have put this test the first, because nothing more clearly marks off the growth of Christianity from that of other ideas than this love towards all those who contribute to its working out. The world has seen many changes brought about by a spirit, or an idea. A race has gathered strength, and marched out to conquer far off lands, that none of its children have seen. Arts, letters, political institutions, have had their time of growth. A general result has been attained, at the loss, very often, of the individuals who bring it about. When the standard of victory has been planted, no one thinks of the soldiers' bones that whiten in the sun and rain, or of the soldiers' blood that will make the crops of next year look greener. When the work of art stands before us in its perfection of calm beauty, it tells no tale of agonising toil, of over-stretched nerves failing, of want or premature decay. The great car advances, and the willing victims throw themselves under its wheels. But of the Church of Christ, those inspired words of Paul would serve as the motto, " I seek not yours, but *you*." (2 Cor. xii. 14.) The great eternal house of God, of which Jesus himself is the head stone of the corner, is built of living stones. By whatsoever the general design of God is furthered by your exertion or mine, by so much are you and I the better, the purer, the richer. No step is taken at your expense. The Church is built up by your effort, but your soul is at the same time brought nearer to God. Every soul of man is an end in this work of sanctifying the world, even though it be also a means. In many a province of nature there is a kind of reason in the poet's complaint —

> " So careful of the type she seems,
> So careless of the single life." *

But not here. Christ is not careless of a single soul. For blind Bartimæus and the widow at Nain the King of Glory stayed his steps, and the healing virtue went out of him. And to love even the least of the brethren with a pure heart fervently has ever since been the bond of the Christian Church. Now here is a test simple and decisive of our Christian state. "Beloved," says St. John, "if God so loved us, we ought also to love one another. No man hath seen God at any time. If we love one another, God dwelleth in us and His love is perfected in us. Hereby know we that we dwell in Him and He in us, because He has given us of His spirit." (1 John iv. 11.) Here love of the brethren is spoken of as the direct fruit of the Spirit of God.

* Tennyson's "In Memoriam."

More than one Christian writer has told us that in the mysterious and ineffable union of the Trinity, the Holy Spirit is the love of the Father for the Son and of the Son for the Father, and that in His manifestation in Christian hearts, it is His special work to unite us in the bonds of love, first with the Father and the Son, and next with all who have shared the Father's promises, and the Son's atonement and the Spirit's sanctifying presence.* If that be so, the absence of love will be a proof of the absence of the Spirit who is love. Now this, my Christian hearers, is a very searching test. Can we say with St. Paul "I seek not yours but you?" Are we living to profit others, or only to profit by them? Observe how easy it is to slide into a state the very opposite of what Christ approves, for want of thought. If you only take the beautiful robe, made in all haste, that some fair woman may look the fairer at a festival, and trace its little history with this light in your hand, you will admit that want of love may creep into transactions where we least suspect it. Could she who is to adorn herself with it, and who thought it no harm to urge on its completion, go up to the garret where the sister-woman lives that made it, and say "I seek not yours but you? I love you more than the toil of your fingers?" Honest lips would not say it. For this might be the answer. "The hours of my sleep are sewn into its folds. In

---

* See Petavius, Dogm. Theol. III. b. vii. ch. 12, for citations, &c.

its seams I have written a record of the aches of my over-tasked frame. I broke the Sabbath for you, because you could not resolve upon the fashion of your splendour twelve hours sooner. As your slave, your means, your instrument, I work and will work, and will not complain; but do not call a cruel use of your position of vantage, by the holy name of Christian love." Ah, my brethren, we do not need the cloven tongues of fire to be a sign of the Spirit's presence; but the Spirit of love, that made the Apostles seekers after and lovers of the souls of men we do surely need. Think over in your minds the different orders of men that come into contact with you in your usual life. To which of them could you say, I seek not yours but you? Servants, companions, children, dependents, are all and each as dear to Christ as you can be. If you use them, and see them grow worse in the using, if your example, your selfishness, your imperious temper, are hardening their souls, you are not showing the Spirit of Christ. Begin to fear lest you should be none of His.

There is another test, the hatred of sin. "Know ye not that ye are the Temple of God, and that the Spirit of God dwelleth in you? If any man defile the temple of God him shall God destroy, for the temple of God is holy, which temple ye are." (1 Cor. †i. 1∮.) It is an inevitable law that we cannot at the same time sin and also see God. We can no more have in our hearts fleshly lusts and the presence of the Spirit than we can walk east and west at the same time. They are contrary the one to the other. I have often spoken here of the destroying deadening power of a single sinful habit. No matter whether it is sensual vice, or avarice, or love of power, that is allowed to defile the temple of God; the indulged sin will overlay the whole soul, until it becomes incapable of bearing any of those fruits of the Spirit of which the Apostle speaks. In an age of outward conformity, when social decorum puts limits to the freedom of action and speech, we are in danger of the hypocrisy which treasures up the religious doubt or the sinful desire in the mind in silence, and of thinking that because society acquits us of the sin it does not see, the sin exists not. But the soul and heart are the Temple of God. There is the shrine; there should we guard against the defilement.

There is yet a third test — that of love and trust in God. "God hath sent forth the Spirit of His Son into our hearts, crying Abba, Father." (Gal. iv. 6.) The many disputes of Christians have done much to weaken the confidence of men in the paternal love of God, and in the power of Christ to save. Are we indeed so near to God, that we can flee to Him as to a loving Father, and pour out our complaints before Him, and show Him our troubles, certain of His love? Did Jesus indeed die for our sins and rise again for our justification? These are questions that some who would fain not doubt are tempted to ask. It is the fruit of a century of controversy in this and other countries. It is the trial of our age, as the Gnostic and the Arian errors were of their day. There is not a difficulty in the gospels—nay, there is not a place into which a difficulty could be thrust, but what has been urged into the service of unbelief, with all the arts that are needed, to make bad reasoning pass for good. We dare not say that this has not made it more difficult for some to turn to their God with that simple faith with which a child betakes itself to its father. And yet without this trust we are not abiding in Him; He is not making His abode with us. Let us pray to Him that He will strengthen the bonds of our union with Him. Let us try to be able to ask Him to take full possession of our souls, to cast out every thought that could set itself against Him, to carry us along the track of his will and purpose, as the wind carries the ship over the seas. Let us ask Him to burn up all the wood and stubble wherewith we have been building in ourselves after a fashion of our own, and build up in us a sincere trust in Him and in His Son. Let us say, " O send out Thy light and Thy truth that they may lead me." For when we can look on God as our hiding-place from trouble, and our shelter from temptation, when we can look up to the Cross on which hung the Son of God manifested in the flesh, knowing that from that death came our salvation, then we are sure that the Spirit of God has not deserted us; for there cannot be in us any faith or any love that does not proceed from Him.

Finally, let this day's lesson for us be — the nearness of our God. If we were taught that the Comforter began His work in the world on the day of Pentecost, we might think that that which began so late might end after a time. But the Spirit of God has never been absent from the world. Before the universe was fashioned, the Spirit moved or brooded over the formless void. Arts and wisdom, and prophecies, have owed their origin to Him under the old dispensation. Just as the eternal Son, one with the Father from everlasting, became, in the fulness of time, the incarnate Redeemer and our Advocate with the Father, so did the eternal Spirit, the love of God, one with the Father and the Son, become, when the day of Pentecost was fully come, the Comforter or Advocate of the Church on earth. And His continuance with us is a fact as certain as that we live and think. Wherever a man loves and reverences the souls of other men (and thanks be to God there are many who do so), wherever there is an abhorrence of sin, and a loving trust in God, there is the Holy Spirit dwelling. No cloven tongues of fire are needed to tell us that He is there. We see Him in His fruits, as we know that a wind has bowed the trees, or ruffled the water, though we cannot see it. Moreover without the presence of that Holy Spirit we cannot rightly live, we cannot safely die. If He is standing near us, waiting to sanctify us, ready to commence His work in us, willing to set up a shrine and make a temple even in these sinful and polluted hearts of ours, and we will not have Him as our inmate, angels might tremble at the audacity of our refusal. Here, on this narrow ledge of time, between two eternities, we stand ready to perish. After a score or two of years all those who are here will have passed into the awful presence of God, and another congregation will be listening to another teacher proclaiming the eternal truth of the Gospel, unless the whole world has crumbled into dust, and the end of all things arrived. And a hand powerful to protect and save is stretched out to us, and we will not take it. And an offer is made to us to commence in us here the true life which we shall have to live in eternity, and we prefer our sins, and clutch our silly toys closer to us, just as we are going to drop into the grave. Father, save us from this unspeakable folly. Pour out Thy Spirit upon us, and bring into captivity every thought to the obedience of Christ. Give us a love of all men, for they are dear to Thee, and a hatred of sin, for it crucified Thy Son, and a loving trust in Thee, whose mercies never fail. So shall we be safe from the evil, and shall know Thy kingdom, which is "righteousness and peace, and joy in the Holy Ghost." (Rom. xiv. 17.)

SERMON X.

GOD IN NATURE.

Genesis i. 31.

And God saw every thing that he had made, and, behold, it was very good. And the evening and the morning were the sixth day.

Between science and religion there is assumed by many to exist a principle of perpetual hostility. The study of nature is supposed to involve over and above those dangers which are inherent in the exclusive and engrossing pursuit of any end whatever, perils peculiar to itself, and snares from which even a good will will hardly save a man. In that atmosphere the seeds of spiritual pride are supposed to float almost invisible, and no soil is so good but that this weed will grow in it. Many religious persons think these dangers so great, that the chances of benefit from the study of natural science do not compensate for them. On the other hand, men of science suspect *them* of a wish to stifle truth and arrest research. Thus it is that science and religion stand aloof in mutual distrust; and the assumption that there is an enmity between knowledge and love, between the truth as seen with the eye, and the truth as felt in the heart, leads to consequences injurious to both.

I. Now, if we were to seek in detail for the reasons of this estrangement, we should probably come first to the false applications which men make of *the doctrine of final causes.* In plainer language, the object with which the great Creator made the universe is often misunderstood. When the six days of creation were finished, " God saw everything that He had made, and behold it was very good." And when it was pronounced *good*, one end of the creation was already answered. His infinite wisdom had found a finite expression in the fixed laws and complex harmonies of the universe; His infinite love had begun to operate in a finite sphere in all the thousand forms of life and happiness among his creatures. The Most High had put forth His hand; had uttered Himself in speech. And when the universe, which had gone forth from Him a finished work, returned, as it were, to the foot of the throne, that it might abide with His approval, or perish at His rejection, then was the great end accomplished, for it did not repent Him that He had made all things. All His work He found to be very good; and there can be no end higher than that of pleasing God.

But here the error of Calvin meets us. The creation is not merely *a means* of showing the glory of God; man is not a mere instrument, as Calvin held, for the same purpose. Man is not a thing; but a moral being, capable of feeling love and wrong; and the lower ranks of creatures are capable in their degree of receiving the benefits of love. It was because the works of God were full of His love, that they seemed to Him very good. For all life was the gift of His love; and the thick covert of the beast, and the cedars of God's planting, wherein the birds made their nests, and the teeming sea, rendered back their mute unconscious thanksgiving for the daily joy and activity which he infused into them. "These wait all upon Thee; that Thou mayest give them their meat in due season. That Thou givest them they gather: Thou openest Thy hand, they are filled with good. Thou hidest Thy face, they are troubled : Thou takest away their breath, they die, and return to their dust. Thou sendest forth Thy Spirit, they are created: and Thou renewest the face of the earth. The glory of the Lord shall endure for ever: *the Lord shall rejoice in His works.*" (Ps. civ.)

The final cause of the creation, then, is, that God's glory may be made manifest through the harmony and beauty of natural laws, and the well-being of His creatures, and that He may approve His own works. Now the common language of theologians, borrowed, I think, from Lactantius (Inst. Div. vii. 4), has led to a great restriction of this definition. The world, they say, was created for the use of animals, and animals for man, and man for God. Hence when proofs of the divine goodness are to be sought for in creation, they are too often limited to direct examples of advantage to man; as if we had established a monopoly of that divine love in which we do so richly share, as if this great universe, this temple of God, wonderful in beauty, echoing with endless liturgies of praise, were a mere workshop for the satisfaction of our wants! The tree whose bark is a sovereign remedy for a stubborn class of diseases, is a blessing to man, and one among a myriad proofs of the loving wisdom of the Creator; but can we say that for this one use, and no other, it was placed upon the earth? Then was it quite useless when it waved for thousands of years along the mountain side, unnoticed in its growth, its bloom, and its decay, before the Jesuit missionaries of two centuries since discovered its healing virtue. "The Lord rejoices in His works." God saw that tree also in the solitude of the forest, and behold it was very good. His wisdom was written upon it within and without; a hundred natural laws ordained by Him nurtured and sustained it. Man comes at last, and discovers here a new treasure of love which he can divert to himself. But if the shivering ague had gone without its appropriate relief, if this remedy had lain hid, as no doubt in the fastnesses of nature many another still escapes us, God would not have been without the little voice of praise which this work contributes to the general hymn. Or again, when it is argued, as we have seen it in a well-known controversy, that one of the great planets of our system is inhabited, because four watchful satellites continue to make perpetual moonlight round it, and if there are none to see, this gift is wasted, the petulant demand that all that is good shall turn at once to human profit, is surely somewhat derogatory, however reverently meant, to the honour of the great Architect. He is not a parsimonious householder that grudges a light until the guests be come. If harmony and beauty be ends in themselves, then there can be in the universal economy no such thing as waste, since there is nothing false or out of place. Let there be some world in which as yet the rough rocks have hardly been won from the receding waters, and the wallowing monster is the only tenant it can sustain, still God sees that this too is very good, good in what has hitherto been wrought upon it, good in its future hopes, good as a constituent in the nice balance of the whole creation, good as bearing the stamp of wisdom, and the promise half fulfilled of love. Now so far as serious persons expect the man of science to confine his search into causes to proofs of adaptation to the wants of our race, so far as all inquiries which do not bring these out are suspected to be beside religion, if not against it, thus far do we narrow the sphere of science unduly, and even deprive ourselves of the helps which science might bring us towards apprehending the wonderful love and wisdom of the Almighty. Nor can the misunderstanding between science and religion be removed, until it shall be confessed that the truths of science have so much in common with those of revelation, that they both reveal to man the same attributes of the divine nature.

II. But if there is some ground for the complaint on the side of natural philosophy, that its opponents would circumscribe its labours to their false impression of the divine intention, there is ground, too, for that fear which seems so widely spread amongst good men, that the conditions of our moral nature and its needs are often lost sight of in the exclusive pursuit of physical laws. Let me sketch, in a most brief and imperfect way, the line of thought in which this danger occurs.

The study of all physical phenomena is a study of fixed laws. With every day's acquaintance with the facts of nature, our confidence in the settled invariable order that prevails there, gathers fresh strength. When some fact apparently exceptional thwarts the application of a known law, no one suspects (provided miraculous agency is out of the question) that there has been any arbitrary interference with the order of nature; the fact is accepted as indicative of a new law, perhaps unknown, and it gives a new direction to research, without abating our confidence in the principle that a fixed order rules the universe. Now it would be a natural inference, unless there be some strong reason against it, that what always is necessarily must be, that what we have never seen otherwise cannot be otherwise than it is. And then, if lower causes are bound to operate, as fire to burn, and matter to attract matter, and a wound to kill, and the like, will not the same be true of higher causes, nay, even of the highest, the divine nature itself? A cause which does not produce effects is not truly a cause. An infinite Being who does not manifest Himself in finite productions, may indeed be conceived of, but we have no knowledge of such a one (thus it is argued) except as a dialectical abstraction. Thus we must not separate nature from the Deity, for we know the one in and through the other. From the bosom of the unchangeable eternity, from the omnipotent Cause, from the unlimited Being, a wonderful variety of finite and imperfect beings is being given off by a necessary law. The divine Being, then, and nature are but two sides, or aspects of one fact, and whether we represent it as the one Being bound to multiply Himself in a thousand forms, or a thousand finite beings depending on and mounting up to one First Cause; whether, to borrow the language of the schools, we conceive of the *natura naturans*, or the *natura naturata*, one and the same thing is before us, the necessary co-existence of the Cause and its created effects, as one great fact given us to know. According as one or other side has been made predominant, the results have been differently stated; now the world has been made to recede till it became little more than a symbol; now it has been brought into prominence, and natural laws, and the various developments of human will, have been accepted as the only accessible form of divine operation. This is the pantheistic line of thought, roughly sketched, which, in its more complete state, has assumed a greater variety of shapes than can even be indicated here.

There are no doubt temptations to this sort of belief; there is even this partial truth in it, that it maintains the presence and the immanence of the divine nature in all the phenomena around us. But it leads us to three appalling conclusions: the god that it leaves to us is not a real god; the will that is in you and me is no real power of choice, but a juggle that we put upon ourselves to disguise the ignominy of a remorseless compulsion; and the evil which perplexed us sufficiently in a world created by a perfect Being, becomes an intolerable contradiction when it is planted in the bosom of the divine Being himself. Yes, we are landed again after our voyage of discovery in the old pagan belief; the gods, said the old Greek, rule us, and fate rules the gods; laws, says the modern thinker, rule us, and fate and necessity rule them. For if the great Creator, whom we have known as One who, by the breath of His word, called out of nothing the stellar universe, and the plant and the beast, and the man, — as One who can withdraw His sustaining will, so that all shall vanish into dust, and the dust itself be consumed away, — is only the powerless hierarch that presides over, but does not control the lower order of causes, then let there be no more worship, for there can be no response to worship, no more reverence or holy fear, for you cannot cry Abba, Father, to the mainspring even of the most wonderful machine; and if all phenomena not only depend on, but are in and part of the divine nature, our power of choice is involved among the rest, and we do indeed, as Spinoza says (Eth. iii. 2), dream with our eyes open, when we think that we can choose or forbear, eschew the evil and seek the good. And it follows that the evil as well as the good is part of the divine nature, and thus the hard paradox of the existence of evil in a world created by the Deity assumes its most revolting form. The knife of the murderer, and the drunkard's babbling speech, and the idolatrous orgy, are all incited by the same compulsion of necessity which urges on the calm march of the heavens, and the yearly cycle of the seasons.

It may be conceded that pantheism in some of its forms has sprung up in connection with physical studies. The contemplation of invariable sequence has suggested necessity; the intense study of the beautiful adaptations in nature has sometimes led to an exaggeration of their dignity and permanence in reference to the Creator. But such aberrations only warn us that the same laws of balance and compensation which maintain the universe apply to the human intellect also; that a falsehood arises from the endeavour to rest in half a truth. A real consciousness of sin would have made it impossible to confound the world with Him who rules it. Look out upon the kingdom of order, where all is sure and settled, where nothing lags or hurries, where the vigilant laws, which are as angels of the Most High, leave no spot vacant, and whence some portion of the serenity that pervades it can hardly fail to be reflected back upon you; such is God's own work, which He pronounced to be very good. Now look within upon the kingdom of confusion; where the weak will utters its behests, and sees them disobeyed, where we can scarcely promise that an outburst of some passion shall not transform itself into a crime, where the light of a better ideal is ever present to rebuke the lame performance of our duty; and then say, "God is not the author of confusion, but of peace." If the ordered universe, in its profound peace, is His work, then my sinful troubled state certainly comes from some other hand; I recognise Him in the peace, I am conscious that the confusion proceeds from my guilty self. Gladly would I feel the identity of my being with His; gladly would I believe my actions were not my own, but were produced by His almighty will streaming through me. But oh, the gulf of guilt and corruption that separates me from such a union! Only in a new creation of my nature can I find my way back to Him. "Who shall deliver me from the body of this death?" Let me find One, if there be any one endowed with such power, who shall be the way, and the truth, and the life to me. Then shall the laws of order penetrate me too; the strange confusion shall disappear, and a deep peace pervade me, such as God loves, and has diffused through His creation.*

III. There is yet a third ground of the distrust between science and religion; it is the fear lest in the immensity of the scheme which science opens out, the means by which man's salvation was wrought should be obscured or even brought into question. " When I consider Thy heavens the work of Thy fingers, the moon and the stars which Thou hast ordained, what is man, that thou art mindful of him, and the son of man that Thou visitest him?" (Ps. viii.) And this danger is perhaps the most subtle of all, and the most likely to stagger even the reverent mind. Some of us may remember the devices by which in the books of Buddhism† the vast extension of space and duration of time are sought to be conveyed. "Enclose," said these fantastic teachers, "the space occupied by millions of solar systems, and suppose it filled with mustard seed, and a single grain taken and cast towards each solar system without the space, and when the seeds are exhausted, not half the systems will have received each its little seed." But are not the realities of astronomy even more striking than these fancies? We are told that our system of stars, of which the milky way is the confine, will appear to

---

* The tendency to materialism is spoken of in other sermons in this volume, and therefore a few sentences on that subject are omitted here. See Sermons on IMMORTALITY and on THE TEMPLE OF GOD.

† See Mr. Hardy's interesting "Manual of Buddhism."

some distant observer a little nebular mass, needing sharp instruments to resolve it even roughly; that all our system, besides the manifold revolutions in itself, revolves in obedience to another distant invisible centre. And no one has ventured, even with a ground of probability, to arrest us as we try to march in thought across what almost seems an infinite universe; no one dares deny that even the most distant body, whose existence we rather infer than perceive, is but as the first step in our progress through the universe. By thoughts like these, our conception of the divine power is exalted, but our notion of the place we hold in the general system contracts in proportion. "What is man, that Thou art mindful of him, and the son of man that Thou visitest him?" The revealed word of God contains at length the history of one transaction, the sin of the human race, and its redemption from ruin. On this little ball of earth, which is only as a sand grain upon the shore of space, did the Most High himself make a covenant with man for his salvation, did truly "visit the son of man" in sending His own Son to bear all human sins, and to purify to Himself a peculiar people zealous of good works, whose King and Shepherd He would evermore continue to be. What is man that such love was bestowed upon him? Has he been singled out from the myriads of races that perhaps occupy the other bodies like this earth, or have the fall and the restoration taken place in other worlds? And if so, what have the means of restoration been? The same as with us, or different? Such questions are apt to be suggested. But neither science nor revelation professes to reply to them. And it is our bounden duty to avoid them; not to allow them to throw doubt either upon divine revelation on the one hand, or the system of the universe on the other. But we *may* inquire whether there exists in us a need great enough to warrant an expectation of divine interference; for it is on this that the belief in atonement and restoration must depend. If souls of men lay shattered and disordered, if their efforts at self-restoration were futile, then there is more than a presumption that the great Ruler of all provided a restoration. For vast as is the universe, there is no hint in any part of it that the sustaining Spirit flags, or that the hand of God intermits doing what each particular case requires. What special medicine was selected for the disorders of other spheres it is in vain to inquire. His wealth is abundant; His love great. The book of revelation does not purport to be a picture of the whole creation. It begins from man, for it is the history of his death and life: even the account of creation, as we read it there, is confined for the most part to the earth, which is our stage of action. Had it pleased God to shorten the researches of science, by granting us a history of all that He had done throughout the universe, its form would have been different, and the space allotted to human affairs probably very brief. Let us follow the example which the Bible sets us; let us dwell upon our own depravity, and the love of Him that hath taken us into a state of reconcilement; and let us not turn aside from the contemplation of these things to fruitless questions about the fate of others. Remember the rebuke that our Lord addressed to a favoured disciple who fell into the same error. Look not up to the heaven, populous with stars and crowded perhaps with beings like ourselves, in order to say, "What shall these men do?" for our Lord will give us no other answer than that which Peter received, "What is that to thee? Follow thou Me." (John xxi.)

These, then, are some of the difficulties to be met with in conciliating science with religion ; a narrow view of the doctrine of final causes, a fear lest the conditions of our moral nature should be lost sight of in the exclusive study of physical laws, and a dread of reducing the earth to a place so humble in the system of things, as to throw a doubt upon its having received the special mercy of redemption. The positive benefits to be derived from the study of the works of God, may well form the subject of another sermon. There is no necessary connection between the pursuit of science and the sin of pride. There is a pride of science, indeed, as there is a pride of religion, or of riches, or of influence, or of strength; that is to say, the sinful egotism of our little nature will peep out in every subject on which our thoughts are engaged. But can we afford to dispense with anything that brings us nearer to that Being who is so far above us, yet whom we must approach since He is our light and life? There are some who would willingly know God only in one of His works, that of redemption. But to learn to reverence Him as the Infinite, the high and lofty One that inhabiteth eternity, we must climb up by the ladder of His works. To comprehend the riches of His love, we must regard Him as the beneficent Father that makes His sun to rise on the evil and the good, and sendeth rain on the just and on the unjust; on whom all creatures wait, whose hand provides them food, whose will gives and withdraws their life. To adore His wisdom, we think on the host of heaven, and the instinct of the animal, and the soul of man, and the mutual adaptation of the parts of the creation, which have ever been the theme of a wonder that does not diminish but increase with the progress of inquiry. Ever on the watch for marks of wise design, we must remember at the same time that ours are not eyes that can be trusted to decide what purpose is wisest; the parts of the creation that seem to us least useful may be as comely in the eyes of the Designer as any that we most admire.

It will be seen from what we have said that error in this subject, as in most others, arises not so much in what we see as in what we pretermit. The materialist sets little store on the life of his own soul hereafter, or on its communion with God in the present; hence he is content with a system in which there is neither Deity nor immortality. The pantheist overlooks the enormity of moral evil. The mystic sees not the realities of the present life, its strife and struggle, and regards it as little more than a symbol of the divine mind, to convey it to the soul of man. Let us be sure, Christian friends, before we embark in this or any other pursuit, that the soul is sane and complete. We never heard of a pious mind perverted by learning how deep are the recesses of yonder smooth heaven, and how infinite in number its shining orbs. We never heard of one who counted his own soul precious, being robbed of all belief in a soul by seeing the knife lay bare the marvellous secrets of an animal structure. In the truest sense " The fear of the Lord is the beginning of wisdom;" because those who fear and love Him look for Him in the realm of order that surrounds them, and they who look find. God is not far from every one of us; every moment of our own existence, every degree and minute of the revolution of the universe takes place by an effluence of power from Him. Do not consent to a divorce between knowledge and religion. I can conceive no sight more deplorable, no portent that more surely marks the corruption of the times which produce it, than that of a philosopher wandering through the universe, and endeavouring of set purpose so to describe the system of the heavens, and chemical action, and the facts of life, and the growth of society, as to exclude the Divine Being from His own work. The only attraction of such a system — that affected precision which is gained by excluding all but facts of direct observation, — is in truth illusory; for at the end it will be found that all the interior facts of the mind itself have been omitted. But we, when we turn towards the Book of Wisdom before us, will read it in a Christian spirit; we will remember that God, and nature, and the soul do really exist, nor shall the study of the one blind us to the other two. Thus shall the pursuit of science confirm revelation. He who is mighty in creation, is the same whom the Bible reveals to us as powerful to save. He whose love and bounty fills the creation with gladness, has also promised that He will not forget the contrite soul. And in the sight of that unspeakable order and repose, the turbulence of our passions, our restless hopes, our unreasonable fears receive their rebuke. We can afford to lay us down in peace and take our rest, for He can make us dwell in safety; for His eyes " run to and fro through the whole earth " which He has made, " to show Himself strong in behalf of them whose heart is perfect towards Him " (2 Chron. xvi. 9).

SERMON XI.

GOD IN NATURE.

Genesis i. 31.

And God saw every thing that he had made, and, behold, it was very good. And the evening and the morning were the sixth day.

The causes of the mutual suspicion of science and religion were the subject of a recent sermon from this place. To discuss the aid which may be expected from a right study of science to the cause of religious truth would be an appropriate sequel to it. The subject is vast and difficult, and needs a special training, but perhaps it has been somewhat too much avoided in our pulpit teaching; and in the silence of those more especially gifted for the handling of such matter, weaker attempts may hope for some indulgence. There is, however, a fear more real than that of man's criticism, the fear lest in attempting to read off the splendid page of God's primeval revelation of Himself through nature, words not intended to be found there, not worthy of Him about whom they are spoken, may find utterance, which, may He, through His guiding Spirit, avert from us!

We are intended to learn from the contemplation of nature, whether scientific or untaught, *reverence* from beholding the power and majesty of God, *love* from observing His goodness, *trust* from seeing His foresight for us, and *humility* from learning His unsearchableness.

I. It has ever been the character of true religion to surround the name of the Lord Most High with awe and reverence. And if it be right to define religion as a deep sense of our dependence on God, no doubt the feeling of dependence can only there exist, where the Divine Being is conceived as One infinitely above and beyond us, "dwelling in light which no man can approach unto, whom no man hath seen, or can see." The false gods of the Greek were little else than Greeks like himself, and their doings were but a transcript of the daily life of the people, somewhat heightened in beauty and poetic colouring, but not more awful or terrible. Close behind every act of life some deity was supposed to be sitting, so thoroughly human, so incapable of affording, even for a moment, moral support, or satisfying the instincts of an adoring mind, that wiser men feared not to approach and examine these semblant divinities, and even dared to pronounce, as Plato did, that it was a scandal and a blasphemy to attribute to gods the passions of men. But when God chose one people to receive a special revelation of Himself, He used the powers of nature to assist their blindness in conceiving of the unspeakable brightness of His presence, He made the thunder and the hail, the fog and the locust agents in their deliverance. They passed through a parted sea into a land where only the Ruler of Creation could have found food for their multitudes. The stormy terrors of Sinai were the chosen evidence that Jehovah was dealing with His people close at hand. God *is not* fire or lightning, but He chose to manifest Himself in using the more potent natural agents, in order that they might know that the Lord, who was King of the Hebrews, was also creation's Lord; and as such did the prophets always make Him known to the people. To take one example — when Isaiah, in the fortieth chapter, pours out for the chosen people the balm of comfort, he reminds them that their deliverer is also the God of all the universe, and that the very vastness of His dominions is a guarantee that He will not forget the smallest part of them. "Lift up your eyes on high, and behold who hath created these things, that bringeth out their host by number: He calleth them all by names, by the greatness of His might, for that He is strong in power: not one faileth. Why sayest thou, O Jacob, and speakest, O Israel, My way is hid from the Lord, and my judgment is passed over from my God? Hast thou not known? hast thou not heard, that the everlasting God, the Lord, the Creator of the ends of the earth, fainteth not, neither is weary? there is no searching of His understanding" (v. 26-28). And thus St. Paul makes it the condemnation of the Gentiles, that they were not without a revelation of God, so long as they had the wonders of creation to proclaim Him. "For the invisible things of Him from the creation of the world are clearly seen, being understood by the things that are made, even His eternal power and godhead; so that they are without excuse" (Rom. i. 20). If, then, Isaiah fears not, at the very moment when he wishes to intensify the sense of divine comfort in the minds of the Jews, to direct their eyes to the wonderful extent of the divine operations, in order that they may be sure of the sufficiency of His power; if St. Paul tells us that the wonders of creation were a revelation to the Gentiles, and should have been their safeguard against atheism, it cannot be wrong to expect from the discoveries of science some aid towards deepening our reverence for the Lord who is our Shepherd, and at the same time the Guardian of the universe, who "shall feed His flock like a shepherd, and shall gather the lambs with His arm, and carry them in His bosom"; yet at the same time "hath measured the waters in the hollow of His hand, and meted out heaven with the span, and comprehended the dust of the earth in a measure, and weighed the mountains in scales, and the hills in a balance."

What, then, have the sciences added to our sense of the awful power of the infinite God? Astronomy, by slow degrees, has advanced from the conception of a single earth, tented over with the jewelled canopy of the sky, to a result which I suppose is as real as any other inference of reason, that the earth is one planet among many in the solar system, and the solar system one among many in a stellar cluster, and the stellar cluster one among many in the visible heavens. It was a great discovery that the sun's apparent motion was an illusion, and his rising and setting were but moments in the earth's revolution. But the sun itself is moving, and with a speed that can be measured, attended by its planetary train, and the narrow scrutiny of the astronomer's glass can tell us how the receding stars converge as we are driven along like the houses on a shore we are quitting. If, as is at least probable, our whole system is revolving round a centre, lurking unseen in enormous distance behind the Pleiads, then may not that very centre itself be subject to the same laws of motion? And where is this chain of thought to end? How far should we travel over immeasurable space before we could reach the point of central rest? If we were to try to express in figures the times and spaces measured in such researches, the usual signs of computation would be meaningless to us from the vastness of the phenomena. Or ask physiology to speak of the abundance of *life* upon our planet, and by fair analogy in other worlds as well. There is no insect so minute, but is truly a marvel of creative power. Each is a little matter, quickened and lighted with life,

with a power which we cannot understand, cannot even define, and which only does not arrest us with adoring wonder, because its frequency blunts our faculties. When the earth was preparing for man, great strata were deposited, in every cubic inch of which lie buried millions on millions of minute creatures which God saw good to make. Here again would numbers fail us, we can hardly carry our thoughts beyond the first step. In one place a whole town stands on the rocky tombs of such a minute population; in another, the shore of a lake is powdered with their remains. Oh the inexhaustible wealth of that creative energy, which poured out on this planet when as yet it was dreary and void, and unfit for the lordly tenant a little lower than the angels, for whom it was being furnished, a mass of living creatures, whose only praise of Him was their life and motion, too small for eye to see, yet each perfect in its kind, and very good! "The majesty of God," it has been well said, "appears no less in small things than in great, and as it exceedeth human sense in the immense greatness of the universe, so also it doth in the smallness of the parts thereof." *
Chemistry, too, would add its record of wonders. How every plant conspires to recruit the air with the element of which the animals have robbed it, and every animal unconsciously requites the benefit — how our food is changed into the juices of life — how the plant wins from mere soil and air its sweet per-

* Hobbes.

fume, its sap with its peculiar virtue, its form of leaf, and the colour of its flower.

Now here are motives for fear and reverence. What bounds can we set to His power? The distinction between miracles and natural facts seems obliterated, for the facts are customary wonders, and the miracles novel ones. And just because the universe is so full and various, do we trust His presence in the smallest part of it. The potter at his wheel shapes the one vessel that he is making, imperfectly; it is cracked, or crooked, or the fire will spoil it, although this, and this only, exercises his faculties. But just because the Most High does so much, do we feel that no part will be slurred or marred. When I see that the starry host in their seemingly irregular profusion are not as scattered sheep without a shepherd, but as a trained army, whose marching steps are all at one — when I think how a moment's relaxation of that will that keeps them steady in their path would plunge them into disaster and chaos, then am I sure that here is one on whom I may look with awe and reverence. Why should it be a thing incredible that He should care for my soul, when I know that all that I am is bound already to Him by the threads of a hundred laws? Why should He leave my soul in hell, if every day bears witness to His care of me? Why should I disbelieve the marvel of my new creation to eternal life, since I am lost in wonder at the trite facts of my creation and preservation? Why should He not have prepared upon earth a special agency for my redemption from sin and death, when I know that ever since I was born, His laws, like angels, have hovered round me, and passed through and through me, mixing me the air I breathe, preparing my elaborate food, warning my senses against what is noisome, conciliating other beings like myself to be my allies and protectors? " Thou hast beset me behind and before, and laid thine hand upon me.... I will praise Thee; for I am fearfully and wonderfully made: marvellous are Thy works; and that my soul knoweth right well." (Ps. cxxxix.)

II. But every argument for His power turns readily into an argument for His goodness. He has made the worlds, we may conclude, that all or most of them, besides the purposes of harmony and beauty they subserve, may be fountains of beneficence, not for man alone, but for every creature capable of receiving and enjoying life. The winds refresh them, the waters give them drink, the innumerable suns cheer them with light. For man the conditions of nature bring not merely happiness but education. Where a bountiful soil and climate render the wants of life easy to satisfy, the human species makes less progress. And so the Almighty has put a lock upon many of the secrets of His love, and has given us faculties to seek the key and open the hid treasure. Everything that has life is a proof of the love of God, and adds one voice to His praise. The minutest of those animalcules we spoke of, all of which are so small, that it is but as yesterday that man has learnt through improved instruments that they existed at all, was endowed with a vital activity; and in placing it where the activity might find room and vent, the Creator made it capable of a certain lower degree of pleasure. And their multitudes must have been so great, that the city most crowded with men would be in comparison little better than a desolate solitude. And though higher creatures now find room in the world, the profuse expenditure of life in lower forms never ceases. The ocean teems with life. Not to speak of the enormous shoals of fish, the voyager passes through miles of turbid water, and discovers that it is tinged with myriads of infusorial beings, too numerous for calculation. No latitude is free from them; they swarm under the hot sun, they abound in the polar cold. They throng the surface, they are found at depths where even the light can scarcely pierce. "O Lord, how manifold are Thy works! in wisdom Thou hast made them all: the earth is full of Thy riches. So is this great and wide sea, wherein are things creeping innumerable, both small and great beasts." (Ps. civ. 24, 25.) Into what depths of truth and beauty, then, does our Lord permit us to look, when He says — "Take no thought for your life, what ye shall eat, or what ye shall drink; nor yet for your body, what ye shall put on. Is not the life more than meat, and the body than raiment? Behold the fowls of the air: for they sow not, neither do they reap, nor gather into barns;

yet your heavenly Father feedeth them. Are ye not much better than they?" (Mat. vi. 25, 26.) Is not the life more than meat? Shall not He who has shown His loving care for us in our creation, continue the life He has begun? If at every moment of our life we are kept suspended, but in safety, over the depth of annihilation, by His will, and that alone, — if the same will, exerted without weariness or distraction, is directed full upon every minutest creature, to sustain it, — then there need be no figure of speech in our Lord's words, " The very hairs of your head are all numbered." The lower creatures wait on God; when He takes away their breath they die and return to their dust. When He sends forth his Spirit they are created, and He renews the face of the earth. Then it is natural to seek in human affairs for marks of His loving-kindness and protection, — to attribute, as the Psalmist does, deliverance from the perils of the storm, and the fertility of the earth, and other such mercies, to the same Divine hand.

And the crowning mystery of Divine love in man's redemption becomes more easy to accept for those who, having observed these things, " understand the loving-kindness of the Lord." (Ps. cvii. 43.) We have said that one difficulty in receiving it lay in our own insignificance. " Will the majesty of the Most High turn aside into this remote corner of the universe to redeem me?" or, as the inspired book itself expresses it — " When I consider Thy heavens, even the work of Thy fingers, the moon and the stars, which Thou hast ordained; what is man, that Thou art mindful of him? and the son of man, that Thou visitest him?" (Psalm viii.) But since the power of God is not finite, since its boundless extension detracts nothing from the completeness of its intension in every smallest part of nature, since He is not far from every one of us, and only the preoccupation of our minds by their own selfish passions prevents us from seeing that in Him we live, and move, and have our being, and to Him owe thanks for all the benefits that He has heaped on us, then we may cease to wonder that He who has begun a good work in us will complete it by our everlasting salvation.

III. Our trust in our divine Father is strengthened by the views which science offers of His providence. Whatever we may think of the abuse of the argument from design, its use is not only scriptural, not only reasonable, but is in fact sanctioned by the common opinion of all ages. When we see things fitted for their uses, we cannot help attaching the notion of design to them. When we find the reptile, the fish, the bird, the mammal, wonderfully adapted to the several conditions in which they must live, then we may infer that their Creator fitted their structure to their exigencies. It is the inversion of the argument from final causes that is unsafe. We may admire the wisdom which has placed animals in a world well-fitted for them, but we must not infer from discovering a world that God must needs have placed animals there. This *argument from parsimony*, which binds, so to speak, the Most High to make a present use of every plot of ground in His dominions, implies a far greater insight into the Divine mind than we can pretend to possess, and it is contradicted by some of the most well-known facts of science. But those opposing facts are themselves an argument for the forethought that rules the universe. Before the earth was prepared for man's habitation, it passed through many stages of improvement. We cannot now turn aside into an exposition of the Mosaic account of the creation; suffice it to say, that the indications of the changes in question are to be sought for, in my opinion, in the Mosaic record, and not in some period anterior to its commencement; and the results of science are not inconsistent, as indeed they could not be, with a fair interpretation of that divine document. But these changes were all so many far-sighted preparations for the state in which the world now is; they showed in themselves order and design, and also laid the foundation of another step somewhat higher, in which other plans manifested themselves, and other phases of order came out. The thread of an unchangeable purpose runs through the various dealings of the Creator with our planet before man was placed there, as it does through the history of man himself. But in order to see the proportions of God's great design, even to the small extent that our powers allow, we must stand somewhat back from the great canvas whereon it was drawn. In the submersion of a continent, as well as in the *Mene, mene, tekel, upharsin* of a kingdom, progress might seem to cease, and the retreating tide of confusion to roll back again; when a juster judgment would show us that no purpose of God can ever fall to the ground. The larger the sphere we can embrace in our inquiry, the more shall we be convinced of this. When the earth was without form and void, it was as truly the destined home of man, as it was after the successive acts of creation had peopled it with all the creatures over whom man should have the dominion. No indication of faltering was there; and the temporary lapses, as they might have seemed, have turned out to be steps in advance. It has been so in historic times. Looking at the history of the Jews, as it were from a distance, we can see how they were made from the first the channel of good to mankind; but when the people of Jehovah made ·bricks in Egypt,—when the theocratic kingdom became a Roman appanage, — above all, when the chosen One of God cried "Why hast Thou forsaken me?" on the tree, the continuity of the Divine purpose might seem to be broken. Now I do not say that we can *infer* from the history of our globe the immortality destined for us. But when we feel the law of duty written in our hearts, and try however weakly to obey it; when we forego pleasure, that we may manifest in some way our love to God; when we assume thereby, as we certainly do, that there is a Lawgiver who has sanctioned this law of duty and approves its performance, then the aspect of the universe, so full of forethought, lends our belief a most salutary confirmation. The attractive forces that dictate their paths to the heavenly bodies, the balance of the animal and vegetable creation, the nice adaptation of our organs to their uses, the abundant materials prepared long before in the bowels of the earth for our present civilisation, supply, if not a proof, a most suasive probability, that that moral law by which we try to live, or which we do not abandon without self-reproach, has its purpose likewise, which a future life alone can satisfy.

IV. It was said in the outset that science, in confessing the unsearchableness of God, might well teach us *humility*. That science has often engendered pride, is but too certain; all that can be maintained is, that whilst a fault of character will peep out in any subject, there is nothing in the nature of physical research to turn a pious heart aside. No one knows so well as the philosopher himself where the limits of his knowledge are fixed. He knows not the secret springs of the universal motion; attraction — gravitation — are convenient names set upon certain facts, but they do not in the least explain the facts themselves. Again, he knows where to apply the word *life*, but he has laboured vainly to define what it is to be alive; still less can he explain the real nature of this mysterious power, which can take up a portion of matter, and fashion it into a complete organism, and enable it successfully to resist the decomposing agents that surround it. Again, he has a clear conception of what he means by an element; it is something which resists the chemist's analysis. But why some substances should resist decomposition and others not; whether the substances now called elements are so really; whether the ultimate elements are many, or few, or one; these are questions on which he dares hardly risk an opinion. So that in the three great realms of physical inquiry, what we do not know is far more than what we know. Hasty observers give men of science credit for a deep research into these subjects, from which nothing lies hid. But those who have entered upon such studies know, that whilst immense results have been obtained for human happiness and good, by careful grouping of facts as they were observed, the products are only superficial in respect of any real inner knowledge of the causes and nature of things. So far, then, is science from bringing us into a proximity with the works of creation dangerous to our piety and reverence, that some slight knowledge at least of the real limits of science is essential to a right conviction of our own weak sightedness. If all that we could know of the Most High lay through the gate of science, we might well make the poet's words our own —

> "I falter where I firmly trod,
>   And fall with all my weight of cares
>   Upon the great world's altar-stairs,
>   That slope through darkness up to God."*

But it is the very "weight of cares" that oppresses us, that should lead us to a higher truth. And here comes in that of which physical science cannot properly take account, the admonition of the laden conscience. The sense of sin has no analogy in the field of physical observation; even the soul that feels it is something set apart, the tenant of matter, but not material, obstinately refusing, in many phenomena, to be assimilated in any degree to lower things. The power to choose, the sense of responsibility engendered by that, the corruptions of our nature that infringe our freedom, without taking away the need of choosing, all connect man with a higher class of facts, which the prudent physiologist will do well to leave out of his province. The sense of Divine behests neglected, whilst yet it is felt that they are as really a portion of the Divine arrangements as the laws of physical motion, lays on us a load of care. And when some one bids us rise and cast this burden on the Lord, and we endeavour to obey, we are taking the first step in a new road to divine knowledge, the road of faith, love, and obedience. It will not hinder us in the work of repentance, to have acquired right ideas of the vast distance which must ever remain even between the most profound philosophers and the august face of God the Lord.

* Tennyson's "In Memoriam."

Nothing that has here been said has expressed the wish that theology should be imported into physical science. The cause of piety will, on the contrary, be best advanced, when science, with a severe self-denial, stops short at her own boundary line. Where physiology has assumed to lay down the nature and destiny of the soul, which must depend in great part on a different set of evidences from any she can command, we are not surprised that materialism, or some other falsehood, should result. Where theology, with a timorous misgiving that natural inquiry may undermine her tenets, has sent a Galileo to a dungeon, or a Bruno to the stake, the world has still gone round, but the cause of a loving Redeemer has been disgraced. But we dare not pretend that there is an antagonism between two sources of truth; dare not believe that the scheme of creation would utter a different voice from that of revelation. What would follow? That the Being, on the lap of whose goodness we rest daily, may not be adored in those very mercies of which we are partaking — must be looked on askance and half in distrust. To what purpose, then, is all this wealth of wonders spread before our eyes? Better, if God is not there, that I were shut up in some dungeon gazing on the blank wall, till God should come and have mercy upon me. But in truth this refusal to behold Him where He is to be found reacts severely on the views men hold of the redeeming work. The condescension of God can only be measured so far as we know His power and glory; the wrong that sin does to His justice, can be best learnt in the regions where perfect obedience to His laws prevails without abatement. If we will not know the creating Father, neither shall we truly know the redeeming Son. But whilst physical knowledge, working in its own sphere, lends light to religion, let it remember that its work is subordinate. There is a voice within us that tells us that we came here to do, and to know in order that we might do. Practical obedience to God's commandments is the chief duty here. And we must not, because spiritual laws are less easy of expression, and allow more diversity of opinion, discard them altogether in favour of the shallow and more precise generalisations of physical knowledge. Just because they lie on the confines of the finite and the infinite, do they admit variety of statement and lead to debate. Hence the difficulty of reconciling freedom and necessity; man's moral action with God's providence. Hence the controversies as to the nature of the Incarnation. But when our minds, possessed with a sincere conviction that practical duty takes the highest place, and that whether its laws are easy or hard they must be sought and followed out, approach the study of nature, they will not fail to read there the glory of Him before whom even the shining stars are not bright, and the power of Him who leads that heavenly host by invisible cords, who has "compassed the waters with bounds, until the day and night come to an end;" and the wisdom of Him of whose works the wisest of men, toiling now for ages, dare not say that they understand even a part aright; and the goodness of Him from whose hand every creature draws life and nurture; and they shall utter with truth the Psalmist's words, "Oh Lord our Lord, how excellent is Thy name in all the earth!"

SERMON XII.

THE HOLY TRINITY.

REVELATION iv. 8—11.

And the four beasts had each of them six wings about him; and they were full of eyes within: and they rest not day and night, saying, Holy, holy, holy, Lord God Almighty, which was, and is, and is to come.

And when those beasts give glory and honour and thanks to him that sat on the throne, who liveth for ever and ever,

The four and twenty elders fall down before him that sat on the throne, and worship him that liveth for ever and ever, and cast their crowns before the throne, saying,

Thou art worthy, O Lord, to receive glory and honour and power: for thou hast created all things, and for thy pleasure they are and were created.

WE are carried by this prophetic vision up to the throne of the divine Ruler of the universe. We hear how He is praised in heaven, where His will is done already, where no evil thoughts war with the love of Him, and where the tongues that praise Him are never profaned by slander or by strife. The images put before our minds are all those of glory and beauty and strength. The voice is like a trumpet. A bow like an emerald surrounds the throne, and He that sits thereon is like precious stones; and from the throne thunders and lightnings and voices go forth. And crowns of gold are on those that worship, and they shine in their white apparel. And the seven symbolical lamps, and the four beasts that lead the worship, carry us up out of the world we know into a world beyond our senses. And we seem to stand in the very heaven of heavens, and we seem to look upon the very face of God and live.

But we do *not* see Him whom the heaven of heavens cannot contain. This glorious world of gems, and fire, and trumpet voices is a world of figures and images. Behind one veil we are permitted to look; but there is another veil still between God and us. The purely figurative character of the vision is evident. Seven lamps may figure, but they cannot be, the seven spirits of God. The number seven is a symbol. The beast like a lion is a type of the destroying and conquering might of God; the beast like a calf, of the power whereby he feeds and nourishes the earth; the beast like a man, of his knowledge and providence; and the flying eagle that makes the safe nest on high for its young, is a type here as elsewhere of the soaring, towering, and protecting strength wherewith

God pervades all things. " Ye have seen," says God himself, "what I did unto the Egyptians, and how I bare you on eagles' wings, and brought you unto myself." (Exod. xix. 4.) And the four-and-twenty elders, the twice twelve denoting perhaps the twelve patriarchs of the old covenant and the twelve apostles of the new, are a type or figure of the congregations of saints that stand in the presence of the Almighty. Out of this world, in which the mystery of God lies hid under every flower that opens, every purple sunset, every storm, we are lifted with the prophet's vision into a world where God, and eternal souls, and the everlasting energy of the heavenly Sabbath of worship, are presented to us under other figures. And we gain by this the assurance that there is another world more real than this, where that worship which we give weakly and scantily is the sole and unceasing employment. But if we would look upon the very face of Him to whom the thrice-uttered Holy is offered, if we think that to our limited minds the book of Revelation can reveal the mystery of the true God, we turn back disappointed. The brightness of the jasper and the sardine stone are but a faint image of the Divine glory, and the halo of emerald light, and the thunderings and lightnings are not His very presence. And we remember that though the vision comes of divine inspiration, it is sent to human eyes, and minds limited and fettered by earthly conditions. And amidst the very voices that come out of the throne, we seem to hear words like these: "Canst thou by searching find out God? Canst thou find out the Almighty unto perfection? It is as high as heaven; what canst thou do? deeper than hell, what canst thou know?" (Job xi.)

Every part of our services to-day reminds us of the mystery of the divine nature. We have professed our belief in the Father, the Son, and the Holy Ghost, the three Persons of the adorable Trinity. We have used words in the creeds which seem like logical definition and explanation of this great mystery; and it may appear to some that this implies that we have comprehended and reduced to the compass of a formula the most mysterious subject on which human thought can be exercised. But this is a construction from which every Christian mind recoils. After all controversies, after the creeds formed upon them, God is still inscrutable to us as He was before. The inspired exclamation of St. Paul still sums up all that we can know of Him: "O the depth of the riches both of the wisdom and knowledge of God! how unsearchable are his judgments, and his ways past finding out! For who hath known the mind of the Lord, or who hath been his counsellor? or who hath first given to him, and it shall be recompensed unto him again? For of him, and through him, and to him, are all things: to whom be glory for ever. Amen." (Rom. xi. 33—36.)

I. The mystery of the blessed Trinity is opened to us in Holy Scripture, not merely in those passages where the three co-equal Persons are mentioned together, but in those which assign to the Son or to the Holy Spirit separately attributes that can only belong to the divine Being. If only once in the course of His work on earth our Lord had spoken of Himself as possessing divine power, and at the same time as a Person distinct from the Father, then every difficulty that attends the doctrine of the Trinity would have been opened up. For example: from those words alone the divine nature of our Lord would be established: " And now, O Father, glorify thou me with thine own self, with the glory which I had with thee before the world was." (John xvii.) Before the creation of the world ($κόσμος$, universe) no created thing existed, and as the Son shared even then His Father's glory, He must be of the same divine nature. But such passages abound in the inspired book. The creation of the world is assigned to Jesus; He is described as able to subdue all things unto Himself; He alone knoweth the Father; He is a searcher of hearts, who knows and will bring to light the most hidden things. Such expressions can only be used of one, that is, of God. If then the equal divinity of the Father and of the Son are asserted in the Bible, and no less strongly the unity of God, then the whole mystery wherewith the Nicene Creed deals, lies upon the page of inspiration already. It is not some new matter imported into theology during three hundred years of controversy; but it belongs to the Christian revelation from the first. The controversies about the divine nature had for their object, not to add to the inspired account, but to prevent a loss. A wrong conception of the Person of the Saviour would have corrupted the view of His work as Mediator; a false notion of the Holy Ghost would have affected our reverence for Him as the Sanctifier of humanity. In the New Testament there is no attempt to draw out the several attributes assigned to the three Persons into an elaborate creed. In the name of all the three Persons were all nations to be baptized; in the name of all the three does St. Paul make his valediction to the Corinthian Church. But a more explicit symbol or creed is not found there, because it was not needed. The divine and human nature of the Son are not in terms described, nor their union defined: but does not the Son live for ever in those inspired pages, in His divine energy and love, in His human sorrows and sympathies? May not the devout heart build up for itself its own creed about Him, saying, "For me He left His glory, for me He showed on earth power such as man could not have shown, for me He bore the insults of the world, and the bitterness of death!" The power and functions of the Comforter are not cast into propositions in the Acts of the Apostles; but the Comforter himself is there. The disciples wait for the promise of His coming, wondering who and what manner of Comforter He must be who can console them for the loss of their Lord; and He comes with the portent of tongues, of which each stranger in Jerusalem shall carry back the news to his own people. And to the disciples He proves a Comforter and a Teacher and a Rock of strength. No pious student of those chapters can ever doubt the reality of that leaven of love that was working in the Church, nor dissociate it from the Spirit of God to whom it is assigned. But when men ask how these things can be, how Jesus could be man yet the eternal Son of God, and whether such an assertion is above or against their understanding, a mystery or a contradiction, then it is necessary to gather out from Scripture all that is told us of His nature, and to fix it precisely in meet expressions. A creed is not meant to be better than the word of God from which it is taken; but it *is* better than the erroneous creeds that must have been in use if it had not stopped their formation or their currency. Precious to us may be the expression, "Of one substance with the Father," even though the precise form of words is not found in the Bible, provided it has protected us from some other words, which would have been scriptural neither in form nor matter, and which would have robbed us of a true belief in the sacrifice of Christ, and made it the offering of a creature for our sins, and not the mystery of the love of God blessed for ever. That Creed which we have used to-day, drawn up at two Councils in the fourth century, and called from one of them the Nicene Creed, is not the fruit of a wanton and too curious logic, needlessly recasting scriptural truths into a new form. It is rather an inscription set up on a field of battle after the contests of three centuries, to tell those that come after what had been the cause of the strife and the fruits of the victory. To the practical knowledge of Christianity it has added nothing; the believer in the time of Constantine knew no more and no less the things that belonged to his peace than the believer in the time of Nero. But the theoretical knowledge of God was guarded against certain errors. Marks were set upon those scriptural statements in which the divine nature was set forth, that they might not be forgotten. Yet after all those struggles, the veil that parts the finite man from the infinite Being that created him was not removed. "Canst thou by searching find out God? Canst thou find out the Almighty unto perfection?" (Job xi. 7.) Are we any nearer to a *complete* conception of the nature of the Most High when we have said that He is eternal, incomprehensible, uncreate? Can we fathom the meaning of our own words when we use them? No. In the prophet's vision he saw the Most High seated on his throne. And he speaks to us of the jasper and the sardine stone, and the emerald glory that circled it round, and the thunder and the lightnings that figure the wrath and power of the Almighty against those that resist Him. But these are not God. Precious stones may be an image of Him; but the brightness of His presence goes far beyond them. Thunders and lightnings may serve for tokens of His terrible presence, as they did when the law was given upon Sinai; but the actual strength of that consuming fire of His wrath none might abide. And when we join in the creed, we feel that we have uttered words that carry us up as near to his divine presence as any words can. But through the darkened glass of our finite state we see not Him as He is, but the jewels and the rainbow and the lightnings that represent Him. Centuries of earnest dialectics have not enabled us to see God as He is; or rather they have not delivered us out of this narrow cleft in which for a few years we are to be imprisoned, and from which we look up to see but a little arc of the heaven that is rounded over us.

And is this all? Do creeds only serve to convince us that the Most High is inscrutable? Are these summaries of the highest knowledge only drawn up to remind us that true knowledge is impossible? Not so. What we know of God is like the pillar of cloud between Israel and the Egyptians, that was a cloud and darkness to the one, and gave light by night to the other. It is at once light to our feet in the path of life, and darkness to our understanding. This seems a contradiction, to say that growth in grace teaches us how little we can know of God, whilst it daily increases our belief in Him, and our love for Him. And yet this is the result of all Christian experience. A man may have studied all the controversies about the Divine Nature, and be able to trace all the steps by which the doctrine of the Trinity became fixed in the creed of the Church of Christ, and yet if he loves not God in his heart, all that knowledge is a pillar of darkness, that separates him from those that walk in the light of divine teaching. But there comes a change; some prop whereon he trusted breaks under his hand. Sorrow produces a consciousness of sin; and the man kneels down before God, and out of the deeps he cries to Him for mercy, and his prayer is heard. The darkness now becomes light for him; in the pillar of cloud he sees the Cross of the Redeemer, and the Spirit, like a dove, ready to come down and make His abode with him. The immeasurable distance between him and his Lord, is now more manifest than it ever was; for he has felt the consciousness of sin. And yet the knowledge of God is now a present light and guide to him, which it was not before. He can say God is inscrutable, yet He is near me; He is invisible, and yet I know that He is present and guides me; He is far above out of my sight, and yet He is feeding me, and guiding me, and watching over me. I cannot see Him, no man can look upon Him and live. Yet in Him I live, and move, and have my being.

These, then, are the propositions to which we should turn our thoughts to-day. In the Bible, the knowledge of the Most High is opened to us. The creeds are summaries of what the inspired book contains. They were drawn up, not to supplant the Bible, but to prevent errors that threatened to prevail. They do not pretend to bring us nearer to the awful presence of God than the Bible does, or to do away with mysteries which the Bible has left. Lastly, the doctrines of our religion only enlighten those who live in them.

When we compare the creeds with the New Testament, we find that the work of the Son and the Spirit of God occupies but a little space in the creeds, in comparison with the statements about the divine Persons. Of the Son we are briefly told in the Nicene Creed, that "for us men and for our salvation He came down from heaven." Of the Holy Ghost, that He is "the Lord and giver of life ... and that He spake by the prophets." In the Bible, on the contrary, we learn to know the Person of the Son by His work on earth. Here is a wide difference; and it proves at once that the creeds cannot supersede the Bible,—cannot educate us in all that we should know of our Redeemer. In the Bible we should study the great mystery of godliness, God manifest in the flesh. There we read that our merciful Father, moved with compassion at our fallen state, sent forth His own Son, made of a woman, made under the law, down to this little earth, to redeem us from the bondage of sin and the doom of death. That Son came, in the form of a servant, taking upon Him the affections, the conditions of a man; He walked about among men, talked with them and answered them, bore with their doubts and their impatience. The love whereof His heart was full He showed them daily.

He spoke the word; the burden of disease was lifted off from the sufferer, the fetters of death were unlocked. By His free intercourse with sinners whom He wished to save, He even drew upon Him the rebukes of the self-righteous. He made it no secret that the end of His pilgrimage would be death, a death already caused by the sins of those whom He came to befriend. He gave Himself up to the training of disciples, who might go forth and teach all nations after He should have returned to His home in heaven. Twelve men of humble birth were treated by the Lord of all things like His very brothers; and one of them was bearing, the while, a treason against Him in his heart. Wherever His feet came He scattered comfort for the sorrowing and hope for the sinful. We can bear to look upon the brightness of the divine glory, reflected to us from the whole surface of a life like this. From the cold bare outlines of a creed the mind may be repelled. But we are invited to live with Jesus, to hear Him speak, to see how naturally perfect human sympathy could be united with divine purity. The school of the Gospels is an easier school than that of the creeds, precious to us as these are. We are able to look upon this glory, tempered to the weakness of our eyesight, and yet to live. And from this mysterious, yet harmonious life, the scheme of the Trinity unfolds itself to our minds. The Creator, and man's first revolt from Him, and the dreary ages of his estrangement; the fulness of time when the Son was sent forth to redeem the lost race; the departure of the Son and the presence of the Comforter, who should build up and sanctify a Church for Him; the exercise of divine power by each of the three Persons, who yet cannot possibly be three Gods but one; all rise up from the accouut of the life of Jesus of Nazareth. Let us bring to the study of that life, not ingenuity, not knowledge of history, but our love and our adoration. Before we argue about Christian mysteries, and profess to determine what our reason ought to accept and what dismiss, let us dwell with humility upon the scheme of salvation as set forth in the Bible. Let us live in those mysteries before we argue about them. Let us believe that that may be a light to our feet which is thick darkness to our understanding. Let us remember that the purpose of revelation is not to give us a scientific theology, but to warn us of the wrath to come, and to call us out of a state of sin unto righteousness and peace, by the atoning blood of the Lamb. We are wise, it may be, we are learned, we have cultivated our reason to the highest point. But as the four and twenty elders that typify the worship of our race, of Jew and Gentile, cast down their crowns of honour before the throne, in token that the kingship belongs only to the triune God that sitteth upon the throne, so let us, when we read God's blessed word in the spirit of worship, cast down whatever we boast of as our crown and pride, and let us fall prostrate before the throne, and without doubt or reservation let us utter our hymn of praise: "Worthy art thou, O Lord, to receive the glory, and the honour, and the power: for thou hast created all things, and for thy pleasure they are and were created."

SERMON XIII.

THE CONVICTION OF SIN.[*]

ROMANS vii. 24, 25.

O wretched man that I am! who shall deliver me from the body of this death?

I thank God through Jesus Christ our Lord. So then with the mind I myself serve the law of God; but with the flesh the law of sin.

So ends one of the most profound passages which ever proceeded from the inspired pen of the great Apostle. Of its general drift no one can entertain a doubt; it describes the divided unhappy state into which sinful desires bring a man. It is the pathology of sin. It lays bare the symptoms of that inward leprosy; and tells us at last the name of the one Physician that can cure it. And many have imagined that St. Paul has done this by simply describing himself; that we are reading, not a general treatise, but a clinical lecture on a single case; that we are studying the nature of sin from the workings of the Apostle's own mind.

[*] This and the three following Sermons form one course, preached in Michaelmas Term, 1860.

And yet against this view there are objections that can hardly be overcome. If from the seventh to the twenty-fifth verse we are reading only the history of St. Paul's spiritual struggles and growth, we cannot safely fix on a time when those words would be true of him, "I was alive without the law once." Attempts are made to explain the words; it was in his childhood, or it was in his early life, before he began to consider the law deeply, and take home its precepts to his own conscience. Yet can we think that either of these states is what the Apostle would describe as life? "I was alive," because I was a thoughtless child, taking no account of divine things! "I was alive," because the law was as yet a dead letter to me, from want of earnest thought! Such language would accord ill with his teaching. And here we may appeal from modern interpreters to those of older date. It was long since seen, that St. Paul often "transferred in a figure" to himself things which really were to be applied to others. He tells us so himself on another occasion: "These things, brethren, I have in a figure transferred to myself and to Apollos for your sakes, that ye might learn in us not to think *of men* above that which is written" (1 Cor. iv. 6). Any scholar could find examples in other books where the writer speaks in the first person, that his hearer may make the application in the third. St. Paul uses this figure of speech very freely. "He constantly treats," says Chrysostom, "of painful subjects in his own person" (In 1 Cor. xii.). He says, for example, "Though *I* speak with the tongues of men and of angels, and have not charity, I am become as a sounding brass or a tinkling cymbal." But who does not see that he is turning the keen edge of an admonition against himself, in order that his hearers may more willingly take it from him, and turn it towards their own hearts? Now in this seventh chapter is the boldest application of this figure. Wherever he uses the word *I*, let us understand the word *mankind*. Let us suppose that instead of the anatomy of a single mind, he is writing the spiritual history of the human race. "I was alive without the law once," he says. Yes, *man* was alive when, in the person of Adam, he stood before God sinless in Paradise, before ever the struggle between the law of God and the law of self had begun. "When the commandment came, sin revived ($ἀνέζησε$, came into life), and I died." Yes, when God laid on mankind, on Adam and Eve, his commandment, they broke it and fell. "Sin, taking occasion by the commandment, deceived me, and by it slew me;" the tempter taking advantage of the sinful tendency to resist a command for the very joy of tasting the forbidden, deceived our first parents to their own destruction. The whole passage from the seventh verse thus becomes an account of what the law was meant to do for the people of God. It was to set a mark upon sin. It was to draw their attention to their own sinfulness. Holy and just and good in itself, it provoked the self-will of those that received it, and became the cause of their fall. But their fall was not meant to be final. The law was to awake in them a sense of the need of something to take them out of their present state, by making them fully conscious of their present wretchedness. All this is summed up in the concluding verses: " I see another law in my members, warring against the law of my mind, and bringing me into captivity to the law of sin which is in my members. O wretched man that I am! who shall deliver me from the body of this death ? I thank God through Jesus Christ our Lord," or rather, I thank God, *who has accomplished this deliverance* through Jesus Christ our Lord.

It is no doubt a bold figure of speech that one man should speak thus in his own person for the whole race of mankind. But instead of seeming to accuse his own nation of being still in a state of sin and discord, from which he had escaped, he speaks for them as one of themselves. No one, perhaps, had felt so deeply the condition he is describing. A zealous Pharisee, alike learned in the law and loving it, he had felt what it could do for man, and after a time had learnt what it could not do. It could reveal God as holy, and just, and good; but from the condition of divided inclinations, of inward resistance and strife against God, it could provide no deliverance. I doubt not that before the light and the voice that arrested him on the way to Damascus, and changed him soul and body, he had often used for himself the exclamation which here he employs for all: "Who shall deliver me from the body of this death?" I see the struggle within him by the very fierceness of his intolerance. He breathed out threatenings and slaughter against the people of God, to conceal from himself his deep dissatisfaction with the system he was defending even to the death. Wretched man that he was, he was seeking rest by doing violence to his own nature. That saying, "It is hard for thee to kick against the pricks" (Acts ix. 5), was addressed to one who felt already that he was not in the way of peace.

From these words of the Apostle, my hearers, which are a kind of comment upon the whole of the Old Testament, let us commence an examination of the nature of sin. And as such a subject must extend beyond a single sermon, we will speak to-day only of one part of it; of that which the text expresses — the consciousness or the conviction of sin.

Now, first, the consciousness of sin is so far a universal fact of human nature, that if any one of us is without it, it is because of some disease, a defect in his own mind. "If we say that we have no sin, we deceive ourselves, and the truth is not in us. If we confess our sins, He is faithful and just to forgive us our sins, and to cleanse us from all unrighteousness. If we say that we have not sinned, we make him a liar, and his word is not in us." (1 John, i. 8, 9, 10.) The conviction of sin may be stifled within us — nay, it is so stifled every day; and yet it is universal. As light is universal, although some may shut their eyes close and admit none of it, so is the consciousness of sin universal, although many believe that they have got rid of it altogether. For this very absence of conviction only proves the incompleteness of their nature. They deceive themselves, and the truth is not in them. They have lost the feeling of sin that was given them as a safeguard. It burns them like a fire; but their skin has lost all sensation. They are sleeping steeped in cold mists and poisonous dews, but they know not the poison because they are asleep. Yet fire burns, and poison destroys, not the less when the senses, that are sentinels against them, desert their posts. Every man whose nature is complete, and awake, and active, knows that there is such a thing as sin, and that he is a partaker in it. The man who has tried for a quarter of a century to pare off from his mind all that does not minister to one chosen worldly pursuit, will be able to deny that he is convinced of sin. But you appeal from such maimed and crippled spirits to the general sense of more complete minds. And the result is the admission that there is a better law, which our conscience admits the authority of, warning against the law of pride, and self-will, and appetite within us, and that the worse prevails against the better, and that the sense of guilt accompanies that wrong decision in every case. So then the sense of sin is not something abnormal, exceptional, that begins in superstition and mental depression, and is kept up by religious teachers by artificial means; but it is the fair and natural result of facts. We know the better way, we choose the worse, and we are ashamed of it; these are three plain facts, which contain all that we contend for. Not those who sorrow for sin are deceiving themselves, but those who deny its existence. The law of Moses, with its strict commands and stern punishments, was not an organised tyranny over the consciences of men; it was the means of bringing them back to a sane state, to a complete consciousness. It set up and kept before them the claims of God and of conscience. When once they had confessed that sin was in them, and that the wages of sin are death, then the work for which the law was appointed was done. It was a great system, having for its one object to bring men to confess. But that act of confession restored men to themselves, gave them back their own nature; reminded them of three words which they were too pleased to forget, of God, of duty, of hereafter. The physician that sees upon a patient the symptoms of a perilous disease, of which the patient knows nothing, that sees him eating the most baneful food, and courting the airs that are to such an ailment most destructive, does well to lay his hand upon his arm, and tell him, though the sufferer's cheek grow white before him, that the poison is there, undermining his life. He is not a malignant enemy for whispering, "The path you are walking on leads to sure death." If the tidings, harsh as they are, give the man a sense of his real position, if they save him from acting like a madman, and set him thinking upon the means of recovery, they are the words of a friend. And such a friend to man was the law of Moses. Without some such admonition the state of man was pitiable enough. Armed in a foolish pride, and pursuing an empty pleasure, and content with a spurious peace, he felt, underneath, the obscure workings of his ailment; and real peace was for him impossible. "When I kept silence," says the Psalmist, "my bones waxed old, through my roaring all the day long." (Ps. xxxii. 3.) To know one's own state and to own it, is to admit truth instead of a lie; and truth is the beginning of light and of the work of grace. "I said I will confess my transgressions unto the Lord; and thou forgavest the iniquity of my sin."

The consciousness of sin, then, is universal. And in what does it consist? It is the consciousness of division and strife within a man. His mind is not at peace with itself. "To will is present with me, but how to perform that which I will I find not. For the good that I would, I do not, and the evil which I would not, that I do. . . . I find then a law that when I would do good evil is present with me." So speaks the voice of inspiration; but all times and nations have found out the same contradiction. "I approve of the good and pursue the evil,"* says one heathen writer. "What is this that struggles against our will," says another, "and will not let us resolve on a thing once for all? We are tossed about on various counsels; we can form no resolution freely and absolutely and for ever."† If any of us will compare St. Paul's description of the state of sin with his own condition, he will see how complete, how true is the picture of the human heart. Last year you formed a good resolution, of diligence and self-restraint. You wrote it down, perhaps; and at some chance moment the note-book opens at the words which were never fulfilled, and reminds you that you are not one man but two. The remembrance of a certain wrong, done long since, sends a pang through your heart when you should be happy, and you mean to set it right so far as may be possible, but you have never braced up your nerves to the effort; and when you persuade yourself that want of time has been the cause, you feel the mere hollowness of the excuse. Some sin was growing upon you; you felt that it was getting the mastery, and forming you from a light-hearted votary into a harassed slave. You determined to break with it; you fixed the day when you would begin the strife. But the wine danced all too brightly in the cup for your resolution, or the words of folly were too enticing, or, in the parliament of your ill-governed thoughts, the votes

---

* Ovid, Metam. vii. 20.
† Seneca, Ep. 52, ad Lucil.

for one more day of idleness prevailed over those for some urgent duty. Tossed on such a treacherous sea, you yet have changed no opinion. The faculty that should rule your mind still pronounces intemperance, and impurity, and sloth to be false and wrong. See what a punishment sin bears with it! We sever ourselves from God, and at once our soul is divided against itself. In our pride we revolt against God, and all our inner thoughts start into rebellion against us. To-day, with its high hopes and promises, passes censure on to-morrow with its foolish outbreaks and lame performance. The thoughts of the closet or the study contrast ill with our acts when we come forth and show as worldly as the rest. "The wicked are like the troubled sea when it cannot rest, whose waters cast up mire and dirt. There is no peace, saith my God, for the wicked." For it need scarcely be added, that the consciousness of sin is a consciousness of deep-seated misery. None can go on in that distracted state and not feel that it is a torment. To know the good, and not be able to pursue it, to sit in judgment on our actions and condemn them; can this be happiness? The great and good beckon us from their graves to follow in their footprints, and we are fain to do it. If we could add a little weight to our will, or abate but a little from the force of our temptations, — but, as it is, the secret record of our lives would be a register of unfulfilled intentions. A living man, chained to a corpse, would feel as the soul does, mated to a body full of unlawful hungers and selfish wishes. "Who shall deliver me from *the body of this death?*" And so great is this unhappiness, that on one side or the other a way of escape must be found. After a time of conflict and suffering, either the soul turns to God, and makes its way to the Redeemer, and through Him finds rest for itself in a renewal of its union with the Father, or else, turning back to the pollutions from which it might have escaped, it puts the better voice to silence and courts death. It is possible to lull that salutary pain of conscience to rest; but "where there is a sense of pain, there is a sense of life;"* and when conscience, drunk with many draughts of sin, sinks into a torpor, truth and knowledge die out with it, and just judgment is taken away, and the man gets peace by drowning all that is best in him. The sting of conscience was like an antepast of the pains of hell; but if there be no pain felt for sin, how shall sin and the wrath of God for sin be avoided? It is better to suffer the extremity of distraction and self-conflict than to lose the last hold we have of the world above us — the conviction of our sinfulness.

These three points, then, have been touched upon to-day, but in a manner most unworthy of their importance. First, that the consciousness of sin is not an exceptional state, but is as universal as the know-

---

* "Ubi doloris sensus ibi etiam sensus est vitæ."—*Ambrose, Apol. David.* i. 9.

ledge of right and wrong; secondly, that it consists in the feeling of a state of discord and division in the soul, which is represented in holy Scripture as a war between spirit and flesh, the law of the mind and the law of the members, the soul and the body, the will and the desires; and thirdly, that such a condition must be one of misery, out of which it is natural to try to escape, either by that door of deliverance opened to us by Christ in His Gospel, or through the gates of death and hell. And all these belong, not to the nature of sin in itself, but only to our consciousness of it. The nature of sin will remain for a future discussion.

But in the mean time there is much for us to think on in the words of the Apostle to which I have drawn your attention. For, after all argument and evidence, many will still think that there is something morbid in the condition which St. Paul describes. People say that it is a real description, but of a state which men would do well to avoid. Why wake up the quiet conscience to lay a burden upon it? Many a man goes through the world, they say, without these distracting anxieties about his spiritual state. He wins respect from his neighbours, he discharges fairly all the duties laid on him by his family or the state, he prospers and is honoured, without having to wrestle down these fears and griefs, without paying any particular attention to any strife that goes on within him. Be it granted that some men do not take full account of their own state. Is that an argument against endeavouring to find out where we are, what we are, and whither we are going? Try it in another case. One friend is sick, but knows it not. The hue of death is upon his cheek; what matter? We can paint it over with a purchased bloom. The plague-spot is visible under his shoulder; draw his garments over it again and hide it. The man will die; but mean time all is well while we can get death to simulate life. This is not the language of the sane! Put together the facts on which we are all agreed, and see whether any honest man can speak thus about them. I will only postulate that death is a certainty, that the soul does not die, and that in the future state our earthly pursuits and pleasures shall not be continued. But who can hold such language as applied to such facts? He who says, "Let us hear no morbid suggestions of sorrow and uneasiness about sin," means in fact, " Let us do nothing to prepare and equip the soul for that condition of things in which it finds itself." Friends, if it be true that in a score of years most of us may have passed into the presence of God, that in two score years perhaps not one of us may be left; if it be true that after time comes eternity; if it be true that there is no power, or knowledge, or wisdom, or device in the grave, whither we are going; then cherish as the most precious gift that conviction of sin which sometimes turns the night into a time of watching, and makes wet the pillow with tears of remorse. Distrust that seeming peace which comes, not from hope, but from the absence of fear. It is bitter to feel the mind distracted by a conflict between conscience and desire. But what if this be the protest against the utter forgetfulness of another life into which we were falling? What if this stern reproval of conscience be the sole link that unites us to God and to the life eternal? It is bitter to cry, "Oh wretched man that I am, who shall deliver me from the body of this death?" but most sweet to thank God for a complete deliverance through the merits and death of His Son. Godly sorrow worketh repentance unto salvation. If you have never felt it, seek for it, long for it, pray for it. Ask the God who has written His law in deep-cut characters on the table of your heart, to break up all your false peace, to pour over your soul the flood of remorse, even though the deep waters threaten to overwhelm you. That remorse, that sorrow, will set you seeking for escape. The wounds of sin ache and tingle; it is better so than that they should mortify without pain. Under the law men longed for deliverance, and looked for it afar off, and did not find it. But for us the Physician is at hand, who will pour balm into those wounds, who will take out of that proud and struggling heart all that resists God and is at enmity with Him; who will create a new heart and a new spirit there, to be a dwelling-place for God Himself through His Spirit, and to be the sanctuary of unspeakable peace.

SERMON XIV.

THE NATURE OF SIN.

LUKE xv. 18, 19.

I will arise, and go to my father, and will say unto him, Father, I have sinned against heaven, and before thee,

And am no more worthy to be called thy son: make me as one of thy hired servants.

THE question that awaits us to-day is perhaps the hardest in which the mind of man can engage. What is sin? We have seen that the conviction of sin is universal; but what is this evil principle which stains every spirit, which disquiets every conscience, and overclouds the most serene life with the shadow of something false and wrong? The answer is difficult, because it leads us into the risk of a contradiction. That which we are in search of is in God's world, yet it cannot be of God; is permitted by the Omnipotent, yet must be abominable in His sight; is suffered within the borders of the divine creation, to make war against that creation's King and Lord. And when we attempt to define sin, that which makes the lips stammer and the thoughts stand still, is, that we fear to set naked before us the definition of something which must be hateful to God, yet which He suffers to exalt itself against Him. Of this difficulty we have no explanation to offer. The pulpit cannot smooth away what the Bible leaves standing in all its asperity. All that we propose is to gather up the statements of holy Scripture that throw any light upon the nature of sin, without expecting that even so we shall be able to comprehend that nature fully. It is something to know the symptoms of a disease, and its causes and results, because they partly unfold its essence, although no physiologist can thoroughly explain it.

I. Now, first, sin is the transgression of a law. The consciousness of sin arises from a man's knowing that he has within him a certain power of pursuing a good object, which power he has neglected to use. We will not ask at this moment whence this power comes to us. What we all know is, that every man, Christian or not, has a will, by which he is able in a sense to direct and fore-order his own life; that this will cannot act as if it were pure caprice, like the flight of a swallow or the gambols of a lamb, but must operate according to some rule or principle; and if the rule by which we act is the highest rule known to us, then the conscience acquits us of guilt; but if it is any lower rule, then our higher and better knowledge, which we have violated, will assert itself and accuse us. Whether at a given time we shall converse, or walk, or eat, or read a pleasant book, are matters indifferent; choose any one of them, and your conscience will not reproach you for having slighted the rest. But if by the walking or the conversing you break a promise or neglect a duty towards some one else, then conscience asserts a right which no one thinks of disputing. You have not lived up to the light that was in you; you have chosen between your convenience and your duty, as though these were two equal things between which you were free to choose, which they are not. You have obeyed the commands of a slave, when you were bound to those of your king. The disloyal act may be palliated; you may silence all misgivings about it, but you never attempt to reward it with self-approval. To state this fundamental fact of our nature in the simplest terms, — we say that there is in us a feeling or conviction that we are bound to do our best, and live up to the highest principle that we know of, and a failure to do so is punished by a bitter sense of frustration, and falsehood, and sorrow. External laws and punishments of man's invention may help to educate this principle of conscience, but cannot have created it; for it goes far beyond them. Self-reproach is often most busy about waste of time or words spoken in ill-will, where law and punishment are out of the question.

Most of the names for sin in various languages bring out this view of its nature; it is the transgression or overleaping of a line prescribed, it is the missing of our aim, or the falling short of our duty. And so far as we have gone, it appears that the consciousness of sin is possible for heathens as for Christians. Conscience is there, if its reproofs are more rare and its sensitiveness less; a higher law of life is there, though far from the highest. It is Cicero, and not a Christian, who speaks these words: "There is no conceivable evil that does not beset me; yet all are lighter than the pain of sin, for that, besides being the highest, is eternal."* Such words are a comment on those of St. Paul: "When the Gentiles, which have not the law, do by nature the things contained in the law, these, having not the law, are a law unto themselves." (Rom. ii. 14.)

II. But we may go beyond this. Sin is disobedience to a known law of God. Without the Bible man could never have known why it is that conscience, which often has not the power to prevent sin, still preserves its authority to reprove it. The conscience is all that remains of God in the soul of the fallen man. Man is strong with God's strength, rich with God's abundance, intelligent with God's light, and he was meant to be holy with His holiness.

* Ad. Att. xi. Ep. 15.

But "by the disobedience of one many were made sinners." (Rom. v. 19.) Resting still in the bosom of the divine love, and drawing on the divine bounty, we have been able to compass the strange mystery of severing our souls from Him. Without God the pulse of my heart would be arrested in its present beat, and darkness would quench my eyesight. But whilst I am beholden to Him for all that I am or have, my thoughts I have taken out of His dominion; and this He has suffered. It is a mystery, indeed; but it is also a ground for dread. Can it be true that the King of all things is present in my heart, and that among my thoughts there is a Judas-thought that would sell Him for money, and a Pilate-thought that would let Him go to death rather than offend men, and a Caiaphas-thought to call the truth which He speaks a lie? Must not the wrath of Him against whom these thoughts offend be already preparing my destruction? "Against thee only have I sinned," says the Psalmist, "and done this evil in thy sight." Face to face with an offended God, all other thoughts about sin disappear. It is no longer a mere imprudence or a folly; it is no longer an injury to a neighbour whom we should not have wronged; it is no longer a brutalising and lowering process by which we are destroying our own mind. "Against thee only have I sinned." It is a defiance of the present God. It is the provoking to anger of One whose anger is death. And in the Bible this representation of sin overpowers all others. It is a defection and a rebellion against God. " Rebellion is as the sin of witchcraft, and stubbornness is as iniquity and idolatry. Because thou hast rejected the word of the Lord, he hath also rejected thee from being king." (1 Sam. xv. 23.) "Your iniquities have separated between you and your God, and your sins have hid his face from you, that he will not hear." (Is. lix. 2.) Between us and Him the gulf of our sins gapes; and whilst He sustains our lives we rebel against Him in our souls, and drive Him thence. In the parable from which I have taken my text, the son wishes to be severed from his father, to have his separate share of his property, and then to leave his father's house, and to spend it in his own way. This is very significant of the nature of sin. But there is always a point at which a parable ceases to hold good ; and the dissolute son did sever himself completely from his home, and in the strange country no father's eye dwelt on the disgusting details of a vicious life. But face to face with our Father we commit our sins. Every throb of our vicious excitement is a wasting of His present supply of our life. The voice of conscience that we madly overpower is His voice, asserting but not enforcing the claims of His eternal law. There is the horror of it. Whither shall we go from His presence? You tell your sins to Him as you do them. You hide them from a sister or a wife, you wish that an affectionate father should not know them. But you take into your confidence the Most High God, the Holy One, in whose sight the heavens are not clean. You borrow of Him the instruments to commit them; for He has fashioned you behind and before, and in His strength your hands and feet are strong. Night, and secrecy, and silence seem safe allies. Above all, sins of thought are out of reach; in the deep chambers of your own mind you may covet, and lust, and recall scenes of foul corruption with a morose delight. Ye fools and blind! If God were not there, how should you have the strength or the life to sin?

This then is our second result. Man's happiness should consist in perfect union with God; in obeying His moral precepts with that alacrity and freedom from doubt with which the world of matter obeys His physical laws. From the time of Adam to that of our Redeemer, this single-minded state was unknown. Sin, once admitted, disturbed the soul's balance; and it could no longer find its sole and perfect happiness in doing the will of God. And yet all was not complete ruin. Had it been so, had evil become the soul's good, there would have been no self-reproaches for sin. But amidst the waste of evil passions, there stood yet in the heart an altar to God, and a few sparks burnt thereon; and the soul, blind and desperate as it was, knew that *there* was holy ground. Still, amidst the confusion of inward sounds, was heard a voice, weak indeed, yet not to be gainsaid, "This is the way; walk ye in it." We would fain obey it; "but," as the Apostle says, "I see another law in my members, warring against the law of my mind; and bringing me into captivity to the law of sin which is in my members." Contrast with this painful description, the language of the 119th Psalm, that describes the state in which the soul would be; and you will be able to measure the difference between life and death. "Make me to go in the path of thy commandments; for therein do I delight. Behold, I have longed after thy precepts; guide me in thy righteousness. I will walk at liberty: for I seek thy precepts. My soul fainteth for thy salvation; for I hope in thy word."

III. But this transgression is often described in the Bible as *death*. Besides the death eternal in which sin issues at last, a present death is spoken of. "Let the dead bury their dead." (Mat. viii. 22.) "To be carnally minded is death; but to be spiritually minded is life and peace." (Rom. viii. 6.) "Sin revived, and I died." (Rom. vii. 9.) "He that loveth not his brother, abideth in death." (1 John iii. 14.) When we add to these passages those in which sin is spoken of as blindness, darkness, ignorance, foolishness, we see that sin is represented, not as something having a real existence, but as a privation of existence, a loss of life which the soul might have had. And a hundred passages might easily be cited from writers of every age, to show how deeply this idea has sunk into the Christian mind.* Evil is nothing in itself, they say. It is a want and an absence, and

---

* See Thomson's Atoning Work of Christ, Notes on Lecture I.

not a substantive state. It is a want of life, of light, of reason, of knowledge, of peace, of the presence of God. When it is objected to these writers, that, if God is the Creator of all things, He must have created evil, they answer with one mouth, that evil is not a thing, but the want of something; and they narrow down the problem of evil to this, that God, having created man, allowed him to bring upon himself a death of the spirit, and to return, so far, towards the nothingness out of which he was taken. And this kind of statement, though often cast in a form too scholastic, conveys a scriptural truth. Sin is death, and can but issue in a death more complete. When the choice between holiness and a worldly life lies before us, it is not a choice between two lives, but a choice between the soul's life and its death. To say that sin is nothing is no play upon words, no logical trick. Men succeed who live without God; they have more brilliant proofs of success to show, than those who possess their souls in peace. They get fame and power, and force the world to take account of them. A little while and they are clean gone, their wealth is scattered among strangers, their cynical books are buried in forgotten corners of libraries or cast into the fire, and no one remembers with love their hard unloving life. And they themselves? The wages of sin is death. If a man spends his life in killing that conscience which was the last link between him and the God that liveth for ever, he has been compassing his own eternal destruction. The blessedness of the dead hereafter will consist in their perfect union with their Maker, in their perfect obedience to His law and love of His commandments. How can we reach that by living in a state of growing death, deepening ever more and more towards complete darkness? "We say," to use the words of Origen*, "that all those who do not live to God are dead, and that their life, being a life of sin, is, so to speak, a life of death."

IV. We turn, in the fourth place, to another group of passages in Holy Scripture, where sin is represented to us as selfishness, self-seeking, self-will. If one was to venture to pronounce what is the most prominent feature in the moral teachings of the inspired Book, one would say that it gives us, above all things, the most striking pictures of the life of seeking God and the life of self-seeking. What is the whole New Testament? A life of one who says of Himself, "I seek not mine own will, but the will of Him that hath sent me" (John v. 30); and again, an account of His followers filled with His Spirit, who said, "We ought to obey God rather than men," and who, to come after Him, denied themselves and took up their cross. And in the Old Testament we have the history of the most self-willed people that has ever been suffered to resist God's purposes. Sure of God's promises, the strength of the Jews was to sit still, to spread their sails to the wind of the divine intention,

---

* Tom. ii. in Joan. p. 69.

and let it blow them whithersoever it would. Yet those wayward children, in the wilderness and when they were settled in their land, ever resisted and thwarted the plans laid for their good. Murmuring and lusting and refusing, making idols to worship under the awful shadow of Sinai itself, they are to us a warning against an indulged self-will. The national character emerges in Jacob, with his base devices to secure a blessing that was his already; and again in Saul, who knew not that "to obey is better than sacrifice." Sin, as we have seen, is nothing in itself, but the soul sundered from God must seek to be something, cannot rest in mere confusion and chaos; will serve a Moloch or a Mammon rather than be without an aim; will set up itself to be God. If we descend into ourselves, we find how this besetting egotism encroaches on the soul whenever we at all relax our vigilance. It whispers to itself about the claims of *my* opinion, *my* ease, *my* special talent, *my* engrossing pleasure; it inclines to appeal from the law of duty to the decision of this selfish "I," that is evermore trying to exalt itself into a god. But these selfish behests cannot be obeyed save at the cost of others, and hence we see the deep wisdom which makes our love of our neighbour a test of our condition as towards God. "This commandment have we from Him, that he who loveth God love his brother also." (1 John iv. 21.) In the war with the worst form of evil, which the faith of Christ must wage before the end of all things, selfishness is one of the chief marks of the evil principle. "In the last days," says St. Paul, "perilous times shall come, for men shall be *lovers of themselves*, covetous, boasters," and so on through the gloomy catalogue of vices. (2 Tim. iii. 1, 2.) The manifestation of antichrist is to be a blasphemous worship of self. "That day shall not come," says the same Apostle, "except there come a falling away first, and that man of sin be revealed, the son of perdition; who opposeth and exalteth himself above all that is called God, or that is worshipped; so that he, as God, sitteth in the temple of God, shewing himself that he is God." (2 Thes. ii. 3, 4.) And if we examine ourselves, shall we not find antichrist sitting in our hearts that are the temple of the Holy Ghost, and exalting himself into a god already? That is our god which we love most and obey most constantly, which we suffer to prescribe the law of our life. The worldly occupation that wholly absorbs us, that has shortened our prayers, and closed our Bibles, and usurped our Sundays, has become our god. It is antichrist and an idol and a lie; but it sits as god in our temple of God, and there is nothing else that we love and obey. Well may we watch against the first symptoms of such a defection. Well may we recall in every hour of trial St. Paul's admonition: "Set your affections on things above, not on,things on the earth. For ye are dead, and your life is hid with Christ in God." (Col. iii. 2, 3.)

These then are the marks of sin. It is a violation

of the law of conscience; it is disobedience to God; it is a state of death; it is a worship of self where God should be worshipped. Be it far from us to think of such a question only as matter of argument, as an exercise of learning and logical nicety. On the contrary, it touches on one great heresy of our time, which whispers to us, "If we sin we shall not surely die." Sin and death are woven together; they are the outside and the inside of a cup; you cannot take one and decline the other. If there is any truth in what has been said of the nature of sin, then, except a man be born again unto righteousness he cannot see the kingdom of heaven. The proud sinner and the selfish voluptuary are not to perish, so men say, in another life! Well, you would save them from the outer darkness and its awful woe. Where will you place them? In the glorious presence of God? He spoke to their conscience in this life through His Gospel, and they would not listen; the truth was pressed upon them perhaps, and then they grew to hate it. All wish to live by it has long died out. And now you would give them an everlasting mansion there, where love of His will and law is the only delight. Again, sin is present as well as future death. All their strength has been given to something which is perishable, which they cannot take out of the world with them. You would transplant them, stripped of everything for which they lived, with their evil inclinations, either dead for want of their object, or turned into insatiable cravings which shall be the eternal chastisement for a life of abuse, into a presence where none of their wants can be revived or satisfied. Your merciful purpose is impossible. It would defeat itself. Heaven would be no heaven to a soul unreconciled with God. What you intended for love would be the most subtle torment; to bring them near to Him whom they love not, and whose presence withers them with rebuke. The wages of sin is death. If we live unto the flesh we shall die. From the nature of sin itself, you cannot divorce punishment from sin. In that most touching parable from which I have quoted, the poor broken prodigal, who had set forth to be his own master and find his own happiness, "came to himself" (as we read), and then resolved to return and cast himself at his father's feet. God grant that we may come to ourselves if we are in the same delusion! For though all men should combine to say, "If we sin we shall not die; There is no great gulf between sin and holiness;" it is still a delusion, out of which we must awake. Our new creation unto holiness is the purpose for which our loving Redeemer wrought on earth. When we come to ourselves and see that we are perishing with hunger, He is ready to welcome back the prodigal, after whom His heart went forth long since, and to put on him the robe of a righteousness not his own, and to create in him a new heart and a new spirit, and to make the rest of his life a training for that life of glory which only those that love God's commandments and wish to live in them wholly can share.

SERMON XV.

THE DECEITFULNESS OF SIN.

2 Tim. iii. 13, 14, 15.

Evil men and seducers shall wax worse and worse, deceiving, and being deceived.
But continue thou in the things which thou hast learned, and hast been assured of, knowing of whom thou hast learned them;
And that from a child thou hast known the holy Scriptures, which are able to make thee wise unto salvation through faith, which is in Christ Jesus.

WE have seen in the two preceding Sermons what is the nature of that sin of which every human conscience feels the painful weight. And so long as we fix our eyes on the page of Scripture we should all assent, I doubt not, to the conclusions there arrived at. It is when we turn to compare them with the opinions of our neighbours that new difficulties are pressed on us. A respect for what is called the common sense of mankind suggests the attempt to reconcile the severe judgments of the Bible against

SERM. XV.] THE DECEITFULNESS OF SIN. 217

sin with the laxity of popular belief. The attempt cannot but fail; but it becomes us to take some account of the cause of the conflict between them. The subject of a Sermon on this point is easily stated in a few words. It is *the deceitfulness of sin.*

No reader of the Bible but has noticed the connection there admitted between sin and falsehood. God says, through Isaiah: " Surely they are my people, children that will not lie" (lxiii. 8); whereas our Lord says that the devil abode not in the truth, but is a liar, the father of lies. (John viii. 44, 45.) " Thou lovest evil more than good, and lying than to speak righteousness" (Ps. lii. 3), says the Psalmist. The violent, he says elsewhere, "go astray speaking lies." " They have taught their tongue to speak lies, and weary themselves to commit iniquity," says Jeremiah. "Thine habitation is in the midst of deceit, through deceit they refuse to know me, saith the Lord." (Jer. ix. 5, 6.) " There shall in no wise enter into heaven anything that defileth or worketh abomination, or that maketh a lie," we read in the Book of Revelation (xxi. 27). In these and many such places the deep connection which exists between God and truth, between Satan and falsehood, comes into view. Every sin is an acted lie. It is a breach of an eternal law. It is a pursuit of empty phantasms instead of real good. It is a distortion of the length and breadth, and height and depth, of all things that surround us, since it brings forward some perishable trifle so that it fills up all the field of view, and loses sight of God, who is all and in all. He who, believing in God, lives wholly for the world, errs not only in heart but in point of prudence and calculation. To admit that there is a God and a future life, and to live as if there were neither, is to sin indeed, but it is also to act upon a falsehood; and every moment of such a life is inconsistent and foolish, as well as wrong. What is the worth of an opinion from a man who lives wholly for money, steeped in the love of it, unscrupulous about the means of gaining it, as to the relative value of this world and another? What is the worth of the opinion of the impure voluptuary as to the wisest mode of spending this short life? What can such men contribute to the common sense or common judgment of mankind, so long as their own lives speak a lie? They own the true God with their lips, and live for an idol. Must not we bid such men to get rid of the crying inconsistency in themselves, before they tell us how sin is to be weighed, and how far it may be safely dared? Here then is the fallacy that lies under that phrase common sense. Common sense ought to mean the general opinion of all men who are capable of forming an opinion. But the popular views about sin are not those of persons capable of forming an opinion; they come from minds tinged with falsehood, from persons professing one thing and doing another, and pursuing as their highest good something which they dare not pronounce to be a good at all. There are questions on which they might advise rightly;

they will tell you where you may safely trust your money, or what turn a war, or a political movement, or a popular cry will take. In all matters of worldly prudence their trained sight is keen. But where higher interests come in, there can be no disrespect in contradicting those who daily contradict themselves. A child might pity the state of inconsistency in which the wicked live; but pity makes no claim on our obedience. False and hollow to the very root, their sinful life can produce no fruits of real knowledge. They wax worse and worse, deceiving and being deceived.

It is thus that we must meet the various errors about sin that prevail in the world. Most of them are referable to these two heads; men say, in effect, either that God is not pure and just, or that there is no guilt in sin. Let us see how such errors can arise.

I. The Most High is of purer eyes than to behold evil, and cannot look upon iniquity. (Heb. i. 13.) When Adam sinned, the relation between him and his maker could not continue. "Who is able to stand before this Holy Lord God?" (1 Sam. vi. 20.) Not one who has wilfully turned aside to sin. The means which God prepared to remedy the evil show the distance that exists between sin and holiness. He sent down His beloved Son, to exhibit before men's eyes the type of a pure life to which He would have them to conform; and to suffer and die in order to bridge over the great gulf between sin and the righteous God. Had sin been a light evil, had men only drawn on themselves the pestilence that destroys life, or the famine, or the war, then the same divine Father who sent the scourge would have arrested it by His mere word as soon as men had been chastened enough. But man has chosen, not suffering, but guilt. He has banished himself thereby from the presence of the Most Holy. Sin is not a mere plague that will wear itself out; it is a change to another nature, it is a rupture of the tie between the defiled and guilty son and his pure Father. To lift up the prodigal from the mire, and take him back without his penitence, without a reconciling sacrifice, and restore him to all he had lost, as though sin were nothing, would be to mislead men as to the very nature of the divine Being. If our faculties are too low to know God as He is, at least we can know what He is not. He is not one that can love sin; and all that painful pilgrimage that ended in the Cross was to witness to that truth. Sin is abomination to God. See what it needs to purge it away! See what a price must be paid to redeem the consequences of it! See who it is who must step first over that awful gulf of death, before the rest of his brethren can be permitted to pass over. Such is the lesson of Scripture; such is not the lesson which we learn from one another.

As soon as we close our Bible and return to the world, we are offered another scheme of morality, the object of which is to conceal that gulf between good and evil. Young men will be passionate; as they grow older they will become worldly and ambitious; and the old are apt to clutch at money with a miser's gripe. We must not expect too much; we must take men as we find them. The good are not all so good as they seem; and in the worst some chord of goodness is ready to vibrate if we can righly strike it. This is the common language; and under the guise of an induction from facts it conveys really the precepts of a new moral code. We are told that it is natural to sin; if the young man, flustered with the usual wine, hurries another into the usual impurity, he is only fulfilling the normal orbit of his life. If the man of middle age strains every faculty, till the brain aches, and the stretched nerves threaten to snap, in beating his competitors in the race of life, sparing no thought for anything higher, this too is natural, nay commendable, for its intensity of self-worship. If the old man, feeling already the chills of death in his veins, keeps watch over his hoard, men smile at the weakness, but they do not feel the wish to whisper to the deluded victim of his own idol, "This night thy soul shall be required of thee."

It is not mere indifference to sin that diffuses this false morality; much of the temptation to it comes out of our more humane and tender feelings. When one speaks to a father of a son's aberrations, one is willing sometimes to give him the countenance of others who have trod the same paths of folly. The man of middle life is worldly, not for himself, but for a family. The old man was kind to us or to those we loved, years ago before he grew so hard. Thoughts like these draw the better sort of minds into over-indulgent views of sin. The wish not to stand aloof from the sympathies of our kind tempts us to see with their bleared eyes and speak with their mistaken language. Many, however, wilfully degrade the truth, that their own sin may find countenance. "How am I worse than others?" This is a question that has served many for an excuse to go on sinning. They think of the Most High as one whose eye cannot find them if they hide their sin amidst a crowd. But be the causes what they may, the morality of men and that of the Bible are not the same, and we must be on our guard against this difference.

II. But we are taught in the world, not only that God tolerates guilt, but that sin is without guilt. Man acts according to his instincts and the condition in which he lives. Because he knows that he forms a purpose, and does not see the secret springs that determine the purpose, he fancies that he is free; and, if free, then he is judged guilty or innocent according to his acts. But how can there be moral guilt in obeying the instincts that have been planted in a man, not by himself? Under other conditions of health, climate, wealth, temptation, he would have acted differently; and how can it be guilt in him to have been born where he is?

False reasoning of this kind passes current because of the few grains of truth that are melted up with it to give it colour. The temptations within and without a man do modify the guilt of his sin. He who sins under the pressure of some sore need will be judged and punished differently from him that in pure wantonness commits the like offence. And we do well not to condemn others in our hearts, when we cannot measure the strength of their temptations. We do well to rescue from dangerous positions the young criminal, the untaught child, the friendless woman; because we shall abate the sin by removing the occasions. But it is when this onesided philosophy is offered us as the whole truth that it becomes a dangerous lie. When God searches and tries you; when the acts of the past that once were pleasures, flushed and crowned and garlanded, stand out bare sins, like naked skeletons, to alarm you; when you feel that there is a graver business to be settled on this earth than any you have thought of engaging in; when you know that there is a certain question about the state of your soul, which must be solved; you will not be so utterly blind as to seek refuge in the state of your body against the sin of your spirit, as to plead that your will was paralysed because your young pulse beat high. You know that guilt is guilt, just as you know that light is light, by what goes on within you. Why is there that inward searching and conflict between you and your God, if there is no such thing as guilt; if you can throw back even upon Him that which we mean by guilt, and charge it to the brain or heart that He made for you, the home in which He placed you, the company that He suffered to come near you? No man ever took comfort, in his moments of real thought, from such resources. When the object is, not to think, but just to sin without thinking too much, men toss such jargon to and fro, and do not know it for the lie it is, because they do not look at it. But if one has once had this thought in his heart that "the wages of sin is death," he has known something which will prevent him for ever from sincerely doubting whether sin is indeed guilt. It is guilt because you have thought and known the guilt of it. And if you say otherwise, you belie, not only conscience, but every law that men ever made against crime. If offences are committed from instinct and through necessity, every punishment for murder has been itself a murder, every prison has been an instrument of oppression, since no man should suffer for that which he did not cause, which is rather the act of the society that made his position for him, and now punishes him for that position, than anything for which he is responsible.

But we are told by another class of thinkers, that the shame and regret felt by the conscience for sin are real; but then they are not connected with the divine wrath, nor do they prove that we are guilty before God. Man's sorrow for sin is a regret that he has acted below the dignity of his own nature, which is ever aspiring to perfect itself. Conscience is not the condemning voice of God; it is the protest of the better part of our nature against a triumph of the worse.

Here is another falsehood by which men strive to extenuate the awful reality of sin. If there is nothing divine in those remorseful workings of the soul, then surely there is no God. Something within you gives you pain when you have swerved from what is holy, and just, and good; but this something you will have to be merely human, the man judging himself. Then what do you leave for the Maker of man to do? Nothing. Will you give Him the charge of the body, and shut Him out from the soul? If He does not chasten man for sin, if man can do this for himself, take the inevitable consequence. Exclude Him from this world as you have excluded Him expressly from the thoughts of righteousness and duty. Do without Him; deny Him. Put some gloss of consistency upon your theory. If there be no God, then the light that is in us must be from some other source. But to take your little rushlight forth into the noonday sun and to say, " It is this little rushlight, and not the sun, that lights up the face of creation," is a transparent falsehood. If sorrow for sin is only our own disapproval of a failure, there should be an intellectual as well as a moral remorse; and pangs of regret should visit us for having faltered in our speech, or forgotten what we would say, or failed to unravel an obscure passage; for these are so many failures in the attempt to exhibit the *intellectual* completeness of man's nature.

But false opinions about the guilt of sin are pushed still further. The sinful tendency is necessary, we are told, to complete and educate the good purpose. Meekness is pride overcome; temperance is a conquest over desire; patience is anger or restlessness kept within bounds. And so through all the graces of character, evil is required by way of contrast to the good. It is the dark back-ground to give the picture more brightness. The existence of evil becomes a necessary condition of the existence of its opposite. All spiritual activity consists in the perpetual conflict of evil with good. Evil, though constantly overcome, appears again in new forms, to be again fought with and conquered. But this theory is against the whole scheme of salvation. It makes the reconcilement of man with God impossible; man cannot cry in the words of the Apostle, "Who shall deliver me from the body of this death?" if the sinful element is one from which he cannot be delivered, because it is the indispensable condition of all the good that is in him. Moreover, it makes the incarnation impossible, for if man is only truly man whilst he is endeavouring to reconcile the contradictions of good and evil in himself, a sinless man there cannot be. A dilemma is offered us which it is almost blasphemous to draw out. If the human nature is such as this, then we must choose between the two natures of the Son of God, the Man Christ Jesus. The divine nature cannot be there if sin is. The human nature, according to this view, cannot be complete if sinfulness is absent. But His life is the refutation of this theory. It is utterly untrue that without the contrast of evil and good in the same soul there would be no spiritual activity. The life unto righteousness, begun in us with conflict, tends ever more and more towards tranquillity. The approach towards the perfection of the Christian character is measured by the degree in which duties are practised without the stimulus of emotion, without internal struggle. When prayer is no longer a strife against wandering thoughts and laziness; when charity is the free outflowing of beneficence without any selfish stint; when it has become a pleasure to do the will of our Father; when our Christian walk is not amongst chained lions that would devour us, but in ways of pleasantness and peace,—then we know that we are regenerate, and that God has begun His good work in us, and is completing it. Jesus prayed all night upon the mountain; He reaped the daily harvest of the sick that were brought to Him from every quarter; He delighted to do His Father's will. Yet no signs are there in that all-sinless spirit of listlessness or languor from the want of an active struggle within. God forbid! When the divine Power possesses us wholly, our activity will not be less than it is now; but it will be calm and constant like the working of the same power through natural laws. As the stone that we release tends to fall, as the rays of light stream out from the source of light, so shall our souls tend towards God, towards holiness, towards heaven. Our life will be free from its early struggles, but it will be possessed by a law that operates for ever, "My lips shall utter praise when thou hast taught me thy statutes."

These scattered hints, on a subject requiring much time for its full discussion, may serve to put us on our guard against the deceitfulness of sin. Hope not, my friends, to reconcile the jarring testimony of all the worldly witnesses upon this subject. You might suppose that as all have sinned, this would be the one question upon which all would agree. But you forget the prejudices that are at work. One witness is struggling to escape from a conviction which threatens to transform his whole life; so he tries to make light of sin. Another, proud of his metaphysical skill, thinks himself bound to look deeper into the mystery of iniquity than any have done before. A third, from a false good nature, would shut his eyes to the fearful judgment of God against sinners, by which so many shall perish everlastingly. And thus upon the subject of the great plague of our race, men utter foolishness, "deceiving and being deceived." "But continue thou in the things which thou hast learned, and hast been assured of, knowing of whom thou hast learned them." Trust no man's judgment; trust not your own conclusions. Right notions of sin are not to be gained from partial inductions or from witnesses suborned by sin to speak falsely. But you have felt for yourself what sin is. You have heard that awful sentence, "Whosoever hath sinned against me, him will I blot out of my book." And your conscience answers to the threat; and fear comes upon you. You confess your sins to the Lord, and pray that He will forgive them for the sake of One who has died to destroy sin and save you. He hears you, and brings you the health you seek; and you die to sin, and feel a new life unto righteousness is begun within you. And after this solemn transaction between you and the Most High, of the reality of which you cannot doubt, you go into the world and find men conspiring with one mind, yet with various desires, to persuade you that sin has no real existence. You find the same lie that has been whispered since the fall, Though thou sin, thou shalt not surely die. The two testimonies are directly opposite. But the witness of God is consistent with itself, and the false witness of the world is not. Those that now make light of sin sorrowed for it once as you did, or at least, if God gives them that great mercy, before they die they will sorrow for it. Oh, believe not that the work begun in you is an illusion! The chastening in the night season, the self-loathing, the terror of a soul that feels itself immortal, about its condition in the life to come, the admiration for that perfect standard of holiness set up for us in God's word; these are not dreams and morbid fancies. No thoughts so real have ever stamped themselves on our minds. They are your sole protection against morbid delusions. They save you from a life of falsehood. We shall all stand before the judgment-seat of Christ. All that believe this and live out a denial of it, are deceived to their destruction. If that great account indeed await us, we should judge ourselves now lest we fall into the hands of the living God on that day. To go on, sinning more and more, and uttering falsehoods about sin, when the day of our death, that may be imminent, will refute us, is to be fools, and to love and make a lie. Trust your own conviction of sin, you that have received that mercy of sorrow. Pray for it, you that have not received it. It is the voice of love calling to you to escape; it is a sorrow that shall be turned into joy. It begins in tribulation. But God would have you know His Son as the Saviour before you are called to meet Him as the Judge. Rich in compassion, that Son does not visit you to bruise the broken reed or to quench the smoking flax; but to tell you of the ransom He has paid for you, that you may draw near to Him with love, and receive the remission of sins. Keep as your dearest possession the conviction of your guilt; it is the one link within your reach of a chain that hangs down from heaven. It leads you up to confession, to atonement, to reconciliation, to a new life unto righteousness, to a joy unspeakable and full of glory.

SERMON XVI.

SIN IN THE REGENERATE.

———•———

LUKE xviii. 13, 14.

And the publican, standing afar off, would not lift up so much as his eyes unto heaven, but smote upon his breast, saying, God be merciful to me a sinner.

I tell you, this man went down to his house justified rather than the other: for every one that exalteth himself shall be abased; and he that humbleth himself shall be exalted.

WE have seen in former Sermons how widely diffused is the conviction of sin, how subtle and searching sin is in its nature, and whence it comes to pass that popular opinion takes so little account of a disease, which, according to the Bible, is universal, and ends in death. Let me speak to-day of the warfare against sin, which goes on in the mind of the Christian man, and of the final triumph of grace over sin. I will suppose it admitted that all men are born in sin, subject to it and all its consequences, and that the work of Jesus upon earth was to redeem them both from the guilt and the death of sin. I will suppose it admitted, then, in order to share this great salvation, each of us must at some time turn away from sin, must be born again, by receiving from God a new heart, new desires, and new affections, and must experience a daily renewal and sanctifying of his heart through the efficient working of the Spirit of God within him. That a man is in this regenerate state can only be proved by one test; if he believes God's promises, and loves Him, then he is abiding in Christ and Christ in him. But now comes the question, which requires an answer. Is sin wholly and completely cast out from the heart of the Christian, as soon as Christ enters in to dwell there? The forgiveness of sin is complete and instant; the repentant sinner is not suffered to groan under the weight of all the guilt which he committed before he knew or thought of the way of peace. The blood of Christ cleanseth him from all sin, so far as regards its guilt and its punishment, so soon as the forgiveness is sought in earnest. "Repent, and be converted, that your sins may be blotted out." (Acts iii. 19.) But our present question is, how far does the act of reconcilement with God through Jesus Christ extirpate sin from the soul, so that it cannot flourish again?

Now, the soul's reconciliation with God must be an inward change. It is not a mere external act. When a king pardons a robber or a murderer, that is an external act only; the man may leave his prison, and repeat his crime the next day. The king could not alter the man's heart; he could only disconnect his former crime from the death or bondage that was its recompense. Not so does our eternal King pardon us. For in the first place our pardon implies a union with Him, and how can He take to Himself a man with all those very sins unabated, which have been the means of separating between him and his Father? But, in the next place, it is a contradiction in terms to say that the punishment of sin can be removed, and sin itself left; for sin is not only guilt, it is punishment. The folly and restlessness and disappointment of sin are a part of that sore burden which we brought to the foot of the cross, and besought the Redeemer to bear. "Sin and grace," says a great English writer*, "cannot more stand together in their strength than life and death. In remiss degrees all contraries may be lodged together under one roof. St. Paul protests that he dies daily, yet he lives: so the best man sins hourly, even while he obeys; but the powerful and overruling sway of sin is incompatible with the truth of regeneration." The pardon of sin, then, is accompanied by an inward gift; and the nature of this will be evident from what we have learnt of the nature of sin, of which it is the corrective. If sin be a transgression of God's law, and a turning aside from the true purpose of

---

* Bishop Hall, "The Believer crucified with Christ."

our life to follow dreams and vanity, and an exaltation of self against God, then the new principle impressed upon us as the seal of our reconciliation will be a certain power to keep the divine law, and to make our life obey the divine will, and to subdue and crucify self, with all selfish lusts and affections. "If any man will come after me," says the Redeemer, not long before His departure, "let him deny himself, and take up his cross, and follow me." Matt. xvi. 24.) To follow our Lord, and to make our selfishness bear its cross, and go out to be crucified, these are the marks of the redeemed of the Lord. And so far there is not much difference of opinion. But when we come to consider that this newly implanted principle does not wholly and for ever destroy the sinful tendency, that the warfare between grace and sin is only beginning, that the medicine and the poison are circulating henceforth in the same veins, and life and death are contending in the same soul, then a new perplexity awaits us. We are amazed at the tenacity of life which sin exhibits; we see how completely it had conquered us before, how it had laced its binding tendrils round the trunk and branches of our nature, cramping, constraining, and destroying us; how, when its root is lopped off, it clings still round branch and trunk, drinking of their life-juices, and striving to finish its work of destruction before it perish. We cried out to be delivered from the body of this death; and forgiveness was deliverance. But are we thoroughly delivered, so long as we have to wrestle with temptations, and suspect the secret ambush of sin against us?

Let us look, then, to-day at the struggle with sin in the believer's mind, for this was necessary to complete our view of the nature of sin, this is wanted to guard us against the Pharisee's shocking boast, on one side, and on the other against a relapse from the new-found peace to our former despair.

Moral actions are the complicated result of several principles. It may be said that there is not a single command which we are able to follow out thoroughly, without regard to time, or persons, or circumstances, so as to obey its spirit whilst we fulfil its letter. It was our Lord who said, "Swear not at all;" it is the same Lord who takes an oath administered to Him by the high-priest. The same divine Teacher says, "That ye resist not evil: but whosoever shall smite thee on thy right cheek, turn to him the other also;" and one of His chief apostles, imprisoned unlawfully, says, "They have beaten us openly, uncondemned, being Romans, and have cast us into prison; and now do they thrust us out privily? Nay verily; but let them come themselves and fetch us out." (Acts xvi. 37.) "Give to him that asketh thee," (Matt. v. 42,) is a holy precept, yet if it be obeyed without thought or discrimination, it will waste the means of giving, so that we shall cease to impart to them that have a claim on our bounty. What then? Is it not true that our communication should be yea, yea, and nay, nay? Are we not to offer the cheek to the smiter? Are we not to give our substance to the needy? Yes: the precepts are ever true, but on each particular case other precepts bear, which must also have their share of observation. Our Lord will not bring the customary course of justice into disrespect, so He accepts the oath which others are expected to take. And Paul will not admit, by misplaced meekness, that it is a crime to preach the Gospel at Philippi; and we, when we refuse to give to every one that asks us, are afraid to abet sloth and vice, by rewarding them equally with honest labour. It is the function of Christian prudence or thought to adjust the obligations of each precept with those of other precepts, to give to each its proper weight. And two persons may act quite differently in the same matter, and yet it may be difficult to say that either is wrong, where it is not clear which of two principles is of the greater importance. In the well-known quarrel between Paul and Barnabas, the contention, which was common to both, was blameable; but whether Paul was right in thinking that one who had looked back from the plough before was not again to be trusted, or Barnabas, who thought that Mark would not so offend again, it would be hardly safe to decide. It would depend upon whether justice or considerate kindness was the principle that should have prevailed in dealing with that particular case. It is so with all the acts of our life. To live aright implies a certain order and good government in the soul. What makes sin, but some wild affection starting forth out of its place, and throwing the rest into confusion? And an act thoroughly vicious from the motives that decide it, may resemble sometimes one that is the result of a deliberate decision upon Christian rules. The obstinate man might have sat still in the Philippian gaol, as Paul did; but that would not have made him like Paul. The miser closes his purse against the prayer of the dissolute, as the Christian may do, but the real quality of their acts is not the same. The same action may be right or wrong, according as it is done in obedience to all the laws that belong to it, or from a blind obedience to some one of them.

Here then is a wide field for that faculty, whether we call it reason, or conscience, or judgment, by which we see the principles that should govern a particular action. Here too is the field on which we have to contend with sin. A new light has been shed abroad in our hearts; but still the flesh lusts against the spirit; still the passions, hot with long indulgence, struggle to be heard. They try to pervert our judgment; they are like a fever that affects the sense of taste, or a jaundice that tinctures all things with its sickly hue. Vicious acts strive to put on the semblance of beauty and holiness: we are tempted to be proud, and call it honest independence; to be cruel, and call it zeal for God; to be lazy, and say we are at peace; to be lavish, and think we are liberal; censorious, and take comfort in our justice.

I speak not now of those who care nothing for God; it is of those who are seeking Him that all this is true. How can it be? Shall He be my guide, and lead me, yet leave me thus to walk amidst pitfalls? Shall even my religious acts be tainted with the worm of corruption? Shall my very morality ensnare me in a Pharisaic pride? Shall my very strictness make me hard and censorious to an erring brother? Shall I, in my zeal for the truth of Christ, be wounding that brother, and hardening his heart against me, and laying myself open to the taunt that I practise a Gospel in which love is not? Sin has thus deceived me with a lie, even though I have come to Him who is the truth. I thought that in the matter before me I was walking in the truth, and have taken some fantastic counterpart of truth instead. "God be merciful to me a sinner."

Yet be not so cast down. Before you came to God you were not suffered to descend at once into the deep mire of sin. By many and slow degrees you found your level in ruin; by painful retracing of your steps you shall reach at last the firm platform and clear light of a complete holiness. Think how much has been done for you already. To recall from its utter estrangement that wicked heart; to wash off all that obscene pollution; to tear up the book in which ten thousand thousand sins were written against you, so that they shall be remembered no more; to put again into your heart the wish and the power to seek anew that God whom you had long deserted,—these are the wonders of atoning love for which your heart should never cease from praise; and they are the promise of blessings to come. You have been born again. You have not started full-grown into another existence; the innate infirmity that taints every motion of the mind, and every fibre of the flesh, has not been suddenly turned to an angelic holiness. The pride and the passion are left in you, like the remnant of the Canaanites in the borders of Israel, that through them God may prove you, whether you will keep His way or not. (Judges ii. 22.) But is there no good in that? Had the change that has taken place in you been like a waking from a frightful dream of sin, remembered only in fragments and then speedily forgotten, would not the painful work of Christ for you have been forgotten too? The present struggle with sin reminds you of the need of his help. Step by step He mounted the climax of His sorrow; set His face to go to Jerusalem, went towards Gethsemane; thence to priest and judge, thence to the cross. And at the moment when He predicts His gradual and protracted labour, He links you with Him by the promise of a gradual and laborious restoration. On the day that He told His disciples that "He must go unto Jerusalem, and suffer many things of the elders, and chief priests, and scribes," He added, "If any man will come after me, let him deny himself, and take up his cross, and follow me." (Matt. xvi. 21, 24.) It was the sense of sin that sent you to the Redeemer; it is a knowledge that a relapse is possible that keeps you by His side. Fight the good fight set before you; count it all joy that you fall into divers temptations. It is your schooling in holiness. You are free from sin, you are no longer its slaves. Christ has made you free, and you shall have your fruit unto holiness and the end everlasting life.

We said in the outset that the existence of sin in a world governed by God was a great mystery. And now in the last of these discourses we wonder at the sinful tendency left still in the heart that Christ has washed and sanctified. Let us think well upon it, for nothing shows us so clearly the power and persistence of our enemy. Man's nature that should be one, is divided into two, and even the power of Christ has not set them wholly at one again. "I had two wills," says Augustine, "an old and a new, a carnal and a spiritual, which warred against each other, and by their discord scattered my soul."* "It is the soul's sickness," he says; "bowed down by evil custom, it cannot rise up whole and complete when the truth lifts it." † It is indeed a wonder. The serpent nature in us, with its head crushed under the heel of the Redeemer, wriggles and defiles and will not die at once. And of this problem men devise three solutions according to their own state. One slides into the condition of the Pharisee. Looking to what

---

* Confessions, viii. 10.   † Ibid. ix. 9.

has been done in him already, and forgetting the doer of it, he thanks God that he is not as other men are. Little does he think of the sense in which his word is true; he is not as other men, for he is falling into the sin of devils, the pride that exalts itself as a god. Another, finding the struggle a hard one, ceases from it, and lives for a time a life as of one neither saved nor lost, hating sin, yet not knowing the sweetness of pardon. A third reads it aright; and trusting God's promise that he shall conquer temptation, he watches and prays, and crucifies his dearest sins, and renounces his favourite pleasure, and abstains from all that borders on evil, and finds himself in time dead indeed unto sin, but alive unto God.

Brethren, sin is in the world; sin lurks in your hearts and in mine; and yet men take little account of it. There was a city visited by the plague long since: and whilst death was busily smiting every household, a few frivolous men and women sought out a pleasant retirement, and there they spent their days in weaving love-tales and playing with compliments; and still the plague was cutting off hundreds at their gate. Just so do we act under our greater plague. Oh, my friends, it is not by hiding our heads, like a silly bird pursued by hunters, that we can escape the keen eyes of our pursuer. The question is—are you willing to die as you are living? Sin has put a great ditch and rampart between you and God perhaps; you have fortified your soul against Him. It is in vain. Vainly the heart denies its own bitterness. Vainly it covers over the aching void where God is not; vainly it tries to construe selfishness into peace. I know not when this elaborate falsehood shall return again into the nothingness out of which you made it. But truth shall assert itself; and the heart that has banished God from it and set up idols, shall know the blackness of its own darkness, the depth of its own desolation. Descend into your own heart. Are you following the truth or setting up and serving a lie? As you value your own souls put the question to them searchingly. God is the end and aim of each man's life; you cannot swerve from Him without perishing. Think how many souls go down the same broad steps of destruction. First the joys of sense, enticing the youth from his better hopes and darkening his better knowledge. Then the cynical manhood from which all such hopes and knowledge have disappeared. Then the tottering libertine, debasing his invenerable age, and denying all goodness to man or woman, and refusing to believe in the future that he fears. Sin is death, and your conscience knows it; if you would let it speak. And you are invited to be delivered from that death. You have heard this week of "the Lord our righteousness." Turn to that Lord. Say to Him, "God be merciful to me a sinner," and the guilt of your sin shall be blotted out. Do not attempt to create anew your depraved heart. One alone can make you a clean heart and a new spirit. Let Him work His work upon you. He will not so change your nature that there shall be nothing left in you to discipline you into a holy state. But He will give you pardon and peace; and an increasing love of Him will attest to you that His work begun in you, is being carried forward. Spend not one day more in searing and corrupting yourself with sin; every act will give you more trouble when you have to break through the custom of it, and love new pursuits, and act on new desires. What fruit have ye in those things whereof your conscience is ashamed? There is neither peace here from them, nor hope hereafter.

And you that have tasted of the heavenly gift, and escaped the pollutions of the world, beware of the last resource of Satan, the temptation to speak as the Pharisee, "I thank thee that I am not as other men!" Miserable man! Such a thought shows that you have returned already very far upon the road to destruction which you thought you had escaped. You are in a far worse state than that of the publican, for you are leaving the shelter of the Rock of your salvation, and he has come to seek it. Christ alone is our righteousness; the publican knows it better than you, for you have come to boast of your own merit. If our Lord should be extreme to mark what is done amiss, who could abide it? If He should call up against us our harshness, our carelessness, our hypocrisy, who could stand? But we will fall on our knees before Him, and confess that we are weak and sinful; we will beg Him to come and fill our hearts with the recollection of His mercy, that we may never be severed from Him, and that gratitude for His love may soften every judgment we pass on others, and repress every swelling thought about ourselves. Instead of boasting with the Pharisee, we will never cease from glorifying Him that loved us and washed us from our sins in His own blood. Remembering the misery out of which He has lifted us, we will own that we can do nothing without Him. Instead of saying, "I am not as other men," we shall cry, "The good that I do is not mine, but the spirit of God that dwelleth in me: but my evil is my own, a return unto my old pollution." We will search every corner of our heart to find smouldering embers of sin and passion that we may trample them out. The corruption in which we were born was great, but the second corruption, of a soul that has known the Lord, is still more terrible. We shall watch and pray against the fatal relapse. Our repentance for sin shall never end but with our life; to the end shall we struggle with the residues and recollections of our fallen state. But whilst we abhor ourselves we know that Christ has wrought much in us, and our sorrow is not that of men without hope, for we already taste in the midst of it joy and peace in believing. We shall say, "God be merciful to us sinners;" but then we know His mercy already, and our confession is not the cry of the desperate man, but the expression of a sure hope. For Christ dwells in us, and we in Him. "He prays for us as our High Priest" (I am quoting the words of another); "He prays in us as our head, He receives our prayers as our God . . . In the form of God He hears us, in the form of a servant He prays with us. Therefore to Him, and through Him and in Him we pray."* And He is with us always even unto the end of the world.

* Augustine Enar. in Psalm lxxv. 1.

SERMON XVII.

THE LIGHT OF THE WORLD.

Matt. v. 14.

Ye are the light of the world. A city that is set on a hill cannot be hid.

When our Redeemer in this sublime sermon sets forth the terms of citizenship in His new kingdom, it is not without design that He begins with the affections of the heart; that He cautions the disciples as to what they must *be* before He commands them to do His work. Are they poor in spirit—mourners for sin, meek, hungry for righteousness, merciful, pure, peacemakers, patient of persecution? then are they blessed, the children of the Father, the followers of the Son, the heirs of the life in glory to come. It is not that affections are contrasted with, and exalted over, holy works; but that no spiritual work can be done, and abide, except where the spirit of the workman is tuned to harmonise with it. The right-mindedness of the disciples is to be in fact one of the instruments, and no slight one, of their work itself. The sermon has begun with the Beatitudes, as they are called, in which all the graces of the Christian character are set forth, in no careless or unfinished fashion, for the enumeration is complete, and moulded into the rhythm of an inspired psalm. The form of expression is general, "*blessed are they*," because for all ages and lands the morality of the Gospel will be unalterable; but in the eighth beatitude, according to the best interpreters, the general purport of the address begins to be contracted. Turning towards His own disciples, rather than to the multitude, He adds, "Blessed are they which are persecuted for righteousness' sake: for theirs is the kingdom of heaven." Then, in order that none might think that persecution was an eternal mark of the Christian, as meekness and lowliness were, He himself restricts its application. "Blessed are *ye*, when men shall revile you, and persecute you, and shall say all manner of evil against you falsely for my sake. Rejoice and be exceeding glad: for great is your reward in heaven: for so persecuted they the prophets which were before you." Clearly it is to the disciples, who afterwards became apostles and teachers, that this directly applies. It is to them, lambs in the midst of wolves, that He is about to give counsel against their dangers. Yet he does not tell them to fight or to flee; does not call for vehement preachers or consummate dialecticians, to talk down the Jewish rabbi and the pagan sage.

He simply tells them that they must be good men, in order that they may prevail and bring men over to the truth. " Ye are the salt of the earth; but if the salt have lost his savour, wherewith shall it be salted ? it is thenceforth good for nothing, but to be cast out, and to be trodden under foot of men. Ye are the light of the world. A city that is set upon a hill cannot be hid. Neither do men light a candle, and put it under a bushel, but on a candlestick; and it giveth light unto all that are in the house. Let your light so shine before men, that they may see your good works, and glorify your Father which is in heaven." It is evident that the Gospel was to operate through the goodness of its professors, as much as through their labour. For good or evil every man exercises an involuntary influence over those that come into contact with him. They must take care that the influence they were to exert was wholesome. The light was to be pure, for shine it must. The salt must not have lost its savour. The city which was to call itself the city of God — the New Jerusalem, would gather men's eyes into one centre ; so the walls must stand firm, and the towers be beautiful, that men might glorify the builder, God himself. Let this subject occupy our thoughts at present; I mean, the unconscious influence which men exercise upon one another, in matters of morals and religion.

I. The principal work of a man's life may, indeed,

be one which does not depend upon moral character. It may happen, for example, that one bent on reforming science, may devote all the thoughts of his prime to the perfecting a better method of research, by which the progress of knowledge in future shall become, in comparison with the past, what the man's firm walk is to the aimless gambols of a little child. The completion of his work may be an epoch in the history of science; and it may be no hyperbole to call him in respect of it " one of the greatest men, and most worthy of admiration that hath been for many ages." And yet the book that makes his name perpetual, and confers on his country a durable good, may be, so to speak, the child of shame. Mixed with the first praises that presage his imperishable fame, may come accusations of justice perverted, and of judgments sold for bribes and revoked for counter-bribes. And a signal downfall may compel him to a shameful leisure; and many a page that could not have been written by the busy hand of the man whom the king delights to honour, may be produced to solace his degradation. And thus it may be ordered by One who, in His wise government, brings many a good thing out of evil, that knowledge and progress may be augmented in spite of, I had almost said *through*, moral delinquency. For an intellectual production is complete in itself; a new principle, a new arrangement of facts, will carry one along with it, whether a bad man or a good, lays claim to the discovery. Depravity of heart, indeed, will react upon the intellect, and prevent in most cases the attainment of any great results. But this is a general rule, far from a universal one. And where the invention is once reached, it needs no certificate of the moral character of the inventor; it stands independent of him. We may, after a time, recollect such a man as I have described almost as two men; and the halo of glory round the philosopher's name may hinder us from identifying it with the obscurer writing that is set over the fallen statesman and venal judge.

But if the object to be attained is the moral amelioration of men, it is easy to see how important the influence of character must be. A teacher proclaims the wrath of God against sinners, the sinfulness of all men, and their need of reconciliation, the judgment to come, and the eternity behind it, the falsehood of all current religions, the forsaking of selfish, lazy, and luxurious ways of life, the impotence of philosophy, the preciousness in the sight of God of every living soul of man, of the publican as much as of the Cæsar, and thus he irritates unavoidably the prejudices of all classes, and stimulates to the utmost their desire to find some excuse for refusing to hear his teaching, though enforced by miracles, and claiming to be a direct message from the Omnipotent God. Let there be found the smallest flaw in his armour, and there the fiery darts of their ridicule will stick. The most trifling sign of selfishness, of a love for the present life outweighing that for the unseen, of lust of power or gain, of a courage less than that of the bold wickedness which it confronts, would be caught at as an evidence against the message itself. And this sharp criticism has been so often successful, that when it fails in one case only, anger must gradually give place to admiration, and those whose hearts are not desperately hardened, will at last acknowledge with reverence the presence of something divine.

We see, then, if this be true, the wisdom of God in the mode in which the scheme of salvation was made known. All its truths were such as related to the spiritual welfare of men; not to political change, not to civilisation, not to science, but to the saving of sinners from a dreadful doom. And they came from a Teacher who presented in Himself the spectacle, unique, miraculous, of one who needed no salvation, who was already in that pure and holy state to which He would raise others. If He called His disciples the light of the world, then might He well be called in the same metaphor the Sun of Righteousness; for meekness, purity, zeal, unselfishness, reverence, love radiated from Him in all that He said or did. You can conceive a greater awe at the announcement of a new religion than that which attended His preaching; for Sinai shook when Jehovah thundered from it, whilst upon this mountain of Beatitudes, crowds of people listened at their ease to the voice of a man proclaiming peace. But that peculiar loving reverence which, by a law of our nature, we can only feel for one like, yet above ourselves, who rules, yet at the same time lovingly goes with and supports us, gathered round Christ when He ministered; and was the cause of the Gospel's strength. "His virtues," it has been well said*, "are all human, and do not quit the earth, or step out of the proportions of humanity. . . He never forgets, in His struggles with the wicked, in the devotedness of His charity, in the most sublime flights of His piety, even in His indignation, He never forgets that He had not taken the resemblance of angels, but the form of a servant, and that He was made in all points like as we are, yet without sin. Man amongst men, He was an Israelite amongst the Israelites, taking part in all the interests of His age and nation, as well as in the worship of His country; suffering His heart to beat with the same emotions which swelled all hearts; 'the last Adam,' as St. Paul calls Him, keeping so close to us, sons of Adam, that He condescends even to weep with mourners at the very moment of a resurrection, as if to authorise and sanctify at the same time our sorrows, our tears, and our hopes." And whenever a self-convicted sinner conceived the wish to flee from the wrath to come, and crept, with that craving for sympathy and guidance which is as much an instinct of our nature as the need of food, to the side of the only One who proffered them, the influence of His complete holiness would surely be

---

* By Athanase Coquerel.

felt. As Luther has said of the divine nature, "God is in all, and yet beyond all; and there is nothing so great but that God is greater, nothing so small but that God is smaller, nothing so high, but that He is higher, nothing so deep, but that He is deeper," so would the penitent gradually realise the infinite holiness of the Redeemer, by finding every transient virtue in himself surpassed by his Master. The disciple might wish to devote himself; but the Master's devotion was so deep, that it reached from the throne he had left, down to the cross, to the grave, to the realms of death. The disciple might yearn to practise the Christian grace of love towards all mankind, but all the Master's life was one mission of love. There was no height of virtue, and no depth of trial which the disciple could conceive for himself, but that One was before him who had soared higher and descended lower. What was it, then, that taught the Apostles to be as their Master? What was it that built up in them the same temper, though infinitely lower in degree, that the Lord Himself displayed? Not a code of doctrines only; surely the influence of His life, when they watched with Him, and saw Him, and brought before Him their doubts and fears, had no mean share in their training. Can we forget, that long after they had felt that influence, and found themselves knit up by it into one brotherhood, their views of the doctrine of redemption were still confused, fragmentary, uncertain? No: God was pleased to work His wondrous work by an appeal to the same principle in our nature as that which makes the child respect the father, and the friend lean upon the greater sense or virtue of his friend, or the city or State turn to those who can guide them best. The influence of man upon man, the insensible impression which his whole moral nature cannot fail to make on others like himself, as distinct from the impression which he voluntarily sets himself to produce by certain tenets, or teachings, or books, must have its separate place, and that a prominent one, among the causes which have planted Christianity so firmly in the world.

Even those who scarcely mention Christianity without a sarcasm or a scoff, are forced to reckon among the causes of its success the pure morality of its professors, although they attribute this mainly to their care for their own reputation as a small community, set apart from a world that watched it with the closest and most unfriendly observation. As if men who were hunted to death for their religion, who professed the faith of Christ crucified under the severest torments, from which a recantation would have delivered them at once, had nothing better to support them in their holy and ordinary life than such motives as the wish to save the reputation of their sect to pagan eyes! It was not then that in the moment of sorest trial they saw with the eyes of faith the heavens opened and the Lord standing in the attitude of succour at the right hand of God, and would not renounce Him:

but that they wished to preserve their own consistency, and keep the Christian name respectable. Surely it is more simple to suppose that they believed in a future state, as they said they did; and living under the solemn presence of that belief, needed not the feebler props of such worldly motives. At least they tell us themselves that they believed, and that all their nature was altered in consequence. They tell us too, that the sight of their purer and more serene life exercised a wonderful power of attraction over others. They have no doubt that many conversions were wrought by the attractive force of holy examples. "Our Lord," says Justin Martyr*, "would not have us resist, nor imitate evil men in this, but He requires that by the power of patience and meekness, we should win all men from the disgrace of their evil passions. And we can point to many among us who, from violent and tyrannical men, have been thus changed by a victorious power, when they saw how their neighbours could bear all things, or witnessed the singular patience of their defrauded fellow-travellers, or came to be acquainted with the conduct or behaviour of Christians in any other relation of life."

"Ye are the light of the world. A city that is set upon a hill cannot be hid." Besides the good or harm we mean to do, we exercise an influence in our sphere, which we do not intend, and cannot

---

* Apol. I. 16, p. 42 ed. Otto.

abdicate if we would. What is called personal influence has a greater share than we can well measure upon our own present condition; but we shall in our turn exercise the same power that has wrought upon us. Tastes, behaviour, looks, gestures, and many a little sign that is observed unawares, reveal to others the various feelings within us. So that we are known and understood, in a degree at least, before we are conscious of having given the least sign of what we are. Those to whom we have scarcely spoken have measured in some rough way our worth, and divined our intentions. Farther, this personal influence is constant; it needs not, like our deliberate actions, the will and the concurrent opportunity to work itself out. It speaks alike to all, whilst our deliberate words only reach those whom we address, and among these only as many as are fitted by education and capacity for understanding them. And, whereas those who do not sympathise with us can be on their guard against our words, and prepare themselves with arguments to refute them, the influence of our life and example takes them unawares, and wins them over before their antagonism is even aroused. And this silent eloquence cannot be arrested by our own will in the same way as the words of our mouth can. Living in free intercourse with our fellow-creatures, we are every day bearing witness to them of our own character and drift. The true and trustworthy, the man whose sense of duty is strict, the frivolous, the vain, the captious, the kind, have never told their neighbour the thought that is deepest in them; but the neighbour has found it out and told it to others, and given us our place in his mind, from which he would not remove us for any argument we could use. There is a perpetual emanation of personal influence from us, which it is impossible to think of without a certain awe. What if we are the darkness of the world? the savourless salt of the world? the ruined city on the hill looking unlovely in its desolation? No one covets such a mission. One neglects his duty, and lives carelessly, meaning hereafter to arrest himself in a career so dangerous: but he does not invite others to follow him. He believes that the consequences are confined to him; he does not try to make proselytes, he is not his brother's keeper. Still less does he give himself credit for so much influence as to affect the tone of his whole circle. Yet if it be true that personal influence is a constant force, uncontrolled by the will, every example will have its value, small or great; nor is the effect less real that we cannot determine its degree. What a weight of meaning, then, is there in the words, "Ye are the light of the world . . . . Let your light so shine before men that they may see your good works." Whether it is felt to be so now or not, there is an intolerable anguish stirred up in the thought that winged words past recall, and guilty acts, and a lavish waste of time, have gone forth from us to do the work of poison amongst our brothers; and that whatever graces of character or gifts of mind we had, only served to make the poison more enticing. Yet there is no resource against it but a good life. If you lecture others to their good, they will smile at the insincere words; if you caution them against your own example, there will be more of that subtle attraction of which I have spoken, in the careless life than in the well-meant caution; because it is more really a part of yourself. If you try to cloak vice with reserve and secrecy, the utter hollowness of your nature will be felt as by an instinct. But if you have adopted, as the rule of your life, the principle of faith, and of duty to God and to your fellows, the result of faith; if, upon that principle, the good Spirit of God is reforming your hearts, bringing order out of disorder, and making sweet the bitterness of self-surrender, then it cannot be but that the same principle of order that is working within you will be felt without you, and show to some one else the beauty of goodness. And, blessed be God, the power of goodness over others is greater than that of evil. Were it not so, thinking men would indeed despair. If my foolish or wicked speech once uttered, were to echo through ages, if my wrong act were to spread in widening circles over the whole current of human life, how could I bear the thought that even my death would not arrest my busy ministry of evil? But in fact the good is eternal; and the evil which is but confusion, is divided against itself and sometimes comes to nothing. The soul that you have turned to righteousness, has received from you a precious seed, which he will watch over to the end of life, which shall flourish beyond the end. But he whom you tempt to evil will sometimes find that the ruin of peace and the prospect of death are all that you have brought him; he feels too that you did not believe in the evil into which you drew him; he discerned in your shame, or in your faltering or your fear of detection, that you were not a hearty advocate of sin, and experience now tells him why. We are thus saved in some measure from usurping the function of the great enemy of souls. Harm, indeed, we may do, worthy to be bitterly lamented, but it does not reach so far as the good we may do. We set the evil going, and that is harm enough; but unless a man "is drawn away of his own lust, and enticed," he will often escape from our baneful influence into some purer one; our power over him, founded only in untruth and disorder, will not pursue him for ever. What amount of influence could ever have framed for any evil purpose such an organisation as that by which the tidings of good have been preached to men since the day of Pentecost? The Church of Christ stands firm, laws last for centuries, good institutions are fostered after their founder has turned to dust, because they are divine, they are the means of order and peace; but the forms of wickedness toss and change like the deceitful sea. Measure not, then, your powers for good by the days of your weakness, when you set an evil example and earned the distrust and contempt of those very persons who lowered their standard of right a little, encouraged by you. There is light and health in the spectacle of a Christian life; every one will feel it, none will forget it. Only work your work as if it were that to which the Father of All had appointed you, remembering that the night cometh when no man can work. Saved by the Cross of Christ, live now by His Spirit. Try with prayer and humility to walk in the light of that most unselfish life. Live as one who seeks to find the saving of his own soul in the pursuit of good to others. Such a life is not silent, is not obscure: it proclaims in clear tones that there is a God over us, and eternity before us, and that sin is death, and the course of godliness life and peace. But in order to *do*, we must also be. Our Redeemer wrought, as we have seen, by the perfect holiness that was in Him, as well as by his preachings and journeyings. And the long preparation for His ministry, the lonely prayer, and the struggle with the Tempter, were therefore part of His work amongst men, although they went on in silence and apart. The period of His ministry grew out of, and rested upon, the longer season of self-communion. Let not the contagion of a busy and emulative age beguile us to believe that outward work is the sole Christian duty. To look with faith on Him who died to save us : to seek food for the life within by prayer and thought about holy things : even to work somewhat less that we may think and collect ourselves a little more, is the most pressing need of our generation. It is the first work of a Christian who would be a light to others to bear in himself the law of holiness, that all who come near may read it. Let him be pure and honest, and just, and a lover of God, and he is already active in his Master's service by the very influence of those gifts. He does not need to keep men at arm's length, lest they spy out his inconsistencies. His life will be simple, sincere, transparent. Everything about him, words and acts included, will show that he is a faithful disciple of Christ; and his light will indeed so shine before men that they will see his good works and glorify his Father which is in heaven on account of them.

SERMON XVIII.

(Preached on the First Sunday after Easter.)*

FAITH AND SIGHT.

1 John v. 4.

For whatsoever is born of God overcometh the world: and this is the victory that overcometh the world, even our faith.

On the day when our Lord rose from the dead, He gave to His assembled disciples a proof that He was risen, by appearing among them. One of them was absent. Thomas was not inferior to the others in earnest devotedness; it was from his lips that those words issued in a moment of unusual peril, "Let us also go that we may die with him." But yet when the disciples told him, "We have seen the Lord," his answer betrayed a mistrust that ill became one who had been a companion of Jesus from the beginning. "Except I shall see in His

---

* Some thoughts in this Sermon are borrowed from Julius Müller.

hands the print of the nails, and thrust my hand into His side, I will not believe." A week later, as on this very day, the disciples were assembled again, and again did the Lord pass through the closed doors to meet them; but this time Thomas was present. This time the visit was to him; the thoughtful Master who had spent such pains on the training of the disciples, came to give another lesson to one of them that needed it. The hands and the side were offered; and his touch recognised the wounds in their ghastly reality, and he could not help admitting that this was indeed his Lord and his God. And we all recall the remarkable words by which Jesus at once rebuked and counselled him. "Thomas, because thou hast seen me, thou hast believed: blessed are they that have not seen, and yet have believed." These words, although they do not occur in the services of this day, belong to it in an especial sense. "Blessed are they that have not seen, and yet have believed." And the words I have taken from the Epistle put before us the same subject: "This is the victory that overcometh the world, even our faith."

I. In what does the blessedness of faith consist? How does faith give us a victory over the world? When Thomas uttered those words of doubt, he was not indifferent to the world above; he had not forgotten his Master, nor ceased to love Him. His want of faith lay not on that side. His was a gloomy and desponding temper, and the horrors

that he had witnessed possessed him wholly, and
left no room for more hopeful thoughts. Those
nails that lacerated the hands which he had so often
seen lifted to heal and to bless,—would the cruel
wounds that they had made ever close again?
That wound that gaped in the side of Jesus, out
of which flowed the blood and the water,
out of which would have passed the life of the
Lord as well, but that he was dead already,—could
aught heal it? Or could one rise, and walk and
speak on whom these five seals of death were set
in blood? Could that body, marred and wrung,
torn with stripes, agonised with all the modes of
pain, ever again be a tabernacle for the Son of God
to dwell in? Thomas would believe it when his
own eye and hand bore witness to it; but no lower
evidence would expel the terrible realities that
pre-occupied his mind. The world had, to all outward seeming, prevailed over the Son of God; it
had certainly overcome the faith of His disciple.
The wounds that the world had made on the person
of the Saviour were real objects of sight; the
evidence for them was real. But there were other
and higher realities than these, if Thomas had
possessed the faculty that apprehends them. The
perpetual out-streaming of divine power which had
marked the Lord's whole ministry, the voice at
His baptism, the glory on the mount, His prophecies
and promises of His sufferings and of His conquest
over them, were facts, as much as were the tokens

of death upon his bodily frame. But before the present horror and fear, all these receded; they were for a time as though they had not been. Faith and trust were suspended; and sight had the dominion and the victory. And what the Apostle craved, to lift him up again, was another sight that might overcome the sight that dejected him, against which he had not the faith to struggle. Thus described, his condition is far from being strange or inconceivable to us. Men that possess faith, but not the faith that can gain a real victory over the world, are in every congregation; and this one can hardly be exempt. If, under God's blessing, we shall be enabled to-day to find a test for our own faith in that risen Lord, whom we profess to believe, the time we shall spend in acquiring it will not be thrown away.

The principal fact on which our faith will fasten itself is the resurrection of our Lord from the dead. If we turn to the Acts, the burden of the Apostolic preaching is always this — "The resurrection from the dead proves that Jesus is the Christ." In the Epistles of St. Paul, the inspired writer insists, with emphasis, upon the resurrection of Jesus, as the fundamental proof of Christianity, and the pledge of our salvation. Our Lord himself implied that this was to be the crown of His ministry; for when the disciples confessed Him as the Christ, He charged them that they should tell no man, till the Son of Man were risen from the dead. In comparing the four Gospels, we find that in the account of the passion they pass through the facts with equal steps, each relating what the others do; and even the fourth Evangelist, who usually pretermits what his three inspired colleagues have recorded, joins his hand to theirs in this place, that our picture of the sufferings of the beloved Lord may be more complete, touched and retouched by four successive hands. But when they come to the resurrection there is a great divergence. Each seems to intend to produce distinct testimony of a fact so all-important — so certain to be disputed — as that of the resurrection; that the evidence may be more than abundant. And as Christianity began to take root in the world, the resurrection was the fact towards which assailants and apologists turned their chief strength. Now the effects of a sincere belief in the resurrection of Jesus Christ will be to give us an insight into another life higher than this, the thought of which will have a perpetual influence on our thoughts and conduct here, and also to give us an interest and a hope in that higher life as something bought for us by the death of the Redeemer.

a. Do we live as if there were a higher life than this? Do we walk by faith, and not by sight? Is it by faith, or by sight, that we are inclined to view the facts that surround us, of science, of history, and of our own inward experience?

α. The laws of the creation are daily more and more understood. Every-day facts that seemed unconnected or discordant crystallise into regular forms, and add a fresh witness to an old law, or give the presage of a new one. The facts themselves are seldom in dispute; but even in this the most certain field of human research, the interpretation of the facts differs widely with different minds. With one every step in discovery tends to replace the thought of a superintending God by that of an eternal necessity; thrusts back farther and farther the epoch of creation into the impenetrable chambers of an almost eternal past; and so dispenses with the thought of a Creator; gives to man a fresh confidence in the predictions of his own reason, in his powers to extract the secrets of nature from her; enriches this life with secrets of health and power and material success, and diverts the thoughts of men *to* these as their proper business, and from the study of a life after death, about which, so it is argued, there is no certainty, nothing but trouble and perplexity to those that allow it to disturb them. Such a line of thinking is indeed the victory of the world over faith; the present life conquering the eternal. It is perfectly natural that mere human eyes that have adjusted their focus by long poring on the things immediately before them, should be unable to see what is beyond and above. But the evidence that we gather from material things is but one kind of evidence after all. And if, whilst we are examining the lily of the field, or deciphering the inscriptions written in the buried rocks before ever the round world was finished, we take with us a real belief in the Father who made all things, and in the Son who died and rose again for us, and in the Spirit of love and wisdom that sanctifies and informs the spirits of those whom He loves, then we are saved from many crude conclusions, from much foolish pride, from the gradual death of all our higher hopes under the chilling shadow of a materialist theory. It is not an inherent fault of all scientific pursuits to lead men away from God, but only of the onesided study of science. If it be true that this world, with its adamantine foundations, with its crown of everlasting mountains, once began because God spake, will one day end because He shall withdraw from it, and now endures from day to day only because the power of His will streams through it in floods of life, and binds it fast together;—then what a miserable pretence of knowledge must that be which leaves out the thought of the divine indwelling. If it be true that the world is a temple of God, and we treat it only as man's store-room and laboratory and workshop, every step taken in this wrong direction must lead us farther from the truth. The whole depending chain of knowledge will partake of the weakness of its first link. It is too common to say that there is danger in the study of nature; that it leads to this and that perversion of truth. Not so. There is danger in the want of religion: it will cramp, and at last destroy, a man, be his pursuit what it may. But ascribing to God the glory of all, we may consider the heavens, which are the work of his fingers, we may study the lilies of the field, which He has arrayed more richly than Solomon in all his glory. "Lift up your eyes on high," says the Prophet, "and behold who hath created these things, that bringeth out their host by number: He calleth them all by names, by the greatness of His might, for that He is strong in power; not one faileth." (Isa. xl. 26.) It is the Lord that set bounds to the sea; that giveth drink out of His springs to every beast of the field, that speaketh even in the voice of the young lions roaring after their prey. Every form of life and beauty in the creation, every subtler harmony that is brought out by the skilful touch of the masters of science, is a fresh witness to Him, and adds to the music of praise that rises from all creation up to His throne. We may pursue with all our ardour the research into natural facts, if we take careful note of ourselves, lest we begin by degrees to banish God from our thoughts, and receive instead some scheme of eternal, irreversible laws. Wherever our researches lead us we are safe, so long as we are able to say with sincere belief, at every stage in our progress— "Oh, Lord, how manifold are Thy works! in wisdom hast Thou made them all: the earth is full of Thy riches. . . . The glory of the Lord shall endure for ever: the Lord shall rejoice in His works. I will sing unto the Lord as long as I live! I will sing praise to my God while I have my being." (Ps. civ.)

β. In the study of the history of mankind faith gives us the victory over the temptations which the world offers us. Those confused struggles of tribes and nations with which all history begins — that fair growth of civilisation, with its poets to grace it, and its philosophers to think it into shape and system, and its patriots to offer their lives for its protection, which bloomed and then vanished in decay—those cities which were once the terror of the Lord's people, and which roused the anger of the Lord's prophets, and now lie buried under mounds of earth, trodden by the unconscious feet of barbarians, until a later age shall exhume their remains; those barbarian inroads which have swept away like a flood the civilisation of many ages even as the sea has swept away the ineffectual dyke, and turned again the smiling plain-that had been wrested from it into a barren lagoon; those records of oppression of free peoples that make even the most patient heart beat somewhat quicker; above all that incurable inequality between rich and poor, which signifies famine and suffering and disease for the one, and (oftentimes at least) indolence and pride, and selfishness for the other, and which has tempted so many thinkers to devise some scheme for reconstructing human society from the foundations, and dividing the goods of the earth anew;— these are phenomena in which at first sight the hand of God does not appear. If in one generation we seem to see the purposes of God in the progress of the human race, we are staggered to find that in the next it halts or is put to confusion. If in the condition of one nation, and one class in it, we discern the bounty of the Most High, who has loaded it with benefits, it is impossible to forget that there are tribes without the sense that would enable them to build a lodging or provide food for tomorrow's meal, or that in the favoured nation there are those, who, in a city full of splendour, find not where to lay their head, and in the midst of feasting see their children weep for hunger. But what does faith teach us? God made not the world in order that man's life here should be the perfect and consummate product of His wisdom. He made it to found here a kingdom for Himself. And when sin entered in, and death by sin, He prepared a remedy for that disorder. The life and death of the Redeemer were this remedy. Round that centre the facts of our history are to be grouped. The world is not a park or a meadow, where human cattle fatten in peace on rich pastures, whilst the strong fence keeps out the wild beast. If this were the divine idea, the actual world realises it not at all. The world is a place where man, once free to choose the good, sinned and fell, and whither, after long preparation, God sent His only begotten Son to preach the kingdom of Heaven on earth, that in it men might find rest for their souls, and eternal salvation. The primeval struggles were the fruits of sin. Not in vain did Jehovah bring out from Egypt a tribe of slaves, and overwhelm the chariots and horsemen of their pursuers in the water flood.; for that race and the land that He gave them were the cradle of the world's salvation. Not in vain did Greek cultivation bloom and perish, for it lent its language to the Gospel message, and its seeds of thought were to fall into Christian soil, and to grow there into a fragrance and beauty more than had been their own. Not in vain did another state subdue and give laws to the world, for the Cross that at first she persecuted so fiercely was soon set upon her banner, and the persecutor became a protector. And though the poor still suffer, the voice of faith alone dares speak to them openly of their lot, for it can tell them, not of some utopian scheme by which, if it can only be realised, as it cannot in their time, their children's children might perhaps eat bread in peace, but of One who ever preached words of comfort for the poor and sorrowful. The voice of Jesus is the true consolation of the suffering; He bids them that labour and are heavy laden come to Him for rest. He speaks of a world where tears are wiped from all faces, and bids them lift up their eyes to that world, and in the strength of hope endure the present sorrow. Thus does faith again overcome the world; it overcomes the difficulties that the world's history presents, it overcomes the temptations that are aimed at it by those who would exaggerate those difficulties. It teaches the suffering to overcome the world by looking

T

upward to a world beyond this, by setting the affections on things above, where Christ sitteth at the right hand of God.

γ. But, lastly, have we for our own guidance in our daily life the faith that gives us victory over the world? We may well ponder on this question; it searches deep into our hearts; its answer is life and death. The Bible sketches for every one of us the chart of our life. We were sinful, born in sin. But the Lord has redeemed us, with what price we all know: with the price of His humiliation, with the ransom of His blood. And now He is risen, and we live a life of hope and expectation. Our affections are risen with Him; we seek to please Him; we expect to join Him. And full of this faith, we are able to overcome the world; we do not lay up treasure in it, for we have no abiding place here, and our home is yonder in heaven. We do not let deceitful lusts sully again the soul that He has washed. Under the eye of a Master so full of love, we cannot but love our brother; before One who left a heavenly throne for the last humiliations that earth could offer Him, we feel that pride in us would be folly as well as sin. This is the type of a Christian life; is it the type of ours? No, my friends, it is not. We believe in a risen Lord; truly and honestly believe in Him. But our belief has not won a victory over the world. We feel that it wants force for that encounter. The impressions of our sight, the facts of this material world, are realities, and have their power over us. Thomas had *seen* the triumph of the priests, and the murder that they had done, and he cried, "Let sight correct sight. Let me see those five wounds over which I wept in spirit, borne upon the body of a living man, and I shall be able to believe that the Lord is risen indeed, and has appeared to you." And we *see* the necessities of this life which claim so much of our efforts. We know that wealth, professional success, the esteem of men, are good; are thought good, even by those that we know to be striving to live aright. How shall we draw our affections off from the near and actual, to that which is afar off, and which does not press upon us with importunity, as do the needs of this present life? Let us first admit that those two phrases, to walk by faith and to walk by sight, are no mere logical subtlety, or empty figure of speech. It is possible to interpret this life as if there were no other, and that is to walk by sight. And it is possible to see it as the training for a higher life, where our inchoate virtues and graces will find their completion, where the gold and the ornaments of this life will prove to be but dross. Even in the life of Jesus himself, the world's Redeemer, one witness probably saw no more than the son of a carpenter, who had no right to teach, having never learnt, and who was put to death lest he should mislead the people. Another sees there the Lord of life, sealed in His baptism, attested by miracles, glorified in the mount, laying down for men the life which no man could have taken from Him, and then rising again, and returning to the glory which He had with the Father before the foundation of the world. Even there the twofold view of life was possible. Men might — ay, and did — look upon that eternal light, and then say calmly it was not light, but only darkness. And who can raise us from the life of sight to that of faith? No resolve of ours, no stoical self-restraint, no determined effort of the will. He alone can raise us who showed to Thomas His hands and His side; our risen Lord and Redeemer. If, indeed, the life of faith be more excellent, if it be better to think and to live as if before us lay the shoreless sea of eternity, rather than to come upon it unawares, then let us pray to Him to teach us how to live. Let us say to Him, Lord, I believe, help Thou mine unbelief! Let us say, "In thee, Lord, we live and move and have our being; oh teach us to live as if we knew Thee. Thy death has given us a pledge of Thy love; Thy resurrection, of Thy divine power. Impress on our lives Thy cross and Thy victory. Teach us to deny ourselves and bear our cross. Make our life a life 'hid with thee in God.' Do Thou, O 'first-begotten of the dead,' set before us daily the remembrance that in Thy life shall we also see life. May we look forward to that awful day of wrath and rejoicing in which Thou shalt judge the world that once judged Thee. Enforce our spirits with that faith which is the victory that overcometh the world, that we may be able to say in that day when the world shall wither up and perish, 'I have fought the good fight . . . I have kept the faith. Henceforth there is laid up for me a crown of righteousness, which the Lord, the righteous Judge, shall give me: and not to me only, but unto all them also that love His appearing.'" (2 Tim. iii. 7, 8.)

SERMON XIX.

THE TEMPLE OF GOD.

1 Cor. iii. 16, 17.

Know ye not that ye are the temple of God, and that the Spirit of God dwelleth in you?
If any man defile the temple of God, him shall God destroy; for the temple of God is holy, which temple ye are.

YE are the temple of God! By this high title the Apostle does not fear to describe the Christians of whom he is writing. The world is reconciled again to God by Christ; and now the Comforter dwells in every believing heart, and the love, and joy, and peace, that bear up each against the hostility of men are His gift, His work; and the awe of His presence restrains the frivolous thought, and puts a watch upon the lips, and makes the walk circumspect; and the whole life goes on as in a sacred presence, and the whole soul is bent into the attitude of worship. The Holy Spirit has made the heart His tabernacle, and His nearness is felt. The fear of offending Him is a daily motive of conduct; the desire of retaining His life-giving light becomes the foremost of the affections. Truly then is He the God, and the Christian is at once the temple and the worshipper, for the Spirit of God, whom he serves, dwells in him.

Did this awful indwelling commence at Pentecost? Was the human soul strange to that hallowing presence from the beginning of time until the day of the cloven tongues of fire? The whole tenor of the New Testament speaks of a restoration to life rather than a creation of it; and as we find in Christ's redemption the antidote of the fall, so should we look in the mission of the Comforter for the restoration of the lost image of God which man enjoyed at first. "God created man in His own image; in the image of God created he him." For if we run through the interpretations of this passage that have at any time found defenders, we shall hardly doubt but that the Spirit of God and the soul of man were acquainted from the hour of creation. Thus "the image of God" does not mean that the bodily organism of man realises the highest and most perfect idea in the divine mind; for, even if the words would bear such a sense, we have no evidence that one even nearer to the angels might not have been made; we dare not say to the rising tide of creation, "Thus high—even to man— mightest thou swell and no higher." Nor must we be attracted by Tertullian's fancy that man's form was the image of God, because it was that form which God would assume when Christ came in the flesh; as he says, "The clay that made us was not only the work of God, but the pledge and promise of God;" for this would make the words that describe man's honour to contain a covert presage of his transgression and ruin. But these forced explanations, and others even more fantastic, give way before the more general opinion among Christian writers, that when God formed man out of the dust and breathed into him the breath of life, it was the Spirit of God which quickened him, and became within him, will, and intelligence, and pure affections. Between the day of Creation and the great Pentecost, the Spirit, we are expressly told, gave strength to the heroes of the chosen people, as to Samson in the fight at Ashkelon (Judg. xiv. 19), and infused wisdom into the artists that decked the Tabernacle, and spake by the prophets, as Isaiah says, "The Lord God and His Spirit hath sent me." The Holy Spirit intervened at the incarnation of the divine Son, was manifest at His baptism, led Him up into the wilderness to His temptation, was with Him in His miracles, went forth with His apostles even during His ministry on earth to plead their cause before the persecutor; "For it is not ye that speak, but the Spirit of your Father which speaketh in you." (Mat. x.) So far the Scripture speaks expressly. And in that passage of the prophet Joel quoted by the Apostle Peter as the promise of the Comforter, it is not the first entrance into the world, but the more plentiful effusion of the Spirit, that is foretold: "It shall come to pass afterward, that I will pour out my Spirit upon all flesh; and your sons and your daughters shall prophesy, your old men shall dream dreams, your young men shall see visions: and also upon the servants and the handmaids in those days will I pour out my Spirit." (ii. 28, 29.) What is this but a promise that the Spirit, known already as a rare and precious gift enjoyed by prophets and chosen ones, shall in those last days spoken of be dispensed more largely, and flow down in free streams from the fountain of all life to all that are gathered out of the world into the kingdom of heaven? The wonder is, not that a new divine agency shall appear for the first time, but that the rare and scattered sparks of divine fire shall blaze abroad and gladden whole nations with their light, and warm the hearts of the lowliest. And not less cogent is the inference that we are forced to draw from passages less express. If the fruit of the Spirit in the Christian Church "is love, joy, peace, long-suffering, gentleness, goodness, faith, meekness, temperance" (Gal. v. 22, 23), then how can we refrain from tracing to the same divine Person the same graces, so far as they manifested themselves before? Does the faith of the Christian proceed from the inworking of the Holy Spirit, and that of Abel, Enoch, Noah, Abraham, and Moses, come from themselves? If "no man can say that Jesus is the Lord but by the Holy Ghost" (1 Cor. xii. 3), then who but the same Holy Ghost prompted the longing outlook of such as under the old covenant expected the same Lord Jesus, the consolation of Israel? If neither love, nor joy, nor peace, nor long-suffering, nor any of the list of Christian graces, was utterly unknown to the times of the old covenant, then as far as one of these manifested itself, ever so dimly and rarely, so far did the Holy Spirit manifest Himself. God did not sleep, though man resisted. Here and there did He, as it were, repair for Himself the ruined temple of a human heart, and enter in and dwell there, although the altar was rent asunder, and the light shone dimly within, and the fowls of the air found lodging there, and the trail of the serpent made it unclean. Even the heathen were "without excuse," because even their condition was not utter blackness and ruin; they too could have seen through the visible world the eternal Power and Godhead; they too had the law of conscience written in their hearts, to teach them the difference between sin and duty. So far forth as they saw the truth, it was by the Holy Spirit's light, for what is there else to enlighten them? This cannot come from Satan, because it is good; cannot come from themselves, because they are nothing; must proceed from Him who is the Lord and Giver of life, because it is the highest and most spiritual element of their life.

Thus much, then, Christian hearers, we may fairly infer from the Holy Scriptures. He who moved on the face of the waters at creation, and was the spirit and breath of life breathed into man, would have remained with him but for sin. And man would have been a temple of the Holy Ghost from the first; he would have felt the consciousness that his own personality, his will, his affections, were eternal and divinely given, shoots growing out of, but not torn away from, the root and stock of the infinite Lord. Communion with God would have been a reality; nay, the only reality of life, because the only mode of treading on the permanent rock whilst the water-floods of a changeful world flowed fast about his feet. And in that communion three principal elements would have shown themselves; love towards God, who had created man's spirit, and fed it with daily supplies of life; love towards other men, because ties stronger than flesh and blood united him with them, because they bowed, each at a different shrine set up in the sanctuary of the heart, to one common Lord and God; and lastly, a deep sense of responsibility in the possession of a gift so excellent: in the words of Job, " All the while my breath is in me, *and the Spirit of God is in my nostrils;* my lips shall not speak wickedness, nor my tongue utter deceit. . . . My righteousness I hold fast, and will not let it go: my heart shall not reproach me so long as I live." (xxvii. 3.)

When the fall of man broke down the altar within him and scattered the fire, and his vision of God became dim, it did not follow that the Holy Spirit withdrew from the world, because the aberration of man's will was allowed to banish him from the human heart. Whatever belonged to him as the giver of life went on still; "the whole creation," says one father, "is surrounded by the Spirit of God."* "The grain of wheat that falls into the ground," says another, "and comes to dissolution, springs up manifold through the Spirit of God that sustaineth all things."† And whenever the veering compass of man's will, utterly perturbed by sin, pointed again to the pole of heaven, and guided him truly, though but here and there and for a season, again was the light seen; the love warmed again, and it was felt that God was still near. The almost forgotten name was recalled in speech, and to the power of the Holy Ghost was the glory given, when words of godly wisdom were uttered, or heroic deeds that helped God's people done, or strains of prophetic music too sweet, too deep, too awful for a harp with earthly strings, were uttered. Here, too, lies one reason that the personality of the Holy Spirit appears more dimly in the language of the Old Testament than in that of the New. It had not then been made manifest how He should become a Comforter to the Church of Christ, sustaining it against the fiercest persecution; how he should whisper comfort to the individual Christian's soul, helping its infirmities, and teaching it how to endure, and what to pray for, and making intercession for it with groanings that are not uttered. As in the Old Testament the work of the Second Person of the

---

* Theoph. ad Autol. i. 5.   † Irenæus, v. 2, 3.

Holy Trinity is shadowed forth dimly in the type and the prophecy, so should we expect that the Third Person, who is to stand in the stead of the Saviour as a present Comforter, should be known most perfectly when His personal work of comfort is most fully experienced.

Now, if this be true, we shall be able to infer from the benefits conferred on all Christians by the Holy Ghost, what was the blessedness of our original inheritance lost by the fall. He guides into all truth; teaches all things; and brings all things to remembrance whatsoever Christ has said. Love and joy, peace and long-suffering, all holy and gentle thoughts does He work in us. So then He pervades the intellect and the spirit of man; all that is distinctive of man as above the other creatures is under His control. Farther even yet does His sway reach. Man's higher powers are grafted upon the lower; the motions of his spirit blend with, whilst they rise above, the laws of his physical life. And He that governs the higher element, controls the lower also. "The Spirit of God hath made me, and the breath of the Almighty hath given me life," says Job. "If He gather unto himself His Spirit and His breath, all flesh shall perish together, and man shall turn again unto dust." (xxxiv. 14, 15.) Life, then, and breath, and the wise thought, and the holy desire, are all from Him. God "is not far from every one of us; for in Him we live, and move, and have our being." (Acts xvii. 28.)

Nor is there anything against this in the passages that speak of the coming of the Comforter as something new and peculiar to the Gospel. The Christian state was new indeed. Old things were passed away; a new heart opened itself to new desires and feelings. The servant of sin ceased to serve it, and obeyed righteousness. Naturally, then, the communion with the all-pervading Spirit into which Christians were admitted was described as a new mission, then commencing. From man's point of view, that which he could not fully know or enjoy was felt to be far distant, and when the barriers were thrown down it seemed to have come suddenly near. The lighting down of cloven tongues of fire was a new manifestation of divine power; but not the first act of a divine Person. Had not the same Spirit descended already in the form of a dove upon our blessed Lord? Yet neither was that the first act of Him who had wrought from the beginning of creation. We know that God the omnipresent does not in truth leave heaven when he would speak on the earth, does not need to move with wings towards any point in that space which He in fact contains, which cannot contain Him. But such representations are concessions to the weakness of our nature; God himself is not limited to this place or that moment, but He wishes our attention to be fixed on the point in time or space where He is about to work for our instruction. The Comforter did *come* on the day of Pentecost, for the door of the heart was unlocked to Him. It had been closed before: sin was as a bar of adamant, and Christ had broken it in pieces with the stone that was rolled from the mouth of his sepulchre. But most unworthy would be our conception of the divine nature if we supposed that the Spirit of God that moved on the face of the chaotic mass, and brought into it life, form, and order, could desert the world He had quickened, and sit in some distant star like a banished angel, with folded wing and hands hanging down, an idle watcher of His own marvellous mechanism, waiting a summons to put His hand to it again.

Christians, it is at the very root of all worship to believe not only that God is near us, but that He has made a temple within us. Every faculty we have is but the reflection of His light in us; our wisdom and our love, that seem so truly ours, are really His; as children believe yon windows are in flame, when their elders know that it is but the beam of the declining sun reflected back from them. All that is good in us, body or mind, is the present work—no past forgotten work—of the Creator; nothing is ours but sin. Are you afraid that this may run up to pantheism? A right conception of sin carried along with us will ever prevent that. We cannot confound God with the universe He has created; so long as we abhor the taint of sin and selfishness that has been permitted, for mysterious reasons, to enter into and defile it. Nay, is it not the best remedy for pantheistic leanings to contrast with the blessed heritage which man wilfully lost, the kingdom of

Satan into which he entered as a slave. From the harmonious action of one common spirit, which might have been ours, into the jarring confusion where each struggles for his own; from purity to vices that cannot bear the day; from a true conception of the divine nature to a fanciful and degrading polytheism; from peace and love, to envy, backbiting, evil-speaking, malignity, murder; this was the headlong descent which man made at the fall. There is nothing about us in our fallen state to foster pride, or exalt human nature to a divine level. There is much to wring from us the cry, "Oh wretched man that I am, who shall deliver me from the body of this death?" And now through Christ, and Him alone, I thank God I am delivered. God abides in me and I in Him. Oh what love must not this awaken in me towards Him who is my Father indeed! What an atmosphere of glory and sanctity invests to my eye every other human soul that is or might be the possessor of the same excellent privilege! What carefulness and circumspection must I not exercise lest I grieve Him by that sin which He hates and will not endure!

But this great truth contains also the antidote to those materialistic tendencies, about which, if I have spoken lately from this place, I shall be pardoned though I speak again, by those at least who know how they are penetrating the scientific and the historical literature of this and other countries.

Man, according to these views, is the product of

the material world, and man's thoughts are strictly determined by material phenomena. "Man," says one writer, "is the product of time and space, parents and nurses, wind and weather, sound and light, food and clothing. His will is the necessary consequence of all these causes, and is bound to a natural law, which we know from its phenomena, as the planet to its course, and the plants to the ground." . . . . "It is hard to make evident to most men the necessity that determines their existence and their actions, because they do not reflect that every impression on the ear or the eye is a motion, which brings with it material alterations; because they do not see that every draught they drink, and mouthful they eat, changes the blood and consequently the nerves, that every breath, every change in the atmosphere, acts on the nerves of the skin, and through them upon the brain."* This is the cheerless theory which men can sit down and honestly write for the instruction of others! From the horizon of our life all the bright hues of hope disappear, and there settles over it a darkness that may be felt; for if all this be true, nothing remains for us but a foolish and aimless game, which we are to play till we are tired, and then lie down and sleep a sleep that is eternal death. Man is in this view the most complex machine, and nothing higher. We thought, indeed, that as surely as we possessed hands and head, so

* Büchner, *Kraft und Stoff.*

surely did we own a will, a power of choice which cannot be defined — cannot even be conceived — except as independent, in some degree, of the incidents of matter; we are to learn that our consciousness of a power to choose is illusory, and age and sex, and temperament and state of health, and diet and climate, drive us, by their joint influence, towards a conclusion as inevitable as the fall of a stone or the burning of fire. We thought that, however manifold might be the sources of our ideas and feelings, there was something within us, one, simple, indivisible, be its name personality or consciousness, to which all impressions, whencesoever arising, were brought and referred. And, we ask, in what part of this bundle of corporeal elements that are supposed to make up man this single somewhat can reside? what among the many material particles in us enjoys this privilege of being the throne of the personal man? We thought that man's peculiar power of setting aside material needs and aims, in order to pursue truth, holiness, beneficence, was an argument that man's work was not limited to matter, and would not perish when the earthly house dissolved from around him; but the materialist is bound to acknowledge nothing but corporeal good, and to call back his instinctive admiration from the martyr and the laborious sage, who have postponed to an ideal good the pleasures and advantages of life. If this theory is true, the whole structure of knowledge must be taken down and rebuilt; consciousness and free-will, and all supra-mundane hopes, must be thrown aside by the builder.

Now, it is remarkable that whilst a tèndency to materialism has often been diffused through a whole generation or country, the writers who have given the tendency a complete shape, and cast it into a system, where principles are pursued fearlessly to their consequences, are very few. Before the last strokes of the chisel have been bestowed on the work, the artist has often shrunk back appalled from his own monstrous creation. It is a hard thing even for the most narrow and partial bigot of a system to sign away his own charter to a place above the brutes; to abdicate his will, and uncover the nakedness of the soul, and trace all his immortal hopes to a timid egotism vaunting itself above its proper bounds. And thanks be to the Spirit of God, who vindicates His work even to the unwilling, the mind often springs back from the enforced conclusion, even when the fallacy of the premises is not exposed. But let us approach the problem of our destiny and nature from the opposite side. Think how matter has been the slave and organ of something higher than itself, ever since this life began. Think how the germ of life, in which is contained, by a mystery that escapes the scalpel and the lens, all that the aftergrowth can develope, has selected, assimilated, or rejected, according to its needs, from the world around it. Think how history, which bears witness, I grant, to the influence of matter over man, records everywhere the cases in which the spirit gains a victory over matter. The woman's weakness made strong, even to bear the torments of martyrdom; the indomitable resolution, carrying a shattered body through laborious duties; the hopes of immortality growing brighter at the end of life, when all the bodily faculties fail and seem to verge towards extinction; the love where hatred would have been the more natural impulse; the joy where the earthly state seems most gloomy; the peace where all earthly circumstances suggest wretchedness; the faith which no trials can shake; all these are protests against the doctrine that matter governs or makes the human soul. But far better is it for us, if, instead of searching history, we can read the records of a spiritual life working within us. Then indeed we shall believe that God the Holy Spirit exists, when we have felt Him helping us. He exists, because He is working within us. *Est quandoquidem donatur.* The man that is weaning his soul and refraining it from its lower wants, and fighting, not as one that beateth the air, with sinful propensities, that so he may be stronger for the duties of life; the man in whom the leaven of Divine love is transforming into something better the anger, and pride, and selfishness, wherewith in his natural state he did battle with other angry, proud, and selfish beings, for very sustenance and life; will never believe that there is no God to have mercy on him, and that he is nothing but a cunning composition of the rain of heaven and the dust of the ground. He cannot deny the life that is in him. There can be no mistake about the existence of that which bears a solid fruit of "love, joy, peace, long-suffering, gentleness, goodness, faith, meekness, and temperance." That which helps us to look beyond this day and place, and in our aspirations after another life gives substance to things hoped for, and evidence to things not seen, is a real power, not subject to matter, able indeed to set it aside. And happy are those who, when every tenet is winnowed and sifted, often by most presumptuous hands, can feel that the sense of God's presence is theirs already; not a vague impression, but a habitual awe and reverence, that keeps God in their thoughts, and teaches them love to other men, and makes them holy in thought, and word, and deed.

But there is also a *practical* or implicit materialism, which is so far from rare that it is the besetting sin of mankind. It is the "living after the flesh" of the Apostle. Having within them two sets of influences, acting from above and from beneath, men abandon themselves to the lower. You see the fruits of it in selfish indulgence; in a contempt of all that try to rise to something better; in a willingness to impute low motives of action to others. It has deeply tainted the literature of the day; and more than one work of genius expresses a disbelief in all high principle, in religion, and duty, and pure affection; treats morality as a conventional arrangement which society has hit upon for its preservation, religion as a lucrative hypocrisy, and virtue as a prudent calculation of consequences ; and arrives at last, by an exhaustive process, at one sole remaining law of conduct,—a vicious self-will, seeking satisfaction here, and looking for nothing beyond. He that feels that this tendency is destructive, because it is earthly and sensual, should protest against it ; should avow, but not obtrude, a higher principle as his own rule; should bear, believe, and hope all things of others ; should never countenance the levity by which virtue, affection, and the love of God are sometimes nicknamed and scoffed away.

" Know ye not that ye are the temple of God, and that the Spirit of God dwelleth in you? If any man defile the temple of God, him shall God destroy: for the temple of God is holy, which temple ye are." Why should we doubt it? Is it because we do not see the mode of His operation upon our human nature — because we do not see angels ascending and descending to keep up our intercourse with Him? Neither do you see the light that passes from the sun to the moon, nor the far-reaching force that keeps the planets true to their courses. Is it that material influences really are strong upon us, and more strong the longer we submit? Surely our memory must supply us with some cases in which we were conscious that we were not all buried in clay, and felt that the body was the seat of the soul, but not its author, and that the temptations of the flesh did not necessitate a decision in favour of Satan. These precious moments are the facts from which we must set out. Love then the Lord God whose breath is in your nostrils, whose inspiration gives you understanding, who has never hid His face from you except when sin lay at the door, who is waiting your repentance that He may come to you and dwell with you, and knit you more closely to God, and be within you the Spirit of adoption whereby you cry, Abba, Father. Love and reverence human nature; and in every man and woman that crosses your path discern a temple of God, either a temple of worship, or a ruined temple needing to be repaired. In the days of thoughtless enjoyment, the soul, bent upon its own revelry, thinks all too little of the dangers which its contact entails on others. Yet if you have made another the hired minister of your folly or sin; if the servant or dependent is silently pleading to himself your example as he apes your vices; if by drinking the crowned wine-cup you tempt him to wallow in its lees; if for you the woman has cast into the mire the precious jewel of her maiden-shame; if the friend transplanted into your baneful vicinity has gone to ruin, and the blossoms of life have borne nothing but the fruit of despair; then, when the scales of selfishness fall from your eyes, if ever that mercy is granted you, oh what pain awaits you! God has given you grace to repent, and you know your heart has become at last the temple of the Holy Ghost. But who shall repair the temples you have ruined? Go to the discarded sot, and see if there be one stone left upon another of the structure which the Creator made for himself. Go seek in the dreary streets for what remains of a woman that once was capable of good, the joy of a home, and bid them lead her into a shelter where, if God so grant, she may find rest for her soul, and practise penitence, and taste the joy of restoration. Oh, terrible punishment that cannot be removed from us, that will press more heavily the more tender our conscience becomes, to see the fruits of our sins spreading after we have come to know the hideousness of sin! Good reason have we to pray that the Comforter may extend His consolation from us to those whose guilt lies hard by our door. The school, the mission, the house of penitence, the hospital, the reformatory, are so many acknowledgments that we are knit together with all that bear the human form, and bound to know them as temples of God; and if we cannot repair the very evil we have done, we may at least, by some of these means, endeavour to turn the balance of evil which was against us. But we shall best guide others to righteousness by walking in God's statutes ourselves; we teach others best by the eloquent silence of a good life. And if we have tasted the excellence of the heavenly gift, we shall fear to lose it. We are washed, we are sanctified, we are justified, in the name of the Lord

Jesus, and by the Spirit of our God. How shall we return to the pollutions of the world, to be entangled in them and overcome? Sin is not a sin against ourselves, it is an offence against a present God! Whenever we are on the point of lending ourselves to a polluting sin, let the Apostle's warning sound in our ears as the voice of the Most High God himself: "If any man defile the temple of God, him shall God destroy: for the temple of God is holy, which temple ye are."

SERMON XX.

(Preached at Buckingham Palace, before the Queen, July 1858.)

THE NIGHT COMETH.

———✦———

John ix. 4.

I must work the works of Him that sent me while it is day: the night cometh, when no man can work.

THESE are solemn words, and every one may make them his own, without drawback or alteration. Every one was sent into the world with a task appointed for him: the path of every one's life leads him before long into the thick shadow and night of the grave. But how wonderful they are as spoken by the Lord Jesus! He, too, owns that He is sent to carry through a work, and that the appointed time for its performance is passing away. Yes: it was even so. The Church which He founded, and which, without sound of axe or hammer, has ever since been growing, with its foundations upon the broad ages, and with converted men for its stones, Jesus himself being the Head of the corner, with the wise spirits of the earth for its pillars, and the prayers of the saints for its incense, this great moral edifice is, so to speak, the fruit of a man's work, even of that of the Son of Man. We are not told that He spake the word only, and it was made: it was not by a voice coming down from a region of sublime repose into the stirring universe, that the religion of Christ was established upon earth, to console the penitent, and repress sin, and build up holiness. In the truest sense, it is the fruit of the labour of Him who cheerfully accepted this as His appointed task on earth. In three years—for such at most was the duration of His ministry—those journeyings, and sermons, and parables, those fastings and night-watchings, those persecutions, those miracles that conquered sickness and the grave, that agony, that death, that resurrection, were all completed. Grappling with the reality of sorrow, facing the baffling opposition which He might have scattered with the breath of His displeasure, He "wrought the works of Him that sent Him while it was day." Truly, He did take on Him the form of a servant, and was made in the likeness of men. The light of His doctrine, of His great atoning sacrifice, of His sinless character, have been shining on the world ever since; and men have been willing to rejoice in that light. But not like the natural light was the spiritual kindled. We do not read, "Christ said, Let there be light, and there was light." He speaks of struggle, and labour, and conflict; He speaks such words as these:—" I have a baptism to be baptized with, and how am I straitened till it be accomplished!" "Now is my soul troubled, and what shall I say? Father, save me from this hour; but for this cause came I unto this hour."

And it is by work that the kingdom of Christ must spread. I speak not only of such labourers as St. Paul or St. Peter, as Augustine or Luther, of those mighty spirits who have been able to write their names on a nation converted, or a great truth fixed permanently in the treasury of Christian thought, or a great error exposed, saying, "This God did through me." There is a work for each and all. Men tell us that in the material world there is no particle lost or useless; not a tiny pebble is there whose mass does not contribute its share to that attraction which keeps planet true to sun, and satellite to planet; not a gust blows, nor a wave falls back in foam from the shore, but leaves its mark upon the changing face of nature. What God has made the law of nature, He wills to be the law of the moral world also. No soul so meek, no will so dependent, but was meant to take a part in that progress of mind and spirit which is moving parallel to the progress of nature. Oh what a misfortune it must be, then, to a man to have a low conception of his duty and work in the world! What a misfortune, if he fancy that he has no work here to do! Parts we are, each of us, of the world that rolls on, neither resting nor hasting, to the end which the Maker has appointed for it. The material frame of man has taken up a portion of the dust of it, and is ever moulding and transforming it; his cogent animal wants drive him to dig and reap, hunt and fish; and so far his work is done. But the gift of an immortal spirit is often entrusted to one who never tries to discover what are the duties that attach to that most excellent possession. What a misfortune that the highest part of us should be the barrenest! that our value as factors in the grand sum of the universe should be only our weight as shaped clods of earth, or our worth as animals seeking for a provision! No one but thinks such a result of life would be deplorable. No one but will pardon a few plain words on a subject which, if it has been handled by ten thousand preachers, can never, so long as the safety of souls is knit up with it, be thought obsolete.

I. All that has been done for the human race in the way of bringing the news of redemption to them, or of freeing them from the miseries that sin brought into the world, has been, by God's direct permission and ordinance, the result of individual effort. Not without reason did our Redeemer choose the way of labour and diligence, as that by which He would approach the Father to make atonement for us. His great example has never been without its fruit from the earliest time. Next to the history of the blessed Redeemer himself, the largest page in the New Testament is that which records the doings of St. Paul. Ceaseless activity, indomitable boldness, a deep love for human souls, brought him into contact with every form of worship, every stage of human culture, every climate that lay within the reach of a traveller at that time. And when, in no boastful spirit, he puts before the Church at Corinth the bare record of his life, which passes as of itself into a rhythmic cadence, we are constrained to confess that that terrible hymn of suffering and labour is surely the meetest praise that ever a mortal man could offer to his God; for it is the plain story of a laborious and much-suffering life, every portion of which was dedicated to the Giver of all life and all good. "In labours more abundant, in stripes above measure, in prisons more frequent, in deaths oft. Of the Jews five times received I forty stripes save one. Thrice was I beaten with rods, once was I stoned, thrice I suffered shipwreck, a night and a day I have been in the deep. In journeyings often, in perils of waters, in perils of robbers, in perils by my own countrymen, in perils by the heathen, in perils in the city, in perils in the wilderness, in perils in the sea, in perils among false brethren; in weariness and painfulness, in watchings often, in hunger and thirst, in fastings often, in cold and nakedness. Beside those things which are without, that which cometh upon me daily, the care of all the churches." (2 Cor. xi. 23—28.) But even the *silent* labours of the other Apostles—for of their doings, except those of Peter, John, and Paul, the New Testament says but little—have their eloquence for us; they, too, travelled and preached, and poured out their blood for a witness, without recording even in the simplest way what they were doing, and what they were about to suffer. But their works remain. There is a record kept by a pen that writes only truth, on a page that no moth nor worm shall eat, until the day of judgment; and there it is written that whosoever else may have abused his talent, they made usury of theirs, and shall enter for ever into the joy of their Lord.

And if we leave the Apostles, men so specially helped by the Spirit of God that their works may seem scarcely to be examples for us, so far above us do they appear, does not every age abound with the fruits of labour of the Divine Spirit working in men an active zeal for God? Individual piety and self-denial raised the village church and the vast cathedral, and bequeathed them to the flock of Christ without money and without price. Individual piety founded the college and the school, expressly dedicated to Christian teaching; and raised the hospital, in order that one prominent mark of the kingdom of Christ, the care for the sick and weak, might there be, as it were, graven in stone. When our prisons had become so many sinks of physical and moral corruption, one man explored the disease and procured the remedy. Two or three persons were able, God helping them, to clear our nation from the guilt of the slave-trade, although the love of gain resisted to the utmost. The movement in favour of education for the poor began but lately and from a few. The rescue of outcast women from a hopeless depth of degradation has been attempted by a few, and found possible. The reformatory for the young criminal, now the subject of interest to the whole country, is one of the latest outgrowths of Christian love, and at first but one or two had found the secret out. And who were these, who, in the Spirit of the Lord, have been strong enough for such heroic deeds, and brought back such rich trophies from the battle with Satan? Were they only the very wise, or the very rich, or the very influential? Far from it. In the catalogue of such heroes we shall find the names of men and women of every grade and station, some of them poor enough, of narrow education, quite unknown in the world, abounding in nothing except patience and love. Who is there who cannot imitate them? Vain are the complaints so often made, that we have no distinct work in life appointed for us; that we stand idle because we have not been called into the vineyard to labour. God has made duties for us, and placed us in the midst of them, just as He has made light for the eyes, and air for us to breathe. There is not an action of our life that may not become an act of worship, if it is consecrated by the love of God in the heart of the doer. But the common round of our common daily life is full of occasions of Christian duty. I think that when Jesus, the Redeemer of the human race, preached the glories and the terrors of the world to come, sitting in a fisher's boat on a retired lake in a province of the Jewish country which was a byword amongst Jews themselves, to an untaught multitude thronging the shore, He showed us not merely that He loved our kind and would save them, but also, that wherever a man's lot is cast, there is the place where God's work should be done. The first words of the Gospel message were confided to a few unlettered persons, who in the beginning understood them imperfectly, and failed to remember them; yet we do not find, because the mustard-seed was sown in obscure Judæan soil, that the tree is weak, or unfit for shelter. Who is he that stands idle because he is not hired? One it must be who can find neither poverty, nor ignorance, nor wickedness at his hand; who cannot influence one person by the Christian tone of his own life; who cannot sweeten the daily life of his home with kindness; who never comes near a sinner rushing headlong to his ruin; who cannot even find a child to encourage in struggling with an evil temper, nor a stricken heart to be consoled by a word of sympathy. On some desolate island, shared only with the bird of the air and the beast of the forest, such an isolated being might possibly be found; but even for that outcast, if he sought the Lord, work would be appointed; and in a closer communion with God, in prayer, and praise, and trust, his soul would find its exercise, and the means of its discipline and purification. The life that is shaped according to the pattern of Christian duty out of a heart full of Christian faith and love, sends up to God day by day a perpetual voice of praise; and whether it comes before men from a high and illustrious position, or hides itself in some obscure corner where few can follow it, the equal eye of God discerns in both cases alike, that here is one working the work of Him that sent him whilst it is day. God grant in mercy to all of us a deep sense of the sacredness of our life, and an earnest resolution to consecrate to Him all that we are, and do, and think!

II. For "the night cometh when no man can work." This truth has been dwelt on by Christian and heathen teachers since the world was young. The pages of the Old Testament are full of it; but never was it uttered with a more solemn sanction than when He spake it who could not be holden of death. The night cometh: to some it comes as the night of nature, with slow, regular, and foreseen steps; on some it drops suddenly, when they thought it was noon; for some life becomes, what with feeble health and blunted powers, one long twilight. For it is not death only which is our night; where the opportunity has been lost, there the night has settled already. Death may be far from many of us: the journey may be long and weary before our sun goes down. But do we take no account of smaller deaths, so to speak? Do we not feel the dreadful suspicion that part of us may be dead already? Are we not conscious of changes that are in their way final? Do we not pass every year on our life's journey some landmark which we shall wish to see again, and shall not be able? That memory which now records for us every fact we entrust to it, night comes upon it, when it will be less faithful. That quickness of conscience, which now punishes with remorse each sin of impurity or violence, night will come upon it if we despise it, and the gnawings of each new sin against the callous heart shall be unfelt. That friend or neighbour with whom we take sweet counsel, let us learn from him all we can, let us pour out for him all the truth we know, and let heart strengthen heart as iron sharpeneth iron; for we may see him again no more for ever, and in his stead nothing but recollections shall remain, overshadowed with the night of a grievous loss. Teach the child whilst he is spared you, for the angel may gather that flower into one of his sheaves, to plant him again in the radiance of the Divine throne, leaving you to the trial of a numbed and benighted affection. Oh, the unspeakable misery that it will be to review all the lost chances of a life that is as changeful as the restless sea! Hope at present with most of us overrules memory; in what we may yet do, we lose sight of all that we might have done. When we reach the confine of life, and no food for earthly hope remains; when before us is nothing brighter than the valley of the shadow of death; then shall the bitterness of all past deaths and losses deepen tenfold the shadow that is settling over us. How prodigal we were of time when we should have been misers of it! How we let the friend drift from us with a careless farewell, ignorant that then and there the commerce that might have been so fruitful for both was ended for evermore! How often we uttered the hasty word, when silence would have become us better! How we kept silence from good words, when an honest expression of opinion would have checked folly or sin! How gladly we saw our precious years buried one by one in the bosom of an eternity that never gives back its dead! Oh, let us no longer squander our treasures of opportunity! God has placed us upon this narrow island of time, with the waters of eternity all around us; and every inch of ground is more precious to us than gold or rubies; for as our dealings with time are, so our share of immortality shall be. And we can make no terms with Him to grant us a longer season to finish the work He sent us to do. The night cometh, and it shall overtake the thinker before he has matured his discovery, and the ruler in the midst of plans of order and improvement. Let us set before us every morning the preciousness of a new day granted to us out of the long night that shall follow, that we may work in it the work of Him that sent us. Let us work henceforth not our own works, but the work of Him that sent us. Let us teach our children to know Him. Let us make our own lives a witness to the truth, as if some light from another world had indeed broken forth for us upon the rough and gloomy places of this, and had guided our feet aright, whosoever else had stumbled. Let us be covered with shame, if in times past we have trifled with our trust. Let us seek to combat those evils which our social state tends to produce, and which, without the mitigating force of Christian love, would reach an intolerable height. Let us try to do men good in the name of that Father who crowns them with mercy and loving-kindness; let us try to turn their eyes to the redemption wrought by the Son; let us promote love among them in the name of the Spirit of truth, and comfort, and love. And remembering that God alone can turn the night that is coming upon us into a most glorious day, if we seek Him here whilst He may be found, let us pray to Him fervently, "So teach us to number our days, that we may apply our hearts unto wisdom."

SERMON XXI.

THE CHARACTER OF DAVID.

Psalm xxx. 6—8.

And in my prosperity I said, I shall never be moved. Lord, by Thy favour Thou hast made my mountain to stand strong: Thou didst hide Thy face, and I was troubled.

I cried to Thee, O Lord; and unto the Lord I made supplication.

In the life of David the king, all the elements that make up human life are found in large measure. Warrior, musician, poet; with a heart susceptible, to its very depths, of all the emotions on which men usually act, of friendship and love, of joy at triumphs, and sorrow at reverses; active to the verge of rashness, yet constantly communing with God, and carrying to the Divine throne all that befell him, to find comfort and counsel there; David is one whose character stirs up some sympathy in us all: for it is a law of our nature, that every one who feels or thinks is drawn to another that feels the same things more deeply, or thinks them more clearly. And as the Holy Spirit, who breathes on whomsoever He will, and is not bound to choose His agents for their natural gifts, has still chosen a Solomon to proclaim the vanity of earthly things which he had experienced, and a Paul to compare and bring into relation the law and the Gospel, for which his early studies were a preparation; so has David been chosen to utter, on the various occasions of his eventful life, those wonderful songs of praise and prayer, which, in the Book of Psalms, have ever furnished, and will to the end, words of support suitable to all the chances and changes to which this mortal life is subject. The life of David was, however, a career of war and bloodshed. On the day when he slew the Philistine, he turned from the peaceful sheepcote to a career of strife, in which he may be said never to have looked back. "The women answered one another as they played, and said, Saul hath slain his thousands, and David his ten thousands." (1 Sam. xviii. 7.) "And all Israel and Judah loved David, because he went out and came in before them" (ver. 13) as their leader in battle. And towards the close of a stormy life, which had begun with warfare, we find his son Absalom arrayed against his father in battle, and routed, and slain. During the intervening time many an enemy had been subdued and treated with hardness; the hospitality of Achish had been received in a way that even the laws of war at that time could not justify; bad men, like Joab, had been employed and trusted; in a word, all the horrors and evils of war had been experienced. There is a terrible meaning in those little words, "David smote the land, and left neither man nor woman alive." (1 Sam. xxvii. 9.) How can it be, it has often been asked, that one whose hands were ever wet with blood, who besides, fell into great sins against God and man, could be spoken of as "a man after the Lord's own heart"? In seeking the answer, we must not forget the context in which this expression occurs. David was chosen king of Israel because of Saul's perverseness and self-will. "Samuel said to Saul, Thou hast done foolishly; thou hast not kept the commandment of the Lord thy God, which he commanded thee; for now would the Lord have established thy kingdom upon Israel for ever. But now thy kingdom shall not continue: the Lord hath sought him a man after his own heart, and the Lord hath commanded him to be captain over his people, because thou hast not kept that which the Lord commanded thee." (1 Sam. xiii.) Because Saul had not ruled his people according to the mind and will of God, but had preferred his own caprices to the Divine commands, the kingdom should be given to one who made it his business to conform his life to the Divine teaching. David was a man after the Lord's own heart, because he strove to do the Lord's will, and not his own. The title does not, and cannot, mean that all his acts and thoughts were what God would have them; first, because we know his grievous falls; and next, because, if the law of Moses could have exalted its children to such a height as to deserve that appellation, the Gospel would have been unneeded. All are concluded under sin; "there is none that doeth good, no, not one;" and one on whose name distinct stains of pride, and perfidy, and lust, are visible, could have been no exception to that general sentence. And that which disturbs our estimate of David's character is, that we do not allow for the difference of times and of dispensations; and try the great men under the law by a Gospel standard. Morality is progressive. The light of Christ has not shone so long upon the darkness without dispelling some of it. The temperance of Jonadab the son of Rechab, the chastity of Joseph, are not so rare in Christian countries as to receive a place in history; for not only do Christians practise them, but even those who are not truly following Christ catch the reflection of such virtues, and what we call the tone of society has become so far Christian. The character of David may be very high, and shine very bright among the Joabs and Abners, the Sauls and Absaloms of his day; yet not stand well in comparison with that of men informed and taught by the Spirit of the Gospel. " Many prophets and righteous men have desired to see the things which ye see, and have not seen them." (Matt. xiii. 17.) They have desired, not to see Christ outwardly only, but to know Him inwardly; to be raised and sanctified, as He alone is able to raise them; but they have not received their desire.

With this proviso, we shall be able to know David as "a man after the Lord's own heart"— as one who really sought and feared the Lord. Besides the temptations of a troublous life, his own disposition was full of danger to him. He was not one of those who sympathise weakly with the world around them. His nature was quick, warm, and susceptible; capable of feeling the full bitterness of desolation at one time, and of utter abandonment to joy and gladness at another. Tempers of this kind, when we see them among ourselves, always cause anxiety, for we know that for them, more than for others, the snares of the world are dangerous. We know how the tide of high spirits will hurry them away from the path of duty; how the pressure of unusual suffering will drive them to all sorts of wild expedients to escape it; how strong social sympathies may give to bad companions a dangerous power over them, and thus their very affections may become gates to let in sin,— some morbid feeling, ambition perhaps, or revenge, or emulation, which quieter natures, that never run into excess, would have escaped. Some of those yearnings which eat up the very heart until they be satisfied, may give a wrong bias to their whole career. These are the instruments which God prepares to work great good, or permits to run into grievous evil. Self-restraint, almost a mere name to those whose sluggish dispositions have scarcely anything to restrain, becomes to them a struggle, real and terrible, between the good and the evil—between the light of religion within, and their natural corruption. David's character surely was of this kind. All the strings of the harp were there: every feeling that a man knows, he seems to have known. Not indifferent to warlike renown, warm in his friendships, hasty in anger, full of interest in the past doings of the Lord's people, rich in imagination,— his was just the nature to make laws for itself, to worship its own idols, to think that right which was agreeable to itself. The homely path of duty must have been more difficult to one who had within himself so much to bring into subjection. So that instead of wondering that the natural man did more than once stumble and fall, we should marvel rather that the grace of God so directed, sanctified, and governed him, as to save him from a life of shame and error, or at least, from frequent falls, and fits of difficult repentance. We see in the son of Jesse one who bore all kinds of fortune meekly, like a son and servant of God; who herded with the reckless and desperate, yet continued patient and full of quiet hope; who endured great provocation, yet behaved himself towards his persecutor as though it had been his friend or his brother; who was exalted to a great kingdom, yet continued humble before God, refraining his soul and keeping it low, even as a weaned child; who, with many temptations to forsake the law of God, many strong feelings to hurry him into practices contrary to it, made it his prayer and his most prevailing desire, that the Lord would give him understanding, and teach him the way of His statutes, that he might walk in that only.

In a word, then, the title "a man after the Lord's own heart" means a godly man, one who strives to find out what the will of God is, and to shape his own by that. It does not imply that David's sin in the matter of Uriah was a light one, or that it was a venial error to number the people. We are not called on to admire his perfidy towards Achish, nor his eagerness to take vengeance on Nabal. Far less are we encouraged to suppose that we, with our lights, and in our position, may fall away so grievously and so often, and yet continue servants of God, and in a state of reconcilement with Him. Our righteousness must exceed the righteousness of the Scribes and Pharisees, must surpass all that the law of Moses can teach; for us the law has been fulfilled, filled up, that is, and completed; "Thou shalt not kill," has become, "Whosoever is angry with his brother without a cause, shall be in danger of the judgment;" "Thou shalt not commit adultery," has been expanded to include even the impure thought and word. Old permissions, conceded to men in a lower state of morality, are rescinded; the wife is no longer lightly to be put away, and the ready oath may no longer be brought in to confirm what ought to need no such support. And all this because the Christian stands upon a higher platform, has deeper notions of duty, possesses his soul in a better state of discipline, sees more deeply into the mind of God than was possible for the Jew. So great is the privilege of coming near to Christ! In the hierarchy of the godly, as our Lord himself described it, John the Baptist ranked above the prophets, and the least of the brethren of Christ was higher than John; because the prophet saw the Lord dimly from afar, and John the Baptist pointed to Him with his hand; but the Christian comes near to touch Him, and lean upon His bosom. In estimating the doings of a good man under the law, let us never forget the difference of the two dispensations; and when one would encourage himself in sin, by thinking of the signal sins forgiven to those under the old covenant, let us recall the words of our Saviour, " Unto whomsoever much is given, of him shall be much required; and to whom men have committed much, of him they will ask the more."

In the services of this day* occur two Psalms which belong to David's two great transgressions; the 32nd, which refers beyond all doubt to the murder of Uriah; and the 30th, which it may be said, with almost equal certainty, refers to the sin of numbering the people. Seldom are we permitted to judge of an outward act of sin by the light of the inward feelings which follow it. Seldom are we able to weigh and measure the repentance of a sinner.

---

* The sixth of the month.

Let us judge of the sins of David with these two guides to lead us.

A blacker act of treachery was never committed than that by which Uriah perished. It has been said that it was the common crime of an Eastern despot to covet the wife of his officer, and to compass the death of the husband for security. The crime may have been often repeated, but none can be darker or seem more hopeless. It was one of the consequences of the polygamy into which David had fallen soon after he was made king. It was no sudden impulse. From this root of perverted affection grew murder and adultery, the worst treachery towards a loyal subject and friend. The whole moral nature of the man seems to be a waste of ruin. But before God's prophet came to him, and with the sword of that well-known parable pierced him to his heart, saying, *Thou art the man*, remorse had begun to do its work. He began to feel the misery of sitting alone with a great unrepented sin. Doubtless in the night-watches his soul went forth to the walls of Rabbah, where Uriah the Hittite, one of his mighty warriors, lay in his blood. The generous soldier, who would not sleep softly in his bed so long as his companions in arms were encamped in the open fields, lay murdered by the master for whom he fought so valiantly. "Set ye Uriah in the fore-front of the hottest battle, and retire ye from him, that he may be smitten, and die." (2 Sam. xi. 15.) Great as was the wickedness of the king, he was not inured to murder; he had not reached that utter deadness of feeling which often punishes sensual vice. And the blood of his dead captain cried out to him from the ground; and about his fevered pillow hovered the thoughts that make men old. Hear how he describes his own state: " Blessed is he whose transgression is forgiven, whose sin is covered. Blessed is the man unto whom the Lord imputeth not iniquity, and in whose spirit there is no guile. When I kept silence, my bones waxed old, through my roaring all the day long. For day and night thy hand was heavy upon me: my moisture is turned into the drought of summer." (Ps. xxxii.) His remorse was as a consuming fire in his bones. The great sin, committed but not yet forgiven,—no, nor yet repented of, for remorse is not penitence,—sits heavy on him day and night. Great as it has been, and much as it has scathed the soul that has admitted it, it has not obliterated the knowledge of right and wrong. The soul sees and feels its enormity. When the prophet comes with his message, there is nothing to break down in order to find an entrance to that miserable heart. David had reached the threshold of repentance by himself, or he would not so promptly have accepted the application of Nathan's story: " Wherefore hast thou despised the commandment of the Lord, to do evil in his sight? Thou hast killed Uriah the Hittite with the sword, and hast taken his wife to be thy wife, and hast slain him with the sword of the children of Ammon." Here is no mere repetition;

murder, and adultery, and treachery, are separately charged against him. All his past remorse gives intensity to his answer: "I have sinned against the Lord." And a real return to God out of sin met a real and a prompt forgiveness. "I acknowledge my sin unto thee," says David in the Psalm, "and mine iniquity have I not hid. I said, I will confess my transgressions unto the Lord, and thou forgavest the iniquity of my sin. For this" (or on this account) "shall every one that is godly pray unto thee in a time when thou mayest be found: surely in the floods of great waters they shall not come nigh unto him." That is to say, "in the time of great judgments and punishments, like the deluge, it shall be too late." And the whole of the Psalm describes, better perhaps than any other part of Scripture, the scheme of repentance from sin, — the remorse, the return, the deep sense of peace and safety, the voice of God in the heart guiding the soul, now subdued and obedient, in the better way, and the joy of righteousness as compared with the blighting misery of sin.

David was again at peace; and loving God as he had loved Him through his life. But Nathan said that the sword should never depart from his house because of his crime: and this punishment was not removed from him. The outrage on his daughter, the murder of his eldest-born son Amnon; the rebellion of Absalom, whom he deeply loved; and at last the death of the rebel, for whom the father would fain have died, by the hand of the same Joab who had been his instrument in the murder of Uriah, were meet punishments for such a sin as his. He could say with truth, "Thou art my hiding-place: thou shalt preserve me from trouble;" but from his lips were yet to be wrung the words of agony, "O my son Absalom! my son, my son Absalom! would God I had died for thee, O Absalom, my son, my son!"

The second great transgression was of a different kind. Why was it so sinful to number the people? In the former case we were dealing with an act of revolting wickedness; here the sin lay not in the act, which is one which every nation practises, which will shortly take place in this country, as it has often before; but in the condition of his own mind. After a time of prosperity it came into the mind of the king to number the people, to gratify the pride of his own heart; perhaps with a view to further conquests and bloodshed. No command from God justified the step. It was an act of wanton self-gratulation. Even the unscrupulous Joab was reluctant to obey: "Now the Lord thy God add unto the people, how many soever they be, an hundred-fold, and that the eyes of my lord the king may see it; *but why doth my lord the king delight in this thing?*" (2 Sam. xxiv. 3.) But the will of David prevailed; the captains of his host went forth and numbered the people, and brought the tale to David. More than a million of valiant men could be drawn out on an emergency, to lend strength to the king's ambition. Proud might a monarch be of such a strength! But "David's heart smote him after that he had numbered the people. And David said unto the Lord, I have sinned greatly in that I have done; and now I beseech thee, O Lord, take away the iniquity of thy servant; for I have done very foolishly." Here again we see how complete is the reaction in his soul against its own sin. It would have been easy to have formed self-deceiving excuses for what might have seemed a mere matter of policy. But if we turn to the thirtieth Psalm we shall see that he sought no such shelter. "In my prosperity I said, I shall never be moved." Such is his touching confession. Here, too, his repentance was accepted, but punishment overtook the sin. As he had been proud of the numbers of his people, so it was his punishment to see their ranks thinned by pestilence, and to know that he had caused it. "These sheep, what have they done?" But the punishment, though severe, was brief. As the Psalmist himself says of it: "His anger endureth for a moment; in his favour is life: weeping may endure for a night, but joy cometh in the morning." God heard the voice of sincere repentance; the plague was stayed, and the sinner forgiven.

In the Psalms of David, then, we have laid before us the inmost workings of a soul that ever was seeking after God. The thirty-second Psalm is the true picture of a spiritual warfare; and therefore those inspired words have come home to many a remorseful mind, in many ages, in various lands. They find out the depths of our hearts, because they welled up from the depths of his. They suit with the moments of greatest mental tension, with great sorrows and with death-beds, because the Holy Spirit drew them forth from the Psalmist in the most agonising crisis of his life. And from the whole career and writings of the royal Psalmist we learn to amend our judgment of sin, to keep the boundaries of right and wrong clear and well marked, and to appreciate the value of repentance. The sin of David in the matter of Uriah was deadly; but it was not the act of a selfish sensualist, deadened to all feeling by a long course of vice. The sin did not represent the whole man, although it was a foul defilement resting on the man. Nathan spoke to what was below, to the David that had striven through a long life of struggle and temptation to make God's word a lamp to his feet, and a light to his path. And the real man answered him out of the depths, from under the filthy crust that obscured him, and said, "I have sinned." Between the cold sensualist, and such a sinner as this, there is a great difference. Again, between the selfish conqueror who, leaving an army strewed upon the plain, comes back to an exhausted country for a new conscription, and treats men as the mere implements and tools of ambition; and David, in a moment of overweening pride, numbering the people, thinking even then that it was God who by His favour had made his mountain to stand strong, there is the same difference. It is the nature of sin to lower the power of conscience, until at last it dies out, and nothing seems to the mind either good or evil. Sins like those of David would argue, if looked at by themselves, that the poison had already entered into the moral system, and diminished its reactive power. But here we have the rare privilege of viewing the whole case. The inward state of the man is before us, and that even more completely than the outward actions. And whilst those acts excite our abhorrence, and show us that the Jewish king was very far from the perfection of the spiritual life, we must admit that one who so long and faithfully sought for the guidance of God, who knew no happiness save in the consciousness of God's favour, and no misery, save in the thought that the divine face was covered from him; who from his backslidings, great indeed and greatly punished, returned at once to the feet of his Father, without reserve or doubting, we must submit that there is a real sense in which David, weak and sinful and imperfect as he was, might be called a "man after the Lord's own heart."

SERMON XXII.

PROVIDENCE AND FREE WILL.

———✦———

Exodus xi. 10.

And Moses and Aaron did all these wonders before Pharaoh: and the Lord hardened Pharaoh's heart, so that he would not let the children of Israel go out of his land.

If it were necessary to fix upon the subject which has received the widest discussion and has issued in the greatest diversity of statement, amongst all questions, philosophical and religious, I suppose that the choice would rest upon the question of the compatibility of human freedom with divine foreknowledge and with the fixed order of the universe. The inspired word of God, in the text and in many other passages, itself suggests the difficulty which eighteen centuries of argument have not solved: and two groups of passages, wrested from their context and arrayed against each other, have been brought to prove on the one side that man was free of choice, and possessed the power to accept or reject the proffered salvation, and on the other that the roll of God's elect had been written unalterably by the finger of God Himself, before the foundation of the world, and that the right choice of believers was made by them and them only, because they alone were appointed to eternal life. Had those passages been studied only in their practical bearing, and as living organic portions of the sacred books whence they are taken, the theory of predestination might have been less logically attacked and defended, but no difficulties in practice would have arisen from their seeming opposition. The devout mind has ever been able to dwell, without finding anything to revolt or offend it, on its own responsibility as a free being accountable for every act, and on its own thorough dependence upon One who by grace had saved it, through faith, in whom it lives, and moves, and has its being.

For more than three centuries the doctrine of grace and free will was held in the Church as it is taught in Scripture, that is, no systematic attempts were made to exalt either side at the expense of the other, and the statements of Holy Scripture were accepted in their completeness, and not selected by the partial light of a theory. There are, indeed, signs of a tendency in the Alexandrian theologians to insist more strongly on free will; whilst the Western Church laid greater stress on the fallen state of man and the need of grace. But this difference arose from the different influences against which the two had to contend; the one against pagan and gnostic views of necessity, and the other against pharisaic and stoical self-righteousness. But the twofold doctrine was held, so to speak, in solution. It did not crystallise into two distinct forms before the date of the Pelagian controversy. And it is worthy of remark, that in the course of that dispute Augustine is obliged to notice letters from two contemporaries * of high name, in which they deprecate the attempt to define and explain predestination as inexpedient for the preaching of the Gospel. But the discussion was then inevitable; and the man they addressed was not one to whom timid or over-cautious counsels were acceptable; and the doctrine of grace, as elaborated by Augustine in that controversy, became, with some modifications, the doctrine of the Western Church. Between the Pelagian doctrine of absolute freedom and the Manichæan necessity, he strove to hold an equal balance. To admit that he absolutely succeeded, would be to say, that for him the laws that limit finite minds had been suspended. But that which has made his arguments acceptable to minds as different as those of Aquinas and Luther; that which has caused his terms to be transferred to creeds and formularies; is the truth which he held so firmly, that man is lost, fallen, depraved; that

* Prosper, and Hilary of Arles.

out of his present condition God alone can raise him; that it is of grace, and not of desert, that he is raised out of it, and that Christ Himself, through faith in Him and His Cross, is the means of his restoration. But the arguments did not set the controversy at rest for ever; it reappeared in the ninth century; it was taken up by some of the Schoolmen; it occupied the thoughts of the Reformers. It has not been confined to the Christian Church, but has always been discussed by schools of philosophy. In one form or another, it has been raised in every age, and certainly our own day is no exception. But without dwelling on its history, I propose to examine what are the facts connected with this subject, and on what evidence they rest.

On the one hand, if I observe my own mind, one of the first powers of which I become conscious is the power to choose. In slight and indifferent matters, where motives can hardly be said to operate, this power is mine without stint or limit. Where motives come in, they act as weights in one scale or the other: and where there is a great preponderance in one, the power of choice is to that extent constrained, and in some cases wholly lost. But even where our unhappy part is only that of yielding to an overwhelming temptation, we are conscious that even that yielding is an act of the will. It is not merely the immediate result of the temptation, for it does not always take place at the moment when the temptation is suggested, but after an interval of struggle; and besides, it is followed by remorse and regret, which implies that it was something in which we had a share, something that by an act of assent we had taken on ourselves. Now, this power, of which each of us is conscious for his own part, we find is universally assumed as the ground of men's dealings with each other. What is all education, religious and secular, but an avowed attempt to emancipate the will from evil influences that would sway it in a wrong direction? What is all law, but a system for enforcing right conduct by fear, where better motives would be too weak to guide the will? What is it which justifies punishments, but the fact that a being capable of choice has chosen wrongly, and is therefore culpable?

And if we now open the inspired Book, we find the same fundamental assumption, that all men have a will and are responsible for its acts. Our Redeemer would have gathered Jerusalem as a hen gathereth her chickens under her wings, and she would not; and her desolation will be the consequence of her refusal. Every sermon preached by the Apostles, every call to repentance, implies a power to obey the call, whencesoever derived. Paul and Barnabas make the Jews themselves responsible for the withdrawal of the Gospel from them: " Seeing ye put it from you, and judge yourselves unworthy of everlasting life, lo, we turn to the Gentiles." (Acts xiii.) And so had Moses long before set before the Israelites life and death, blessing and cursing: " Therefore," he adds, " choose life, that thou and thy seed may live." " There is joy in the presence of the angels of God over one sinner that repenteth " (Luke xv.); but what can be the ground of the joy, but the fact that repentance is something that he may choose or refuse? " To him that knoweth to do good," says St. James, "and doeth it not, to him it is sin " (iv. 17). In short, all through the Bible, exhortations to holiness, warnings against eternal death, offers made and withdrawn when rejected, presume the existence of a power of choice, whencesoever derived, and howsoever loaded with the weight of sin and ignorance that detract from complete freedom.

On the other hand, it is a fact as well attested, although by a different kind of evidence, that God is the king of all the earth. He that feeds the fire of the sun, and maps out the tracks of the planets, must be the same as quickens into life the worthless thistle seed and the ovum of the insect that we brush aside from our path. It was an idle question, whether there could be a *providentia circa minima*, often as it has been asked; because nothing is either great or small, hard or easy, to one whose power and knowledge are infinite. A prince of this earth may select what he will attend to, and neglect what is too minute to need his care; because his powers are limited and he is conscious of some more pressing needs. Not so One whose command all things obey, and to whom one thing cannot be more important than another, since He needs nothing. All who believe that there is a God, will also attribute to Him all the laws by which the universe is governed, and the harmony which they maintain through all its parts. Nor will they refuse to see in the course of history, which is the record of man's operations, the same power shaping our doings towards ends that we did not dream of; or in other words, overruling by laws even the vagaries of the human will. Cyrus thought not, as he passed almost dryshod through the channel of Euphrates to take possession of Babylon, that his glorious conquest was a step towards the restoration of the captive Jews, and the appearance among them of a Prince greater than he, but not of this world. Between the fall of Constantinople in the 15th century, and the revival of letters and arts in the West, the study of the languages of Scripture and the Reformation, we can discern the links of connection; not so those who lived through the events, and believed that they were leaving the impress of their will upon all that took place around them. A hero rises; men bow before him, his acts are sung in epics or said in histories; we measure our strength beside his, and find that he is as a giant, far more brave, more resolute, more strong of purpose than we are. God the sovereign of the world takes that man, and sways his footsteps as we do an infant's, lifts his weak hand towards this work or that, carries him whither he knows not, makes him effect what it never entered his mind to do; and thus even the wicked are made unconsciously to subserve the eternal purposes of Him against whom they are at war. Who was it that brought about the scheme of redemption, by which God showed His ineffable love for the world? It was those who cried, "Crucify Him;" it was Pilate, who left a just man to perish; it was the chief priests, who bought Him for thirty pieces of silver; it was the disciple, who sold and betrayed Him with a kiss. Children of hell conspired to complete a work for man, which angels look on with admiration as a prodigy of goodness and love. What was it that spread the Christian name abroad over the earth? Did not the first persecution, that drove the disciples from Jerusalem, diffuse the knowledge of Christ, as men try to trample out a fire, and only scatter its live embers amongst the stubble? Nero and Diocletian knew not that their persecutions would only redound to the glory of Him who had given such faith and constancy to men; that they were in effect promoting the Gospel which their hearts abhorred. All things serve and obey the King of all the earth; and the most hideous acts of wickedness, whilst they crush the souls of those that do them, are moulded by His hand, so that the filthy clay becomes a vessel of beauty and honour. "All the inhabitants of the earth," said the king of Babylon, returning to his right reason, "are reputed as nothing; and he doeth according to his will in the army of heaven, and among the inhabitants of the earth; and none can stay his hand, or say unto him, What doest thou?"

(Dan. iv. 35.) Here then is the second truth at which we may arrive without much disagreement. The world is governed; the laws of matter, of life, of individual and social action are so arranged as to produce order and harmony; and we may infer that they were pre-arranged with a view to such condition; nor is there any presumption of a contrary kind, that order would follow without the intention to produce it, without the guidance of a Being capable of foreseeing and foreordering it.

Now these two facts, that there is a will in man, and that the universe shows marks of providence and design, are so evident when taken singly, the one from the immediate witness of our own consciousness, and the other as an inference hardly avoidable from the facts which science and history bring before us, that we ought to suspect any attempt to obliterate one or the other, by bringing them into collision. I speak not now of pious efforts to make them explicable together, to enable us, if I may say so, to put our finger on the point of contact between man's will and the divine power that acts upon it: such phrases as irresistible grace, unconditional decree, co-operating grace, will at once serve to recall them to most of my hearers, and to suggest their difficulties. But any one who watches at all the drift of the current of modern thought, will see another set of influences at work.

The reality of the human will, and consequently

of responsibility, is attacked on different sides; here on physiological, and there on historical grounds. Arguments such as the following are used. We are told that as social science has enlarged its inductions, it comes out that there is a regularity in moral phenomena as in physical; that facts connected with the human will admit of exact calculation and prediction, according to what is termed the law of averages, and that consequently the doctrine of free will, which was never capable of proof, must be displaced by a doctrine recognising the certainty of human action. It is perhaps well for the interest of truth, that this kind of notion, which has long floated about our literature, has lately taken a definite shape in a well-known book.[*] The answers to such a hasty conclusion will hardly have escaped some of my hearers.

First, the belief that man has the power to choose is so far from wanting proof, that it has all the force which universal consent can give it. Not only do all laws and all educational institutions assume it, but it is worthy of note, that in all the theological discussions to which allusion has been made, when men's powers had been tasked to the utmost by the greatness of the problem they were attempting, and its momentous bearing upon our condition before God, they have never cut the knot they were seeking to unloose, by giving up altogether that which we

---

[*] Buckle's History of Civilisation, vol. i.

call the will. They have felt that a person of ordinary honesty and understanding could as soon deny the possession of hearing, or sight, as of the power to choose in some sense between good and evil. So that if social science has discovered any new class of facts bearing on this question, one set of facts must be set against the other, for comparison and reconcilement. But social science has discovered no such class of facts: it has only given precision to the common-places of moralists and statesmen, which have been handed down from distant generations. If it can be proved, and this is one of the facts most relied on, that in a given nation one person for every eight or nine thousand, will in a given year be convicted of some crime; this only attaches a numerical value to an expectation which every statesman in every country has entertained, which indeed is implied in the very fact that there are criminal laws. And supposing, which is not the case, that the one person annually condemned is dragged by irresistible motives into the position of a criminal, we must infer that the vast number who escape such a condition are under no such compulsion, and so far enjoy the privilege of free choice as to be able at least to escape from crime. If, however, instead of the one criminal being a doomed creature, whom no effort could have saved from the operation of irresistible motives, he represents rather the net result of loss, after many a struggle in his breast and that of others against temptation, then even as to him, free will was not abolished. Others, perhaps, stood on the brink of great crimes, and were snatched back in mercy from them ; and this one that is now condemned was perhaps less likely to fall, but a weak moment admitted the tempter, or an outburst of violence hurried him into sin. If that be so, the whole argument disappears. No one ever identified will with lawless caprice. If in men similarly circumstanced the operations of the will are, upon the whole, uniform, this is what we should naturally expect to find.

But this average which is supposed to rule the will like a rod of iron, is itself the most variable. It yields under the hand like tempered clay. It is not the same in London and in Paris ; it varies even in two adjoining counties; it alters with time and circumstance. We ourselves may alter it. We are doing so in teaching our poor, in finding them employment, in protecting female chastity, in curbing male intemperance. I do not see how that which our will is now acting upon, which varies in different countries because the will of man has made different laws there, can be conclusive against the doctrine of free will. The average of human conduct is only the expression of the results of many human wills ; we have made the giant, which, according to this ingenious writer, is to fall and crush us. The study of the law of averages, so far from paralysing philanthropic exertion, will only assure us of the wide scope allowed us for success, and if it shows us a regularity and certainty in the recurrence of evil, it will encourage us to think that the same regularity will appear in the good results that may follow from honest endeavours after good.

Let us hold fast, then, both these vital truths. God governs this world, governs you and me, down to the very depths of our being. And we possess the power of choosing right and wrong; right by the grace of God, and wrong by our failing to use that grace; and as responsible for such a power, we shall be summoned at last before the judgment seat of Christ. At present the two are hard to reconcile; but if each by itself is a proved truth, let us wait patiently for the reconcilement hereafter. Do not suppose, that because attempts to reconcile them fail, neither the one nor the other is eternally true, but that both are principles laid down to guide us for the present, instead of some truth which we could not now apprehend. The Apostle tells us that now we see through a glass darkly; but he does not say that we are only gazing on a painted screen, from which we cannot form any notion of the things behind. Both Providence and the will exist; what we see is real, though we only know in part, and wait for the time when that which is perfect shall come, that we may see face to face.

Two thoughts occur which in leaving this subject ought not to be passed over. First, our Church, in her article on Predestination, draws a distinction between the effect of the study of it on the good and on the bad, the sincere believer and the unbeliever. To the godly it is "full of sweet, pleasant, and unspeakable consolation;" whilst it leads the carnal to "wretchlessness of unclean living." Our own hearts tell us that the distinction is just. There cannot be a more perilous symptom of the moral state, than where men profess to abandon the struggle with their passions, because they think they have no choice but to succumb; thus clasping to their arms that loathsome body of death which they were intended to escape from through Divine aid. On the other hand, it does not detract from the sweetness of self-approval to ascribe to God alone all the good that we find within us. That is the Apostle's language: "By the grace of God I am what I am: and His grace which was bestowed upon me was not in vain; but I laboured more abundantly than they all: yet not I, but the grace of God which was with me." (1 Cor. xv. 10.) For it is the highest reward that a Christian can receive in this life, to find that he is in act and wish united to God: that he loves to walk in the course of duty, which was once hard; that the good which he does is no weak achievement of his own, but flows from something divine which is being formed in him. Without rashly concluding from some beginnings of good that we have fought our fight and assured to ourselves a crown of glory, we may find sweet and unspeakable comfort in believing that God has stretched out to us the hand of His mercy, and is leading us out of our natural selfishness into a higher purer life, and bringing us more near to Him.

Lastly, the remarkable words of the text are not without their warning. "The Lord hardened Pharaoh's heart, so that he would not let the children of Israel go." This does not mean that the long succession of warnings to Pharaoh was a useless form — that his sin was hopelessly confirmed, and his doom sealed from the beginning. It means that God, who punishes sin with death, sometimes punishes sin with sin. Each new plague was a new warning; and had there been kindled in Pharaoh a spark of remorse—of real penitence, the grace of God might have made that the means of softening him and turning him into a better way. The Lord hardened Pharaoh's heart; that is, He withdrew from it His grace, without which it must needs be hardened, because the lost king did not wish to retain it, and had hardened himself in stubborn resolution against the Lord. Sin, then, is sometimes punished with sin. If any one begins to neglect prayer, he finds it day by day easier to do so without compunction. If ony one is pursuing a course of sensual vice, he feels that the protecting sense of shame grows daily weaker in him, and the craving lust more imperious. And at a certain stage in his dreary, downward course, the Lord hardens his heart. God is not responsible for his sin; but when he has repelled the voice of conscience and the warning of his Bible, and the entreaties of friends, then grace is withdrawn from him, and sin puts on a judicial character, and is at once sin and punishment. Oh, beware of that cumulative power of sin! Human actions admit of three degrees; where the choice is perfectly free, as it is in light and indifferent matters; where the choice is fettered with motives hardly resistible; and an intermediate condition where motives exist to sway but not to coerce our choice. Every sin we commit adds weight to the motives that endanger our freedom. See the folly of those who allow themselves to continue in sin, believing that hereafter, as their passions cool, they will forsake their evil ways. It is a fearful danger to immerse the moral nature in uncleanness, meaning to escape from it at a future time. Every day makes repentance more difficult; and who can tell when the face of God may be wholly averted from you, so that He will harden your heart? and even if you escape this, the bitter recollection of many a past sin will cleave to you even after your repentance. "Thine own wickedness shall correct thee, and thy backslidings shall reprove thee." (Jer. ii. 19.) Shake off the yoke of that shameful bondage before the iron of it has eaten into the flesh. Do not let a corrupted will be still further enslaved. Believe not that the force of passion is a bondage past escape. In order that the strength of sin might be broken, Christ suffered on the Cross for us. And the same Lord who for a punishment hardened Pharaoh's heart that was already obdurate against him, invites us to return to him and become part of His chosen people. " Let the wicked forsake his way, and the unrighteous man his thoughts, and let him return unto the Lord, and He will have mercy upon him, and to our God, for he will abundantly pardon." (Isaiah lv. 7.)

SERMON XXIII.

LOVE OF THE BRETHREN.

1 JOHN iv. 16—21.

God is love; and he that dwelleth in love dwelleth in God, and God in him.

Herein is our love made perfect, that we may have boldness in the day of judgment: because as he is, so are we in this world.

There is no fear in love; but perfect love casteth out fear: because fear hath torment. He that feareth is not made perfect in love.

We love him, because he first loved us.

If a man say, I love God, and hateth his brother, he is a liar: for he that loveth not his brother whom he hath seen, how can he love God whom he hath not seen?

And this commandment have we from him, That he who loveth God love his brother also.

Two kinds of love are spoken of in the New Testament, the love of believers towards all mankind, and their love towards one another. Both are mentioned in such passages as these, "Add to godliness brotherly kindness, and to brotherly kindness charity." (2 Pet. i. 7.) "As we have therefore opportunity, let us do good unto all men, especially unto them who are of the household of faith." (Gal. vi. 10.) And wherever the phrase *to love one another* occurs, it is evident that a love between Christians is meant — a love which can be bestowed and requited on equal terms, which is founded on common hopes and interests; for this alone is mutual love. The love enjoined towards enemies and towards indifferent persons that need our help is of another kind, and is spoken of in the Bible in other terms. And this distinction arises from our very nature, for it is not possible for a human being, however refined and purified by grace, to act precisely in the same way towards the man who hates, derides, and despises him, and the man who requites his love, shares the same feelings, bears the same burdens, and proposes to himself the same end and aim of life. There may be the same good-will towards both; but in the one case it can scarcely find expression, except in some rare opportunity of doing a kind action; in the other, every word, every wish, the indifferent acts of daily intercourse, acquire a meaning, and pour life, and strength, and courage into a brother's heart. When Jesus parted from His disciples He gave them a new commandment, the same which is alluded to in my text, that those whom He called His friends, His little children, should love one another. (John xiii.

34.) To love was no new invention reserved for those last days; but to love as Christians and for Christian motives, became first possible when the scheme of salvation through Christ had been completed. A new and special love, to distinguish members of Christ from those without, founded in the recollection of the love of the Lord for us, strengthened by the daily interchange of sympathy and support, and by the assaults of enemies from without, this is the subject of the new commandment which is more than once recalled in the Epistle I have been quoting. Love is no new thing; but such love as that of Jesus for man is new, and must have new and special consequences. Observe how our Lord makes Himself the motive in the very words in which He gives the commandment: "A new commandment I give unto you, That ye love one another; as I have loved you, that ye also love one another. By this shall all men know that ye are my disciples, if ye have love one to another." And in that sublime prayer wherewith the same discourse is concluded and summed up, He says, " Neither pray I for these alone, but for them also which shall believe on me through their word; That they all may be one; as thou, Father, art in me, and I in thee, that they also may be one in us; that the world may believe that thou hast sent me." (John xvii. 20, 21.) Love, then, a special love of Christians is to be, as Tertullian says, the mark to know to whom the flock belongs. Not merely love, but the same kind of love that Jesus showed for them was to be conspicuous in their conduct. The recollection of the benefits derived from Christ was to tinge and soften their whole life. As St. Paul says, "Be ye kind one to another, tender-hearted, forgiving one another, even as God for Christ's sake hath forgiven you. Be *ye* therefore followers of God as dear children; and walk in love as Christ also hath loved us, and hath given himself for us, an offering and a sacrifice to God for a sweet smelling savour." (Eph. iv. 32; v. 1, 2.) Now there are in the text three propositions which appear to involve or sum up the doctrine of love contained in this Epistle; and it will be convenient to speak of each separately. God is love. He that dwelleth in love dwelleth in God, and God in him. Perfect love casteth out fear.

I. *God is love.* Are these words easy to say with sincerity? To look up to the host of heaven, to look at the earth bursting forth everywhere in the sudden life of spring, and to say that God is power, is not difficult. But to think of the pestilence that destroys men's lives, and the hunger that keeps down the strong man's strength and stunts the growth of the child, and the strife that sunders a family, and the drunkenness that betrays to crime, and then to say, God is love, is somewhat hard. Go to the wretched mother, that sits amidst her children crying for bread; go to the father, almost ruined and quite disgraced by the riot of a prodigal son; go to the wife, who has laid her husband's body in the grave, and in that grave has buried the joy and affluence and affections of her own life; go and pronounce the words *God is love*, and you will see whether in every case they carry an instant conviction to the sorrowful soul, and stanch the tears and lighten the face with smiles. If that mother, and father, and widow know nothing of the Gospel, you will find that the feeling in their hearts is of a different kind. "God is strong. Fate is irresistible. What we cannot heal we must learn to bear. We see not God's love, but His anger in men's suffering." So spoke the poets and sages of the heathen peoples, teaching a proud and stoical submission instead of resignation. And no man can truly feel that God is love unless God himself hath taught him. He has created men not to sorrow, not that they may perish in sin, but that they may see and know Him, and find eternal rest for their souls. When they turned to sin, and by their sin filled the world with sorrow and death, He sent His Son to restore them, that they should not perish. To those that seek Him, the present trials and sorrows, even if they should be life-long, are no proof that God is not love. For the range of our vision is lengthened till it reaches into eternity. And if the present trials are an education—if they have any power to make us meek, lowly, unselfish, they cease to be evil. They are part of the careful education of a soul for its eternity of life. They are medicines to purge out gradually its inborn corruption, which would otherwise perhaps break out in sore diseases and destroy it. There is no evil in the world but what comes from man's evil will. All that God sends is simply good. He sends the fruits of the earth in their season, and the sweet voices of children to us, and causes the home affections to blossom into goodness round our hearth, and adds to us friends, and power, and esteem. And then lest we should wax wanton, he plants the little thorn in the flesh, or saddens the home with sickness, or even, as in the case of Job, takes back one by one the blessings He has given. But as He that sends the storm and the ripening sunbeam is one and the same, so is it the same God of love who sends the joy and the sorrow: "The Lord gave, and the Lord hath taken away, blessed be the name of the Lord." Have we learned that this life is neither a feast nor a sleep, but a school to prepare souls in their childhood to bear themselves well in an immortal maturity? Then are we prepared to understand that God is love; and that nothing that befalls us here is without a purpose, and that the love of God for us miserable sinners shapes every purpose towards our good. But this great step towards wisdom must have been taken by the help of the Spirit of God. It is no natural inference from our observations to say that God is love—is nothing but love. Nay, even for a man who has begun to love God it is very hard to admit in his own case that sorrows are blessings in disguise. He can console his friend's sorrow thus, but he writhes under his own. He tries to persuade his neighbour that the loss of one nearest and dearest to him will tend to perfect his soul; but when the blow falls on wife, or son, or daughter, under his own roof-tree, he cannot yet call that affliction that extinguishes the light of life, and robs his pursuits of all savour and colour, a new mercy from a most merciful Father. To know that God is love is the first lesson of Christianity; to know it perfectly and feel it thoroughly, is the very last attainment of a Christian character.

II. The mystery of redeeming love is far above our natural comprehension. That God was wroth with men, and because of the self-devotion of His own Son to death laid His wrath aside; and that the Son sent the Spirit of adoption into the hearts of men, whereby they were able to call God Abba, Father, these are high and mysterious truths, which cannot be touched and handled. There is no handbook to make them easy; no mathematical expression can render them more precise. How shall I so seize and appropriate them as that they shall have a practical bearing on my life? This is the question we are tempted to ask. Where is the faculty of my mind, by which I can lay hold of these high truths? By faith alone can they be apprehended; we must believe that which we cannot explain by reason, but which yet supplies the deepest wants of our hearts. But the faith must be an active faith, not a mere feeling or sentiment. And the Apostle tells us in my text in what direction it ought to act.

"If a man say, I love God, and hateth his brother, he is a liar; for he that loveth not his brother whom he hath seen, how can he love God whom he hath not seen?" Here the Apostle does not say that it is easier to love men than God, but that it is easier to love the seen and known than the unseen. Woe to us, if after all that we have learnt from the Bible, from sermons, from prayers, the redemption of our souls from death seems to us no nearer—comes no more home to us—than might something transacted far off in the boundless space of heaven! And this is just our trial; we are to love God whom we have not seen. But the Gospel teaches us what temper we must cultivate in order to bring that mystery down from the heaven above us into our very hearts. Unselfish love of our brethren shall be the way to know and admire that great work of self-sacrifice. If with the shadow of the Cross upon us we can slander our brother, if we have a keen and greedy eye for his faults, if we care not whether his soul perish, if we have never tried to take a temptation out of his way, if we store up the memory of some wrong that he has done us, hoping one day to reckon with him for it, it is plain that our eyes are blind to the Cross, that we see not Him that hangs upon it, that His words "Why hast thou forsaken me?" do not suggest to us the most wonderful depth of self-devotion and sacrifice. How could we carry into that presence our petty and wicked malice, if we knew the presence in which we stood? When angels are praising Him who for our sakes left His glory and endured all sufferings, how could we, if we had ears for that heavenly chorus, break in upon it with the hoarse discords of our hatred? How could the servant in the parable be hard with the fellow-servant who owed him a hundred pence, whilst the words of his own forgiveness of an almost infinite debt were ringing in his ears! Christian friends, faith is a moral more than an intellectual quality. We could not see the sun, said a great thinker*, if our eye had not about it something sunlike. The ear must be practised, before it can judge of music; the sense of form and colour must be cultivated before the masterworks of painting can be at all understood. And thus, loving disciples can best feel their Master's love, and thank Him for it. Those who are always pouring out their strength and their heart upon the good of others, will read with a light that never shines for the cold and lazy, the history of our redemption. "When we were yet without strength," says St. Paul, "in due time Christ died for the ungodly." (Rom. v.) But who can doubt that those simple words—Christ died for the ungodly—acquired for that great Apostle an ever increasing weight of meaning, as his own labours ripened him more and more towards a perfect unselfishness? All those journeys of his in which Christ was with him, those chains

* Plotinus.

and stripes which he bore with psalms of joy, those zealous efforts to build up the churches in the faith, strengthened the spiritual eyesight of the man to see deeper into the hidden things of God. The worst foe of the Christian faith is not the sceptic, with his astute objections, for these cannot touch the man who has tasted of the grace of God in Christ;—is not the persecutor, for the early Church grew and was purified by persecutions. It is the selfishness in which we indulge ourselves. When the covetous man and the self-important, and the slanderer, and the cruel man meet together and recite the words of our creed, where in such hearts as those can there be any taste for those high virtues? There is no more worship in their words than in the roaring of the sea or the gibbering of apes in the forest. "He that loveth not his brother abideth in death."

III. But the last of the three propositions which I selected, described the state to which Christian love would bring us. "There is no fear in love ; but perfect love casteth out fear; because fear hath torment. He that feareth is not made perfect in love." The Christian life begins in fear. Waking up to the consciousness of sin, the soul sees before it death and judgment, and above it not a God of love, but a God who is a consuming fire. All do not feel this fear, but it were well for them if they could. They are sleeping through their time of danger; they will never know the terrors of shipwreck till the rushing waters pour around them and destroy them. And yet the course of the sun towards its setting is not more sure than the course of our lives towards the grave. And after the grave, there is much to hope or much to fear. But the course of the sun towards the west can be computed; our life often dashes down suddenly into darkness, like a meteor from the zenith. We shall all die; yet many of us do not fear, and do not hope. In this at least bravery is pushed beyond the bounds of madness. But, suppose that the thought of an offended God and of a polluted soul has brought a wholesome fear at the outset. Suppose that the truth has been reached that God is love, and that He wills not the death of a sinner, but has provided the means of reconciliation. There must be doubts at first. The atonement of the Lord Jesus is complete, but will it reach me in my depth of sin? Shall I that have served sin, be able to keep steadfast in the better way unto the end? But as the discipline of the Cross works more and more in the heart, these fears begin to vanish. Loving men and helping them deepens the love of God. And as the spiritual eyesight clears, it sees the Father no longer as a God clothed in the terrors of judgment, but as Him, who loving the Son, yet loved us so well as to give His only-begotten Son to die for us; it sees the Son as loving the Father, and striving to bring back all men into their share of that Father's love, the first-born of many brethren. It sees the Holy Ghost in the love of the Father and the Son, and the bond of divine union between them, dwelling in all who believe, and thereby uniting each of them to the Father and the Son. To have seen and known these high truths carries along with it a certain measure of assurance that they will never be lost. The promise of Christ is seized on and kept : " I give unto them eternal life, and they shall never perish, neither shall any man pluck them out of my hand." (John x. 28.) But besides outward promises, held fast by a believing mind, the indwelling of God in such a mind is a reality. In sober truth, and not by a figure of speech, do the Father and the Son come to him and make their abode with him. In such communion fears are dispersed like mists before the sun in the morning, and the peace of God which passeth all understanding is shed abroad in the heart, and nothing can take it away. And the fountain of everlasting water springs up clear in the soul; and whatever trials may threaten him in this life, the conviction that no evil can happen to the just is more than a defence against them.

This is a rude sketch of the growth of a Christian soul. And the instrument of its education is love of the brethren. Is that love easy to practise? All our souls know the same sinfulness, look up to the same cross of deliverance, expect the same judgment, and desire a seat in the same heaven; here, at least, is the community of interest that would make friendship easy. Yet between Paul and Barnabas, engaged at the time in a mission for saving souls, a sharp contention arose, so that they parted asunder. In truth it is very difficult for human creatures to reconcile great zeal and activity in any cause with perfect love and agreement. Wherever there is a great work to be done, different views will be taken of the mode that should be followed; and good intentions will not always prevent errors from creeping in. Did Paul at Antioch withstand Peter for what seemed to be time-serving timidity? Ever and again shall one man justify to himself as prudent, conduct that another thinks wavering. Do Paul and Barnabas part asunder, because one will forgive Mark for turning back, and the other sees him as a deserter? Again and again will a man's heart burn with indignation at seeing a good cause imperilled by good-natured indulgence. And who dares to say that love of the brethren—the love of Christians for the sake of the name they bear and the profession they make—is realised amongst ourselves? Does it not seem as if we had invented a special Christian *hatred*—as if those who prayed to the same Lord were more strange to us because of some point in dispute, than the heathen or the godless? Yet the Bible is true, and it is true that he that hateth his brother abideth in death. My brothers, let us not thus give the right hand to Satan; let us bear and believe and hope all things of those who believe in the same God and the same Cross, and the light of the same Spirit. Gathering clouds all round us, warn us of storms that shall beat upon the temple of God. The personality of God, the immortality of the soul, the atonement, the sinfulness of sin, all these are brought into question; and we are weakening our cause and lowering the tone of our spiritual life by our janglings and suspicions. I pray you, avoid such wickedness and folly. Turn your eyes within. What are you doing that comes of love of the brethren? How are you practising love on this earth, that ye may the better love God in heaven? When the rains shall descend and the floods shall come, it will not be the censorious, and quarrelsome, and backbiting brethren that will be a foundation for the house strong enough to bear the storm, but the believing and loving spirits, that can seek Christ and his peace in sincerity. Tremble so long as the house of God is a house divided against itself. Do what you can to heal its divisions. Give no encouragement to that specious hatred that calls itself Christian zeal. "He that loveth not his brother abideth in death."

SERMON XXIV.

THE DOOM OF JERUSALEM.

Matt. xxiii. 37.

O Jerusalem, Jerusalem, thou that killest the prophets, and stonest them which are sent unto thee, how often would I have gathered thy children together, even as a hen gathereth her chickens under her wings, and ye would not!

Behold, your house is left unto you desolate.

For I say unto you, Ye shall not see me henceforth, till ye shall say, Blessed is he that cometh in the name of the Lord.

We need not be told that these words are the outpouring of a profound compassion; we need no expositor to show us the love that they express; we know that such tenderness towards a city of many sins about to be punished with many sorrows, from one whom it had wronged more than it had wronged even the slain prophets, is more affecting almost than any other passage in the Sacred Book. It is not put before you now as if any such reflections as these were needed, but rather to suggest to us a subject often brought before us in Holy Scripture; I mean, the moral responsibility of cities and communities, as distinct from that of the individuals who compose them. For, not to speak of Nineveh, of Tyre, of Babylon, is it not plain to us that we can trace in our Bibles, as it were, the personal life of Jerusalem, its hard and cruel youth, its depraved and callous maturity, its time of moral trial, its great guilt and many falls, its destruction brought about at last by its own crimes? And this personality (for I can find no nearer word) of the city of Jerusalem is truly distinct from that of the several moral beings that made up the whole society. The city was at different times better and worse than the men it contained. The city was a malignant murderer of the prophets; the men oftentimes intended to do God service when they cast the stones that slew them. In the death of the Lord, which was the crowning crime of her wicked life, the community seemed to pursue the Redeemer to His death as with a settled malice; there never was a time when He was safe within her walls; and the meshes of the hunter were drawn closer and closer round the divine prey until He was taken and destroyed. Yet it may well be doubted whether any class of the people had formed a settled purpose to put Him to death from the beginning. Sometimes the common people seemed about to believe on Him;

sometimes the fear felt by the priests was stronger than their wounded pride, and they left Him unmolested; but however persons, and even classes might waver, we see that the face of the city lowered and frowned upon Him more and more, until His sacrifice was accomplished and His warfare over.

Why do we dwell on this? Because we see that it is verily true that a city or a country may have its time of trial before God as well as a man; and that that city may be London as well as Jerusalem. Christ, the beloved of God and the lover of the souls of men, stands looking down on *us* from a sublimer height than that whereon He stood when His compassion took its last survey of the doomed Jerusalem; and from the right hand of the Majesty of the Eternal, He says, "Thou that despisest the prophets, and crucifiest afresh by thy sins the Saviour that was sent unto thee and all the earth, how often would I have gathered *thy* children together even as a hen gathereth her chickens under her wings, and ye would not! Behold your house —" No: perhaps there the parallel stops; that part of the sentence is still unpronounced.

Consider then this subject—the responsibility of a city; for it is not to point a rhetorical figure that our Lord has personified Jerusalem, nor is it true that a city has no life save that which belongs to each man that dwells within it. Consider it with reference to ourselves, as a theme of real anxiety and sorrow.

I. Consider, first, the enormity of the sins of which a society may be guilty, beyond the will of any individual man to be found there. Jerusalem had slain the prophets; she had overlaid the law of God with human inventions; and the phylactery of the Pharisee, inscribed with texts, was taken instead of the writing of the Word of God on the fleshy tables of the heart; and in the Court of the Temple, in which God had promised His presence, traders chaffered and bargained noisily about the price of an offering. The Scriptures told them of Messiah, and He passed before their very eyes, yet they could not see Him. When an impure woman was to be condemned, our Lord saw that there was not, out of a crowd of accusers, even one whose conscience would not reprove him as guilty of the very same sin.

And are not the sins that deface our own city very grievous? How thoughtless she is about the sore needs of those that minister to her luxury, her pomp, her splendour! Hard by her lines of palaces are rows of dwellings, parcelled out room by room among the families of the poor; and in the one room's compass are packed the father's trade and the mother's sick bed, and the infant's cradle, and the children's playground. Disease works like a ferment when once it gets entrance to that mass, until the whole is leavened. Moral purity is difficult to guard where the outward decencies of life are impossible. Knowledge and virtue are not apt to be the aims of life, where the struggle is for mere bread and shelter.

I do not say that all this is easy to remedy. But are we even seeking a remedy? Is not this great evil accepted as a fact, rather than regarded, by most men at least, as a problem? The hard unfeeling city wakes and sleeps, eats and drinks, and thinks not of the divine image so cruelly marred by want, of the souls born to be heirs of light and life, yet left full of darkness. The ministers to her great luxury cry, and their cries "are entered into the ears of the Lord of Sabaoth," but she hears them not. Then how unscrupulous she is in her passion for gain! You ask for bread, and she sells you a stone; in some branches of trade words have lost their meaning, and promises are held out which it would be almost a sign of imbecility to credit. Then how many souls fall victims to her impurity! At the corners of her streets sin in hideous shapes flits under the doubtful lamps of night; and you shudder to think that thousands of castaways are perishing in soul and body, the hopeless victims of one single form of sin. Think, too, of her godlessness and idolatry! Children grow up who have never learnt to call on God, or look up to a Saviour. Those who are better taught forget to live by the moral rules of the Gospel. Their heaven is a higher social position on earth; the Sinai of their law is that little eminence which they call "society." "Shall I not visit for these things, saith the Lord, and shall not my soul be avenged on such a nation as this?" (Jer. v. 9.)

II. It is remarkable, too, that the social state is

worse than any one man, even the wickedest, would wish to make it. In the ancient and the modern city alike, each offender knows that his particular form of vice can only be practised so long as it is not too common, and each is ready to condemn the vices which he does not affect. The man who packs ten families into the room of five, without regard to health or morals, because ten can pay more than five, and because houses are a kind of monopoly, is not the man who gambles on the Exchange, or who sweeps the poor man's savings into the coffers of a ruined bank; and both would look on the seducer or the profligate with detestation. Yet when these various forms of selfishness work together, they do in fact strengthen one another. The hard struggles of the covetous make poverty more oppressive, and poverty offers to the trafficker in woman's virtue more easy terms. And on the great aggregate of human wickedness the watchful eye of the Almighty looks down, not with pleasure; His wrath is kindling against us as a consuming fire. But He spared Nineveh when she repented; He bore long with the wayward Jerusalem. He bears long with us.

III. But this guilt, real as it is, is often accompanied by a profound unconsciousness. In Jerusalem, now when the signs that the face of Jehovah was being averted from them were patent enough, when the very worship of the temple was carried on under the eyes of a foreign garrison stationed in a neighbouring tower, and the very money of their daily dealings bore the impress of a foreign king, whilst the throne of David and Solomon had been overthrown, they were as proud as ever of their national descent. Inheritors of the promises of God, they thought not of prophetical threatenings, far more applicable to their backsliding condition. They went on unsuspecting, following the blind guidance of the Pharisees, towards the destruction which was soon to overtake them. They rejected Him who alone could save them, and chose Barabbas the murderer instead. Little did they know that in this act, so readily done at the bidding of their priests, so easily forgotten, they were passing sentence on themselves. They chose a robber, who had made an insurrection and committed murder; and robbery, and murder, and insurrection, were the portion of their city during its last troubled years, and brought it at last to utter destruction. Little did they suspect, when famine and rapine were devouring their besieged city within, and the army of the Roman pressed it without, that the rejection of Jesus was their ruin. They could not have put their hand upon the precise point in their history when the term of their trial ended, and their judgment was pronounced. "If thou hadst known, even thou, at least in this thy day, the things pertaining to thy peace, but now they are hid from thine eyes." (Luke xix. 42.)

And the state of the modern city is only too similar. We, with our well-meant cant about national greatness, and the blessings of a Christian country, and the like, do shut our eyes wilfully to fearful signs of evil within. In what chapter, I pray you, of the blessed Gospel do you find it written that with tens of thousands of children left ignorant, and therefore godless, with streets that for patent wickedness are a whole world's wonder, with a commercial morality deeply depraved, you are to sit down in complacency, and say, Behold a great and understanding people! Behold the working of the Gospel of Love!? Rather mourn that the rules of the Gospel of Jesus are still so far from being the law of a country that professes to uphold that Gospel in its purity. Rather repress every boastful word whilst such enormous evils cry to God against us. It is remarkable, too, how insensible we are of danger to us from our sins. This is the common characteristic of all wickedness indeed; it shuts its eyes against the hour of retribution. "They think their houses shall endure for ever." Why should not this nation grow as it has been growing, become richer and richer? why should not the arts of luxury advance continually? I know not: but this, my Christian hearers, we do know, that God has ordained a law, and neither you nor I can set it aside, that every evil contains within it a germ of destruction. God is indeed long-suffering; he gives the man time to repent, and his mercies to him are new every morning. He gives the city or the state time to turn from its wickedness. Wonderful are those words in the history of Jonah, as applied to one who cannot change ; when the people of Nineveh repented, "God saw their works that they turned from their evil way; and God repented of the evil that He had said that He would do unto them: and He did it not." (Jon. iii. 10.) But when the man or the people refuse to repent, there comes a time when the sun of His beneficence is hid by the thick clouds of displeasure, and the man dies and goes to judgment, and the place of the city is taken away for ever. And are there not in the very sins of which we have had to speak, the evident seeds of future evil? Are we not most vulnerable in those two points—our commercial credit, and the industry of our working classes? Yet we do little to relieve the extreme pressure under which our artizans and workmen live. Too often — I know how shocking the words will be—they are worse housed, worse fed, worse cared for than the brute beasts that we employ. And a gross infidelity is whispered into their ears, and finds them willing to listen: " You *are* as the beasts that perish," it says; " you are a cunning combination of bodily organs, and what you call your soul is only the product of your brain and organs. When death dissolves the body, the soul is no longer. Eat and drink, then, for to-morrow you die; and every sensation of pleasure is something snatched from an approaching annihilation." I appeal to those who know the under-workings of society, whether this does not go on. Nay, can we wonder at it? If no man seems to care for their souls, they are laid open by that very fact to a temptation to believe that the soul may perish.

Oh, terrible fire of evil that is smouldering under the flowery and smiling soil of society! terrible retribution that it may one day work by some volcanic outburst, such as history has often described for us!

IV. It is true, then, that a nation goes through a moral probation, as a man does; that up to a certain point she has her opportunities of retrieval, and after this, sin is finished and brings forth death. Jerusalem slept not less soundly the day after the crucifixion than the day before, nor were her markets less thronged, nor the proud carriage of her priests at all abated. Yet the transactions of one week had altered utterly the condition of that place. When our Redeemer entered into the city, they cried Hosannah before Him, they greeted the meek and lowly One with the titles of a king. Glimpses of faith were breaking in upon their minds; there was hope yet that they would not reject Him and destroy themselves. But when they cried "His blood be upon us and upon our children," all was changed. The blood that was to save the whole world sealed them for their destruction. All that follows is but an account of the thickening of the clouds of ruin. "How hath the Lord covered the daughters of Zion with a cloud in His anger, and cast down from heaven unto the earth the beauty of Israel, and remembered not His footstool in the day of His anger!" (Lam. ii. 1.) It is so indeed with men. The texture of a man's life seems smooth and even, each day the twin-brother of that which went before. We cannot see, perhaps, when the last spark of hope dies out into darkness; but there is—there must be—a crisis at which the man's fate is decided, and if he fails there, he is dead thenceforth even while he lives, and the words of hope are a lie to him, and all attempts to reclaim or comfort are as the idle wind. You will answer, that there are no signs that our country is approaching that condition. There are no legions encamped against us, as at Jerusalem; robbers are not plundering and murdering within, and dashing the children against the stones, as they were in Jerusalem at its fall. God does not deal with all cities alike: perhaps he may spare London and England for a thousand years to come, to adorn or deface the earth, as it may be. In God's hand is the sudden thunderbolt, that shatters in a moment, and the decay that eats slowly for centuries. But once more, evil itself is punishment and destruction. Fraud and wrong-doing are the bandits that steal about and rob you; drunkenness, gambling, and impurity, are the monsters that dash your sons and daughters against the stones. Let any of us lay aside for an hour our preconceived notions of our social condition; let us look beneath the varnished surface of society, and every word of boasting will be silenced. Whether this city is better than others, or worse, it may be hard to say; but that it groans under enormous evils, of the kind that have been the ruin of other countries, is as certain as that its atmosphere is dimmed with smoke, and its river polluted.

And on this day*, when we are called on to remember the triumphal entry of the Redeemer into His own city, it seemed not unnatural to set aside for a moment considerations of individual responsibility, and think of our duties as parts of a larger whole. In this last week, so to speak, of the Saviour's earthly life, He seems to deal not with this or that man, but with the people as a whole. He comes to His own, meek and lowly, yet with enough of state to show them that He claims them as His own. It is the King coming to His subjects; yet, as Augustine says, His entrance is not so much the triumph of a king as the procession of a victim to the sacrifice. And that is the time of their trial. An unusual emotion stirs the people; not this man or that, but the people of Jerusalem cry Hosannah, and greet Him as the Christ in the well-known words of a Messianic psalm. They strew the palm-branches in the way; their fervour cannot be repressed. They have forgotten their ancestral character; Jerusalem, the slayer of the prophets, is moved at the presence of the Archprophet into an ecstasy of holy joy. Let but three days pass, and that flame of zeal will have died out. The busy priest and Pharisee are putting into their mouths words of another spirit. And when Christ is arraigned before the whole people, it

---

* Sixth Sunday in Lent.

shall be the voice of Jerusalem that will cry out, "Not this man but Barabbas! Crucify him! His blood be on us and on our children!" Thus it has come about that the city receives and rejects Him; that the people, the "daughter of Jerusalem," as it is sometimes personified in the Old Testament, deals with its Christ and King as one person might do. Let us, my Christian hearers, accept the suggestion. Throughout this week we shall think of the crucified Saviour of the world more than at another time. Spend not the time in sorrow for Him. "Weep not for me," He says, "but weep for yourselves and for your children." See Him coming as amongst us, not in regal triumph, but a victim carried about in procession before it is offered for sin. It was to cure sin that He came and died; not the sins embalmed in histories, but yours and mine, and those of every one that shall sin and suffer on the earth. Cannot we do something to lighten, even if but a little, the load of evil that makes unbelieving London but too like the self-doomed Jerusalem? The amount of evil seems enormous, and the strength of a man but little; but the Word of God rebukes our dastardly hesitation. Had there been ten righteous men in Sodom, it would not have been destroyed. Thirteen Apostles, creeping as it were from out the falling walls of Jerusalem, the city that they could not save, built up the Church of Christ in all the lands. Often the sacred pages set forth the account of one solitary man contending against general wickedness. Fear not then to take part in the conflict, for the strength is not your's but God's; and weak as you are He can wrest the victory for you. "Lord, thou wilt ordain peace for us, for thou hast wrought all our peace in us." Not one voice uplifted against impurity or fraudulent dealing, not one attempt to reclaim the outcast or to comfort the suffering, shall fall to the ground. Seek out the weak places of the social state into which you are thrown; make common cause with those who are trying to heal them. Remember that sin, great and potent as it seems, is a conquered kingdom; it looks menacing, its numbers are legion, but the victory gained over it by our Lord was a real victory, and its strength is ready to crumble away when it is touched in earnest. All the good that is actually being done around us bears witness to the fact of Satan's downfall. Daily some are snatched out of his grasp, rescued from vice, taught, clothed, brought to Christ. Rays of light from the Divine throne may be directed into the deepest gloom of sin, and poverty, and wretchedness; and the sweet voice of Him that sympathises with all that labour and are heavy-laden will reach and cheer them. Blessed are all those who make themselves instruments in such a work of love. Blessed is the city where such works are largely done. He whose deeds on earth are prompted by the heaven-sent Spirit, by faith in the Son that suffered the bitterness of the cross, by love for all that God the Father has created, has built upon an eternal foundation, which shall endure after the city in which he dwelt has become a wilderness, and its glorious palaces are a heap of dust.

TWO OCCASIONAL SERMONS

SERMON XXV.

SHE IS A SINNER.*

LUKE vii. 39.

Now when the Pharisee which had bidden him saw it, he spake within himself, saying, This man, if he were a prophet, would have known who and what manner of woman this is that toucheth him; for she is a sinner.

"SHE is a sinner!" This is the Pharisee's compendious trial and verdict and sentence of one in whose soul, it seems, the sore but wholesome struggle of repentance was actively going on. "She is a sinner;" accursed from God she is and must continue. There is abomination in her touch, and falsehood in her tears. All that a prophet can do for her is to pass her by on the other side. Let her not come here, to shame by her presence those who know her infamy;

---

* Preached at St. James's, Piccadilly, for the *St. James's Home*, an institution for fallen women of the more educated class.

let the lost herd with the lost; and the dead bury their dead; and let us, the saved and living, be free from their intrusion. Thus reasoned a sincere respectable man among the Jews; not a monster of intolerance, not a brutal scorner of the suffering; but a respectable Jew of the most exact sect among the Jews, speaking in the interests of society, and echoing an acknowledged social principle. And thus reason many sincere and worthy men amongst ourselves, almost two thousand years after the Lord has taught lessons of another spirit and a more loving wisdom.

Social rules are general, not universal; and our danger lies in building on them more than they will bear. I suppose that experience has taught most of us that it is as difficult to retrace the steps along the broad way of sin as it is easy to enter it. It is no very common thing for the confirmed drunkard to conquer his depraved yearning; nor for the dishonest man to become trustworthy; nor for the violent and brutal to learn gentleness. It is no common thing for a woman like her who came to wash the Lord's feet, when she has turned all God's gifts to the uses of folly, and scattered all her mind and spirit in vanity, and learnt to disguise under gay speech and a defiant manner the anguish of an inextinguishable shame, to sit down sober and in her right mind, and repair the rags of self-respect that still cling to her, and alter the tone of profane defiance for the tears and exclamations of the contrite. And society for its own protection makes a rule, somewhat rough and inexact, that all who have lost their *character* shall stand under a social ban, which shall not be removed at all, or at least not without the most patent proofs of recovery. Loss of character, so to speak, is the leprosy of morals; and the unclean shall not mix with the clean; they shall bear the marks of their ailment upon them; and the conditions of cure and re-instatement are so remote as almost to preclude hope.

Nor must we expect that this will ever be completely changed. Men see not with the eye of God; the heart is hid from them, they can but judge the acts. The most determined murderer may plan and secretly execute his destroying work in the midst of us, and it is not until some miscalculation of his, or some unusual vigilance of others unmasks him, that the social circle recoils from around him in horror. What can we do, then, but watch the actions, and rate men by the only standard, to speak generally, to which we have access? But our measure is very inexact, the sentences we pronounce often wrong. How different is the judgment of Him who came to seek and save the lost! What would have become of the whole human race, if the broken and contrite heart had been despised by Him, because it had once beaten with the pulses of a guilty excitement? if He had been as ready as we are to break the bruised reed of a weak will, and quench the smoking flax of an incipient penitence? For just observe how the harsh judgments of society tend to increase the sin which they condemn. No one at first throws himself or herself headlong into guilt, sinning with all the heart and soul, without casting one look backward upon the state of comparative peace he is leaving. The descent into the gulf of lost souls is a stair and not a precipice, and upon the first steps the feet falter, and the hands grope vaguely to meet the firm grasp of a friend, if haply one will arrest them before they disappear from the face of day. If the sinner, at the moment when return is possible, sees behind him only faces of scorn, and hears only the hum of many voices crying out shame, he prefers too often the sympathy of vice to the austere rebuke of self-satisfied virtue, and hastens on to the level of those who are worse than himself; where, at least, there are none to point the finger of scorn at him. And yet how various are the grades of offence which the world includes in one sweeping condemnation! "She is a sinner," says the Pharisee in the text. One word suffices to classify all that have gone astray; he makes no inquiries; draws no distinctions; indulges no hopes. It is all one to him, whether a depraved will or a giddy vanity made her a willing victim, or the sheer pressure of starvation drove her to ruin. It is all one whether every day when she rises, and every night when she lies down, she hates herself, and in bitter anguish compares the thing she is with what she was; or acquiesces in her own destruction, and does all she can to hasten the darkness that is settling down upon her moral nature, and to welcome the perfect night. It is this fatal precipitation in judging; it is this loose and general estimate that we are too lazy to correct; it is this want of hearty faith in the Healer of Spirits which makes us stand with our hands hanging down in the midst of an appalling amount of sin, some of which, at least, if we would only copy our Redeemer, and deal with our erring fellow-creatures in the spirit of mercy in which He deals with us, we should be able to remove. We pass our hasty sentence upon thousands and tens of thousands of erring beings, not considering for a moment how many among them are devoured by an unspeakable remorse; how many are capable of sorrow, though they stave it off; how few comparatively are the hopeless children of perdition, lost in this world and the world to come.

Now there are two facts which may well make us pause ere we adopt the hard and thoughtless rule of society in dealing with guilt; and they *are* facts and not mere surmises. The one is incontestably proved by the careful inquiries of sensible and benevolent men. It is, that society is in a large measure responsible for the very sins which it so readily condemns and casts out. If we could deduct from that astounding total of guilt, which so shocks the moralist and utterly perplexes the statesman, all that has been brought about by the pressure of positive want, and by treachery and deceived hopes; if, in a word, we could strike off all that has been caused by the very classes which are so prompt with their condemnation, the sum of what remained would be small indeed by comparison. It may be said that society is not answerable for the poverty which is the most frequent cause of sin; I will not dispute this wide question, but whether we have taken every pains to teach poor people to guard against thoughtless habits, whether we have seen that the labour we employ is fairly remunerated, so that none who work for us shall have the dread alternative offered them of sinning or starving; whether the lawful claims of the poor to a maintenance are always fairly met,—are questions upon which, to say the least, two opinions might be held. But all that I now argue for is, that if the operation of social rules has in any measure caused sin, we that make and uphold social rules should deal considerately with the sinner. Even if it be an imperfection, and not an inherent wickedness in our social arrangements, that causes them to generate sin, we must not be too ready to visit on the erring, guilt which is only their own in part, guilt which they groan under, and perhaps would fain be delivered from. Imagine a friendless woman in this great city, working from the dawn of one day till the strokes of midnight announced the next, to earn at the week's end a sum that might almost be told in pence; think of the time when, after bearing up long against hunger and weakness, hope gave way, and the fruitless industry was abandoned; think of the misery endured by a mind tutored for better things in eating the bread of sin, whilst it was known that the wages of sin is death. Follow her as she rushes forth some inclement night, clutching to her side her child, the one humanising influence left to her by a merciful God, determined to turn from sin, and hide herself from besetting temptations in no better sanctuary than a workhouse. See her sink down in the snow at a door, her child's feet frozen to her side, and she fainting from starvation. And when the good Samaritan that lives there has opened the door, and set food before her, and rubbed back the life into the numbed limbs, she shall go on her way and seek entrance at the workhouse door, which would be to her as the outer porch of the gates of heaven, for sin would be shut out behind her; and she shall be rejected, no doubt by rule, for some formality which has not been complied with; and she shall fall back again into the old life of guilt, shame, and sorrow. And the well-dressed passer-by, wearing on his back the labour of her fingers, paid for at the rate of threepence for nineteen continuous hours, avoids her path, and whispers "She is a sinner." Did I say *imagine?* It is a true tale, to which not even one particular has been added. She, indeed, escaped at last, for great is the mercy and love of God; but others have suffered and not escaped. And when we are told that not in one case, but in hundreds, this tragedy is being acted over and over again — the incident different, the catastrophe the same — we must, if we are honest, change the

Pharisaic formula, "She is a sinner," for one that is more humane. "She is a great sufferer, sick in soul; may the Lord take her to the arms of his mercy!"

Now let us give due weight to the other fact, that there is hardly any escape for those who have once entered the path of sin. Where should a woman like this one of my text betake herself for a shelter, when she tastes the bitterness of her degradation, and longs eagerly to escape from it? The door of her home is often shut against her; the home affections that once refreshed her flow no longer towards her. Unblemished character is an indispensable condition for almost any safe employment; and the most sincere and heartfelt repentance would not stand instead of it. We seem to bid her fill up the measure of her sin; we will not help her to escape. "*She is a sinner;*" no one will take her into a blameless home to employ her; no one will visit her and give her counsel. The consciousness that she belongs now to a class of outcasts fills her with shame; and the more that feeling exists, the less likely is she to return into the presence of those who might be able to restore her. Thus does one step in sin utterly destroy one whom God created to serve and praise Him. God bids the sinner turn from evil ways; and we will give her no chance of turning. Christ came to turn every one of us from his iniquities; and we interpose against one form of sin. He was sent to bind up the broken-hearted, to proclaim liberty to the captives, and the opening of the prison to them that are bound; and who are we that we should neglect a breaking heart and its agonising cry, and leave captives groaning in a bondage of sin worse than death? There is not perhaps one point upon which the world of professing Christians has more strongly resisted the Gospel than this. We tend the sick because our Lord has bidden us; and there is not one large town without its hospital. We teach the poor; we build churches for worship; we set up clubs and charitable institutions for physical wants. But very few have been the Houses of Refuge in which a penitent woman may hide her shame, and find, instead of scorn, some portion of that spirit in which our Saviour said of one like her, that came and shed the tears of repentance upon His feet, and wiped them with the hair she had once been vain of, " Her sins, which are many, are forgiven, for she loved much: but to whom little is forgiven, the same loveth little."

Within the last few years earnest efforts have been made to grapple with this great difficulty, and to efface this black stain upon a Christian nation; and the Institution for which your aid is asked to-day has this to interest us, that it marks the second epoch in the history of penitentiaries for fallen women. It is the first attempt in this country to *classify* the cases of moral disease. The prisoners in a well-ordered gaol are all parted into classes; in every workhouse, in every hospital for the sick, the same principle is applied. In all these cases the principle of classification was adopted late, after the attempt to do without had been found, after experience, to fail. You might see even now in a foreign prison, as I have done, the professional thief and the student whose only crime has been a copy of verses or a declamation on liberty, shut up for months together in the narrow precincts of a single room; but no one can well doubt that the student will come out a worse citizen for that so-called correction; every hour and minute of which has been a moral torture to him, such as no power has the right to inflict on any man. The attempt to classify, to separate dissimilar cases, and provide appropriate treatment for each, is a sign that the work has made progress, and that experience has been gained in dealing with it. This "Home for Penitents" has been opened for two classes of the fallen; for those who have descended from a somewhat higher station in society, and for those whose career of sin and shame has not been so long as to harden them to the utmost. It is not at all intended to establish in the former class what may be called an aristocracy of guilt; nor to countenance the notion that sin which has retained some small vestige of refinement, is on that account less heinous, less deplorable. The Committee, in an excellent Report, tell us that "their experience leads them to fear that the higher the birth and education, the more depraved must be the nature to occasion a wilful wandering away from the path of virtue, where temptations to wickedness are so few." It is not because they are better, then, but because their treatment is more difficult, that they are to be set apart. Many of them are quite unfit for hard work; they have lost all that is best in a woman, but retain a woman's repugnance to coarse manners and speech. If they were placed in an ordinary refuge, to spend their time in hard manual labour in the company of those who have received no education and are further brutalised by vice, their resolution to amend never very strong, would give way sooner or later. In a work so difficult as the restoration of a sinner, let us remove every obstacle that will give way to human hands: if this separate treatment will save one sister the more, let it be fairly tried. But up to this time the experiment has not been made completely. Besides the Home itself, a little way removed, it is very desirable to open one or more houses into which, upon the first impulse of remorse, the sinner may hasten and find shelter and encouragement and strength. Most of these unhappy beings are incapable of forming a fixed purpose of good. The moral nature is utterly broken down under a course of shameful excess. An assumed joy, attained too often by the help of poisonous stimulants, alternates with the deepest depression. The actions are impulsive as a child's. Whether the lost one shall come in to the Christian comforter that would bring her back to the ways of peace, or crown her sins by suicide, depends upon an impulse, not upon a choice.

Open the door, then, of some house where, at any hour of day or night, the daughter of sin may find herself welcome. Let her know where it is — let it be near the haunts where the fallen act out their life of guilt — let them point at it as they flaunt past with a smile or a sneer; some of them will remember it one day when their hearts are too heavy for sneers, and it may be their harbour of refuge from a devouring sea. This is what we are called upon to aid in by our alms to-day. This is what is needed to put this excellent institution in possession of the complete means of good.

Let there be no extravagant expectations of the results of such an institution. The task it proposes to itself is hard beyond description. In a hospital for the body a few days often suffice to work a cure; the moral diseases are all chronic, and need a patient treatment. Sometimes the hope that new habits are forming is suddenly disappointed by a relapse; but still the course of repentance has in many cases resulted in a restoration to piety and a virtuous mode of life. In this Home, just established, the results are small as yet, yet they are real and definite. If only one had been rescued from perdition since it has been at work, all the cost and the devoted labour that have been bestowed on it would have been richly repaid.

Now, is there one that can hear of an institution like this, without giving it his sympathy and his prayers? We are verily guilty concerning our sister;

there is no escape from that. We have set traps in her way that she may stumble, and made it most difficult for her to rise again. And when once that most excellent workmanship of God is defaced, hard indeed is it to restore the divine impress, and recover the lost proportion. The affections deadened, the temper soured by scorn, the mind becomes frivolous and fickle as a child's, the tastes degraded. Such are the details of ruin, and the process of restoration must be slow, because it must be systematic, and time is required to show whether any permanent good is really done. The desultory exhortation will do little here, and the occasional kind word. What is required is an education wholly new. How can this be given unless the patient, sequestered from all impure associations, and safe from fear of want, shall be trained for a year or two in habits of virtue? It is plain, then, that without a house for penitents, private exertion would do little or no good. So that this is the only mode in which the rescue of the fallen can be attempted with good hopes of success. Man, whose own sins have been visited by no social penalty, though peradventure not less in guilt than those which have consigned her to infamy and a grave, do what you can for restitution. Doubtless there is a God that judgeth the earth. And if man sins, and woman bears the fearful punishment, all that we know of the world's government tells us that that at least cannot be suffered to continue to the end. In the class of cases with which this institution is to deal, are found not so much the victims of poverty as of man's falsehood and deceit. The woman, perhaps, was drawn from virtue by professions of a love which she hoped would be both lawful and perpetual. She lives for a few years in luxury, to be the toy of his leisure, to whom she has given up all her heart. By and by the dream ends. The man marries another, and the woman begins to descend through all the grades of ruin. The man is looked up to by an innocent wife, though there is one dark chamber in his past life into which he dare not let her peep. Innocent children gladden his home with their voices. Where is the woman who listened to his first vows? A drunken maniac, blaspheming in the midnight streets, with all her beauty blotted and defaced; in a year or two she will be forgotten in a pauper's grave. Yet doubtless there is a God that judgeth the earth, who will not suffer this unequal measure to continue for ever. That two should sin together, and one should bear a twofold portion of the punishment, that the back of the other may be safe from the smiter, this cannot be just, cannot be the plan of God. What will you do for restitution? Will you make up again that defaced image to its former beauty and purity? You could as easily put back last year's leaves upon the trees again, or curtain the bright sun with last year's eclipse. But this you can do; you can help the efforts that are made to snatch such as she is out of ruin. You can tell other men that the destruction of women rests in fact with them, and that to have taken any part in that foul conspiracy of the strong sex against the weak is not what will bring a man peace at the last. Be not so ready to take a desponding view of the condition of the fallen; is not Christ the well of life, out of which fountains of recreative water flow; and cannot He who recalled Lazarus to life, and made the deaf hear and the lame walk, work wonders of renewal in the breast of the repentant? Woman, whose earthly happiness lies in the honour and love of husband, children, friends, do not fail to recollect that of the outcasts of society who lull the incommunicable pangs of shame to sleep by the treacherous anodyne of drink, and who look with longing, as to a bed of down for the weary, upon the deep water that rushes under the bridge,—many a one began life with better promise, perhaps with as fair as yourself. Round her cradle affectionate hopes gathered, and the prayer of a mother sanctified her sleep; and the first lisping words were shaped into prayers. And as she grew, her very presence was a household blessing; the old man sitting at the hearth would part with all that he possessed to save her from the contact of dishonour. All is gone now; the day that opened so fairly is now the blackness of darkness. Nothing remains but to take the lost sister by the hand, and speak to her the strange words of comfort; to awaken her to the godly sorrow which worketh repentance unto salvation, and so issueth in true peace. Our benign Lord has taught us that even the lost may be gathered back; that even when men, too indolent to inquire and discriminate, pronounce the ruin final, the Divine Spirit can rekindle the scattered sparks of love, and warm the cold heart. Let the magistrate or the legislator, who knows well that our political institutions consult for the happiness of each citizen, and are so far imperfect as they fail to do so, remember how unequally they deal with this class; how careful they are of human life there, how prodigal here. We have often seen able judges and consummate advocates occupied for days in the trial of one criminal; and we may be proud, that, although the voice of the people may have already pronounced for his guilt, prejudice has been laid aside, and the guilty wretch has received the same dispassionate hearing as if his case was absolutely new. So careful are we lest through prejudice the life of an innocent man should fall! And yet, such is our impotence, that where we see thousands of poor creatures treading the path of certain destruction, we can devise no law to prevent or even palliate the social grievance. The task has been found too difficult by every legislature. But not to offer facilities for the return of those who have found how bitter is the fruit of that whereof the conscience is ashamed, would be a criminal supineness. But God be thanked for it! what the law could not do, the private exertions of the good are beginning to bring about. The pure and refined devote themselves to the care of the lost; they bear with many cases of disappointment; they suffer wayward tempers, and are content with the slow dawnings of good. And they ask for the help of all Christian people, for the prayers of all who love the Lord Jesus Christ in sincerity. If we have known any consolation in Christ, let us aid in bringing the lost sheep back to their true Shepherd; that instead of the torments of remorse, and the fear of a dreadful future, they may hear the word pronounced by Christ, "Her sins, which are many, are forgiven."

SERMON XXVI.

THE SECOND TEMPLE.*

HAGGAI, ii. 9.

The glory of this latter house shall be greater than of the former, saith the Lord of hosts: and in this place will I give peace, saith the Lord of hosts.

WE are all aware that these words refer to the first and the second temple at Jerusalem. The temple built by Solomon had stood in its splendour more than four hundred years, when Nebuchadnezzar destroyed it by fire. It was not a vast building, not to be compared in that respect with many a building to

---

* One of the sermons preached on the consecration of St. George's Church, Doncaster, in October, 1858. The old church was destroyed by fire on the 28th of February, 1853. The new one, which is, perhaps, the finest work of its architect, Mr. G. G. Scott, was erected at a cost of 40,000*l.* raised by subscriptions. On the day after the consecration a humbler, yet hardly less beautiful church, was consecrated in another part of the town, built by the Great Northern Railway Company, chiefly from the design of Mr. E. B. Denison, Q. C., for the families of its workmen. These particulars will explain allusions in the sermon.

which we have access now; but whatever wealth and skill and commerce could procure to decorate it was lavished there. Beautiful carvings covered the walls, and every part of it was overlaid with sheets of gold. For thirteen years of Solomon's reign the skill and resources of the Jewish nation were taxed to adorn this house for the Lord of Hosts, for it was to be, in a sense, the one single church for a whole nation. Every Jew had his share in it; every male was bound to repair thither at three solemn seasons of the year. That feeling which amongst us makes every parish look upon its church with interest and with love, was there extended, yet not diluted, over a whole country. If any one would understand its nature, let him read the 122nd Psalm. "Pray for the peace of Jerusalem," says the Psalmist, "they shall prosper that love thee. .... For my brethren and companions' sakes I will now say, Peace be within thee. Because of the house of the Lord our God I will seek thy good."

But it was not the beautiful structure alone that called forth this feeling of love; it was the manifestation of Jehovah there that made the chief glory of that "First House." When the ark of the covenant was placed within it, " the cloud filled the house of the Lord," (1 Kings viii. 10,) and Solomon knew it to be a token of God's presence. "The Lord said that he would dwell in the thick darkness," (ver. 12;) and from that hour it was in an especial manner the seat of God; it was the spiritual heart of the Jewish people, from which the blood of life was to circulate through them. There were the tables of stone, written with the finger of God on the awful mountain of Sinai. There was the Shechinah, the light of glory which Jehovah had chosen to be a symbol of His presence. There were the Urim and Thummim, manifestation and truth, by which the mind of God was revealed to the high-priest. And these tokens of the divine presence surrounded the temple with an atmosphere of love and reverence. It was not the shimmering of the plates of gold; it was not the craft of the workman that carved out of wood the gourds and flowers, and the cherubim with extended wings; it was not the countless vessels of gold and silver, nor the priestly vestments gleaming with precious stones, that made that house glorious. But there the God of heaven and earth condescended to set His name. "A fire goeth before Him, and burneth up His enemies round about. His lightnings enlightened the world: the earth saw, and trembled. The hills melted like wax at the presence of the Lord, at the presence of the Lord of the whole earth." (Psalm xcvii.) Yet He dwelt amongst His chosen people in the house that they had prepared for Him. Well might Solomon exclaim, "Will God, indeed, dwell on the earth? Behold the heaven of heavens cannot contain Thee; how much less this house that I have builded?" Splendid as the edifice was, it was prepared for One who had made for His pleasure the shining stars and the blue vault of heaven, whose storms ruffled the sea, whose word bade the birds fly, and the lions roar after their prey;

who brought round summer heat, and winter frost, and seed time and harvest in their succession. No wonder, then, that Solomon felt that the habitation was unworthy of Him for whom it was prepared.

This first temple, as we know, was burnt by the Chaldees, and the wall of Jerusalem was broken down, and the people carried captive to Babylon. And it was more than fifty years after that the foundation of the second house was laid. It was an occasion to stir up mixed feelings among the people. The glory of their nation had passed away. They came back as exiles, by the permission of a foreign power, to the land that their fathers had conquered. Hope and recollection struggled against each other, when they dwelt by turns on the state from which they had been cast down, and on their hopes of restoration. "And when the foundation was laid," to use the words of the Bible, "many of the priests and Levites, and chief of the fathers, who were ancient men, that had seen the first house, when the foundation of this house was laid before their eyes, wept with a loud voice; and many shouted aloud for joy: so that the people could not discern the noise of the shout of joy from the noise of the weeping of the people." (Ezra iii. 12, 13.) Well might they weep amidst the joy of the more hopeful. The ark of the covenant had perished in the fiery destruction of the first temple: the treasures that adorned it had the spoiler taken. Jehovah would not manifest Himself in the same degree as He had done before, to a people who were suffering the punishment of their backslidings: and the house they had built Him was but a poor copy of the temple that had perished. "Who is left among you that saw this house in her first glory? And how do ye see it now? is it not in your eyes in comparison of it as nothing?" (Hag. ii. 3.) Such are the words of Haggai the prophet: yet he added a promise that this second temple in its poverty should be more glorious than the first, because the Desire of all nations, even Christ himself, should come to it, and the Lord of hosts should fill it with glory. And how was this prophecy, repeated also by the prophet Malachi, fulfilled? The presence of Christ, offered in the temple at the Purification, and afterwards teaching there, a meek and lowly man among men,—this was what made the second temple glorious beyond the first, even with its cloud, and its bright light of glory, and its speaking oracles. For these things were but signs and types of God; but Jesus was God himself manifest in the flesh. Those who thronged upon our blessed Lord, or jostled Him even in the press in the court of the temple, felt no such awe as those had done ages before that saw the cloud filling the temple. But the cloud was but a token; and our Lord was a divine Person, and one who held in His hand the keys of their salvation. The stone tables of the old covenant were lost, but then the Author of the new covenant was there. The Urim and Thummim no more gave its token upon the breastplate of the priest: but the tongue of Him who spake as never man spake was heard uttering words of divine wisdom in the spirit of divine love. Truly "the glory of the latter house was greater than of the former."

II. And does not this teach us, my Christian hearers, that it is not the house, but the presence that sanctifies the house, that constitutes its glory? Here we are assembled in a second temple, not perhaps less glorious than the first, as a material structure. But whether it shall be a glorious church, or whether the abomination of desolation shall brood over it, is not a question for architect or workman, but for the consciences of all of you. God dwelleth not in temples made with hands; but in your hearts He will dwell if you seek Him. You are the living stones out of which the real church in this place is to be built; the wood and stone that make this noble pile are but as the outer casings of the spiritual church within. Do you not feel that it is so? Recall for a moment the state of the church at Jerusalem after the ascension, before it had even come into men's minds to raise a building set apart for Christian worship. Think of the devotion of those poor men. Think how they threw all their worldly possession into one common treasury for the use of Christ's flock; how they were of one heart and one mind; how fervent they were in prayer, and how their prayers were answered; how fearless they were before magistrates; how strong was their faith in God; and say whether the Most High had not found here a temple, a temple raised without axe and hammer, in which God delighted to manifest Himself. Take, on the other hand, some great church in the corruptest times of Christianity, when the love of God had almost died out, and a taste for pagan arts and letters was the only intellectual life that seemed to remain. All the mechanism of worship was there. The house of God was beautiful; it was crusted with marbles, and the light came in upon it laden with rich pictures of the most sacred scenes and persons. The voices of priests were seldom silent; the swinging censer perfumed the air with incense; yet perhaps there was no temple there for God, no real worship, no manifestation of the Divine presence. The house of prayer had become a den of thieves; thoughts of lust, and envy, and avarice crept in, where there was no real spirit of worship to burn them out. And the words of prayer went up, but God cast back the heartless offering again; and the strong pillars bore up the stately fabric, into which perhaps some great architect had compressed all the thought and skill of a life; but there was no real church there; nothing in the sight of God but a hollow sepulchre, in which the dead chanted empty words to their dead. Truly, "God dwelleth not in temples made with hands." "Thus saith the Lord, The heaven is my throne, and the earth is my footstool: where is the house that ye build unto me, and where is the place of my rest? For all those things hath mine hand made, and all those things have been, saith the Lord: but to this man will I look, even to him that is poor and of a contrite spirit, and trembleth at my word." (Isai. lxvi. 1, 2.)

Here, then, is a question which each person who means to frequent this holy house may well put to himself. Can I contribute to make it more glorious than that which preceded it? I doubt not that mixed feelings, much like those of the Jewish exiles, have arisen in those who have seen the old structure, and now meet to worship in the new. There has been, in the heart at least, the voice of weeping, mingled with the shouts of joy, and hardly distinguishable from them. Within those former walls, you were sealed for Christ at the font; you were confirmed in your Christian position, with the laying on of hands, solemnly devoting yourselves at the same time to God and to his Christ. You entered upon the family life there by a religious act, and went forth joined in the tie of marriage with words that raised and sanctified to the utmost the union which death alone could dissolve, and the effects of which not death itself could efface from the soul of wife or husband. You brought here all that remained of a parent, or a brother or a child, and you set down the ashes of the lost one in the aisle; and you checked your sobs and tears to listen to the Apostle's account of the resurrection; and you went back believing that that which had been sown in corruption, should be raised in incorruption, and looking forward with hope to the time when death should be swallowed up in victory, and praying God to deepen that sacred hope in you. I know they were but brute and senseless stones that looked down there upon your joys and sorrows; that God could have dealt with you, both in His bounties and His chastisements, if this parish had had no stately church to be the focus of all its religious feelings; that the smoke of the fire which burnt it up dimmed not the eye of God, which alone has truly seen you all along, nor its flame consumed even one page of His book in which all your happiness and all your sorrows were written. But so men have been made by their wise Creator. So spoke the captives who had seen the walls of Jerusalem rased and its temple consumed. "How shall we sing the Lord's song in a strange land? If I forget thee, O Jerusalem, let my right hand forget her cunning!" So think many of you, as you recall the first house, growing every year more weather-worn, yet more girt about and adorned with memories and associations. It is no sinful regret that you feel. But it rests with you whether the glory of this latter house shall be greater than that of the former. It rests with you whether the Saviour shall manifest Himself here more than there; for He has promised, "If a man love me he will keep my words, and my Father will love him, and we will come unto him, and make our abode with him." (John xiv.) If in this house of God the words of truth shall so come home to you as to awaken your conscience from a long sleep, and to give you a real insight into the peace of God which passeth understanding; if, in a word, you shall be turned to God here, and cast off the works of darkness; will not that one fact endear this church to you more than all family associations endeared the old? There will be the birth of the soul to a new life, its death to old corruptions, and its union as one member of the Church to Christ Himself the bridegroom. "In this place will I give peace, saith the Lord of hosts," and it was that giving of peace that was to make its transcendant glory. Seek peace here; come unto Him, all ye that labour and are heavy laden, and He will give you rest. You shall not have to weep, as did the Jews, because the holy of holies is emptied of the mysterious light by which Jehovah gave sign of His presence; that instead of the ark of the covenant, and the tables written by His finger, there is only a stone. None shall ever come here to seek Christ, and find that He is not here. Come, then, to this new temple with new hearts, and a new energy of devotion. You have made great efforts to replace the former building by another more costly and magnificent. You have restored the temple in its material beauty; that is but half the work. Fill it with a congregation of devout Christian people. Let the incense of fervent prayers ascend to the foot of the throne. Try to weary Him with the ardour of your supplications. Be not satisfied till He shows some token upon you for good. Come here to ask for peace, and refuse to go away unsatisfied. Claim His promise; tell Him that He promised to love you, and manifest Himself to you, on a condition which you are eager to fulfil. Say to Him, "Lord, I believe! help thou mine unbelief." Remind Him that even the dogs are fed by the crumbs that fall from the master's table. He will assuredly hear you. He who came by His Spirit to His disciples, now under the outward sign of cloven tongues of fire, now under that of power to heal the sick, now under the form of Christian graces vouchsafed them, as humility, charity, untiring zeal, will come to you with the Father, and make His abode with you.

Christ will be present here. But is there not another form in which we may meet Him? We have seen that He will give peace. But what if we behold Him with a scourge of small cords in His hand, with terrible wrath in His looks, prepared to cleanse His temple, and saying to us, "My house shall be called the house of prayer, but ye have made it a den of thieves?" That must have been a great sin against which He put on the appearance of a man of wrath! The meek Redeemer, of Whom the prophets had said that He should not strive nor cry; Who was gentle as a lamb in the hands of those who slew Him, Who bore with the Pharisees, Who was not provoked at the mistrust of His disciples, nor at the accusations of His enemies, was moved twice to anger at the desecration of the house of God. There is a terrible significance in that phrase, "the wrath of the Lamb!" (Rev. vi. 16.) By thus casting aside His habitual gentleness,—and scarcely on one other occasion during His earthly ministry is such a feeling attributed to Him,—He did set a special mark of abhorrence upon one great sin, that of polluting what is sacred, by importing sin into it. "My house shall be called the house of prayer, but ye have made it a den of thieves." No one will plant in a church the money-changers' table, but many a thoughtless one has done his worst to make a Christian church a den of thieves. The thoughtless woman has decked herself to attract, and spread abroad her nets to catch foolish eyes, whilst the worship of the Most High was the pretext for her presence; and men have come to church even for motives whose impurity would not bear the light. The man of business lets his thoughts run upon his bargains, whilst his lips are uttering the confession of sin. Neighbour watches neighbour with jealousy. The Lord's Supper has been eaten by lips fresh from draughts of sin. Even the minister may be tempted sometimes to let his thoughts turn aside from the glory of God to the display of his own talents; or may shrink from rebuking a dangerous vice, lest some powerful member of his congregation might take offence. All these have set up their idols in their heart; "Shall I be inquired of at all by them?" says the Lord. (Ezek. xiv. 3.) Lost is the labour of those that built and set apart this noble church, if spiritual abominations are to pollute it. Better would it be that it was all cast down into a hideous ruin, than that people should only come here to tempt God by offering Him the sacrifice of devils — the lust, the pride, the frivolity, the indifference of their own hearts! But, my brethren, we are persuaded better things of you. Amidst the incessant calls of worldly occupation, amidst the ever-increasing claims of the world, with a competition in all callings, with a tide of news poured in upon us from every quarter of the globe, there is one place which still claims to be the home of peace, from which all outward signs at least of worldly strife and turmoil are excluded. Think how precious a boon that is, and do not allow your own thoughts to rob you of it. We want rest for our souls. We want hours in which the selfishness that grows from a constant struggle with our neighbours, may be corrected by the thought of God and the remembrance of another life. We need such help to keep the petty concerns of this life down to their due measure. On the other hand, is there not a defiant mockery of God in treating this great blessing with contempt? Did you ever think what it would be if every one were compelled to utter aloud his wandering and wanton thoughts, conceived in God's house? Mingling with the humble words of confession, with the tidings of forgiveness and peace, there would be heard the malignant slander; the scheme for gaining an advantage in the morrow's bargain; the devices of lust; the boasting of the rich, the beautiful, the successful. Would such be the utterances befitting a house of prayer, or the den of thieves? And do not suppose that there is any difference with God between the thought and the outspoken word. Even the furtive *look* of impure desire flashes out before Him; even the covetous thought speaks with a trumpet's loudness against him who harbours it. And will you first build the house and dedicate it to the Saviour and the Prince of Peace, and then turn it into a harbour of devils? Guard well against such great wickedness. Watch over your minds, lest any thought come in which would be a discord in the harmony of worship. For not only the uttered confession and the psalm and prayer will ascend as incense to the throne of the Most High; but with them all evil thoughts and passionate wishes, as a testimony against those that admit them. Watch and pray, then, against such intruders. Say with Jacob: "Surely the Lord is in this place. . . . How dreadful is this place! this is none other than the house of God, and this is the gate of heaven." (Gen. xxviii. 16, 17.) Not the temple of Solomon, with its magnificence, its thousands of golden vessels, its splendid array of priestly vestments, and its smoke of offerings evermore ascending, could be half so glorious a house for the Most High, as a humble village church might be, in which all the congregation, how small soever, were filled with that poor and contrite spirit on which God delights to look, and offered as one body their prayers to Him, no discordant wish or thought coming in to mar the still small voice of their harmonious worship, as it went up for a memorial to the throne of grace.

We have seen, then, what makes the glory of the temple; it is the presence and the work of God therein. We have seen that it rests with us to help or hinder that work, according as we seek God here in earnest, or let our hearts go after their covetousness. You have done much for God's glory, by the zeal you have shown in restoring His house. In this town two churches have been consecrated on two successive days, and I know no other place that can point to such a proof of its zeal for God. Many who hear me have witnessed this day a proof of care for the spiritual wants of the poor, in the completion of a church expressly for their use. Two churches, each in its kind most beautiful, have been conferred on you, not without much strenuous labour, and some sacrifice. But the spiritual church within, of which you are the living stones, must go on building, and our Lord is the Master-builder. Where so much has been done by private hands, I feel sure that the importance of the work and its true meaning have been deeply felt amongst you. May God in His mercy grant that our feelings of devotion may be strengthened day by day! May God hearken to the prayers of His servants which they shall offer in this place, and forgive their sins! May He show His power in bringing many to the knowledge of

His blessed Son by words spoken in these walls! May you all be brought to know that in a spiritual sense the glory of this latter house is greater than of the former, and that in this house God has given you peace!

THE END.

LONDON
PRINTED BY SPOTTISWOODE AND CO
NEW-STREET SQUARE

www.ingramcontent.com/pod-product-compliance
Lightning Source LLC
Chambersburg PA
CBHW050846300426
44111CB00010B/1143